Lecture Notes in Computer Science   9871

Commenced Publication in 1973
Founding and Former Series Editors:
Gerhard Goos, Juris Hartmanis, and Jan van Leeuwen

More information about this series at http://www.springer.com/series/7410

Gilles Barthe · Evangelos Markatos
Pierangela Samarati (Eds.)

Security
and Trust Management

12th International Workshop, STM 2016
Heraklion, Crete, Greece, September 26–27, 2016
Proceedings

 Springer

Editors
Gilles Barthe
IMDEA Software Institute
Pozuelo de Alarcón, Madrid
Spain

Evangelos Markatos
Department of Computer Science
University of Crete
Heraklion, Crete
Greece

Pierangela Samarati
Dipartimento di Informatica
Università degli Studi di Milano
Crema
Italy

ISSN 0302-9743   ISSN 1611-3349   (electronic)
Lecture Notes in Computer Science
ISBN 978-3-319-46597-5   ISBN 978-3-319-46598-2   (eBook)
DOI 10.1007/978-3-319-46598-2

Library of Congress Control Number: 2016951694

LNCS Sublibrary: SL4 – Security and Cryptology

Printed on acid-free paper

This Springer imprint is published by Springer Nature
The registered company is Springer International Publishing AG
The registered company address is: Gewerbestrasse 11, 6330 Cham, Switzerland

Preface

These proceedings contain the papers selected for presentation at the 12th International Workshop on Security and Trust Management (STM 2016), held in Crete, Greece, during September 26–27, 2016, in conjunction with the 21th European Symposium on Research in Computer Security (ESORICS 2016).

In response to the call for papers, 34 papers were submitted to the workshop from 17 different countries. Each paper was reviewed by three members of the Program Committee, who considered its significance, novelty, technical quality, and practical impact in their evaluation. As in previous years, reviewing was double-blind. The Program Committee's work was carried out electronically, yielding intensive discussions over a period of one week. Of the submitted papers, the Program Committee accepted 13 full papers (resulting in an acceptance rate of 38 %) and two short papers for presentation at the workshop. Besides the technical program including the papers collated in these proceedings, the conference featured an invited talk by the winner of the ERCIM STM WG 2016 Award for the best PhD thesis on security and trust management and by Dr. Bogdan Warinschi.

The credit for the success of an event like STM 2016 belongs to a number of people, who devoted their time and energy to put together the workshop and who deserve acknowledgment. First of all, we wish to thank all the members of the Program Committee and all the external reviewers, for all their hard work in evaluating the papers in a short time window, and for their active participation in the discussion and selection process. We would like to express our sincere gratitude to the ERCIM STM Steering Committee, and its chair, Pierangela Samarati, in particular, for their guidance and support in the organization of the workshop. Thanks to Panagiotis Papadopoulos, for taking care of publicity. We would also like to thank Javier Lopez (ESORICS workshop chair), Sotiris Ioannidis (ESORICS workshop chair and ESORICS general chair), Ioannis Askoxylakis (ESORICS general chair), and Nikolaos Petroulakis, Andreas Miaoudakis, and Panos Chatziadam (ESORICS local organizers) for their support in the workshop organization and logistics.

Last but certainly not least, thanks to all the authors who submitted papers and to all the workshop's attendees. We hope you find the proceedings of STM 2016 interesting and inspiring for your future research.

September 2016

Gilles Barthe
Evangelos Markatos

Organization

Program Committee

Spiros Antonatos	IBM Research, Dublin, Ireland
Myrto Arapinis	University of Birmingham, UK
Elias Athanasopoulos	Vrije Universiteit Amsterdam, The Netherlands
Davide Balzarotti	Eurecom, France
Gilles Barthe	IMDEA Software Institute, Spain
Gustavo Betarte	InCo, Universidad de la República, Uruguay
Stefano Calzavara	Università Ca' Foscari Venezia, Italy
Cas Cremers	University of Oxford, UK
Jorge Cuellar	Siemens AG, Germany
Hervé Debar	Télécom SudParis, France
Carmen Fernández-Gago	University of Malaga, Spain
Sara Foresti	Università degli Studi di Milano, Italy
Michael Huth	Imperial College London, UK
Christian Damsgaard Jensen	Technical University of Denmark, Denmark
Martin Johns	SAP Research, Germany
Dogan Kesdogan	Universität Regensburg, Germany
Marek Klonowski	Wroclaw UT, Poland
Daniel Le Métayer	Inria, France
Yang Liu	Nanyang Technological University, Singapore
Giovanni Livraga	Università degli Studi di Milano, Italy
Javier Lopez	University of Malaga, Spain
Evangelos Markatos	ICS/FORTH, Greece
Fabio Martinelli	IIT-CNR, Italy
Sjouke Mauw	University of Luxembourg, Luxembourg
Catherine Meadows	NRL, USA
Martín Ochoa	Technische Universität München, Germany
Evangelos Ouzounis	ENISA, Greece
Nineta Polemi	University of Pireaus, Greece
Erik Poll	Radboud Universiteit Nijmegen, The Netherlands
Michalis Polychronakis	Stony Brook University, USA
Silvio Ranise	FBK-Irst, Italy
Michael Rusinowitch	LORIA, Inria Nancy, France
Alejandro Russo	Chalmers University of Technology, Sweden
Pierangela Samarati	Università degli Studi di Milano, Italy
Steve Schneider	University of Surrey, UK
Rolando Trujillo	University of Luxembourg, Luxembourg
Edgar Weippl	SBA Research, Austria

Fabian Yamaguchi   TU Braunschweig, Germany
Stefano Zanero   Politecnico di Milano, Italy

Additional Reviewers

Arp, Daniel
Christou, George
De Capitani di Vimercati, Sabrina
Degkleri, Eirini Aikaterini
Deyannis, Dimitris
Engelke, Toralf
Ilia, Panagiotis
Imine, Abdessamad
Issel, Katharina
Jhawar, Ravi
Kasse, Paraskevi

Papadopoulos, Panagiotis
Polemi, Nineta
Ramírez-Cruz, Yunior
Rocchetto, Marco
Roth, Christian
Sciarretta, Giada
Smith, Zach
Traverso, Riccardo
Troncoso, Carmela
Yautsiukhin, Artsiom

Contents

Towards a Personal Security Device

Christof Rath[✉], Thomas Niedermair, and Thomas Zefferer

Graz University of Technology, Institute of Applied Information Processing
and Communications, 8010 Graz, Austria
{christof.rath,thomas.zefferer}@iaik.tugraz.at,
niedermair@student.tugraz.at

Abstract. In Europe, eID and e-signature solutions are basic building blocks of many transactional e-government services, especially in
citizens-to-government communication. Many European countries issue
smart cards to provide eID and e-signature functionality on a high assurance level. However, to access these tokens, security-critical code has to
be executed on the client platform of the user. If the client platform is
compromised, an attacker may gain access to credentials of the user and
subsequently be able to issue electronic signatures or access protected
resources. To address this problem, we present the concept of a personal
security device. It is an isolated, low-cost, single-purpose device to execute security-critical code of eID and e-signature tasks. We developed a
concrete implementation on a RaspberryPI and evaluated the solution
via an external application. Our solution increases the security of eID
and e-signature processes by mitigating the impact of a compromised
client platform.

Keywords: Electronic identity · Electronic signature · Signature
creation application · Trustworthy user device

1   Introduction

In the European Union (EU), electronic identity (eID) and electronic signature (e-signature) have gradually evolved to central building blocks of transactional e-government services. This especially applies to citizens-to-government
services, where citizens use their eID to identify and authenticate, and rely on
e-signatures to provide written consent in electronic form. The relevance of eIDs
and e-signatures has also been backed by a strong legal foundation on European
level for many years. For instance, the EU Signature Directive [10] has provided
a basis for legally binding e-signatures in the EU early on. Only recently, the
EU eIDAS Regulation [11] has been enacted. This regulation repeals the EU
Signature Directive and represents the current legal foundation for legally binding e-signatures in Europe. Furthermore, the EU eIDAS Regulation defines a
framework for the application of eIDs in a pan-European context.

Representing the legal basis, the eIDAS Regulation defines relevant requirements for technical implementations of eID and e-signature solutions in Europe.

G. Barthe et al. (Eds.): STM 2016, LNCS 9871, pp. 1–16, 2016.
DOI: 10.1007/978-3-319-46598-2_1

For instance, the regulation defines requirements for qualified electronic signatures, which are legally equivalent to handwritten signatures. While pure software solutions are unable to meet these requirements, smart cards have turned out to be an appropriate technology for the creation of qualified electronic signatures. Accordingly, various European countries have started to issue personalized smart cards early, which can be used by citizens to authenticate at e-services and to provide written consent in electronic form [14]. Examples are the roll-out of the Citizen Card in Austria [17] or the eID card in Belgium [4]. Recently, mobile eID and e-signature solutions that rely on mobile technologies as a replacement for smart cards have also attracted attention [23]. Surveys on the European governmental eID landscape show that 18 countries have implemented smart card based eID and e-signature solutions and only 4 countries provide additionally mobile solutions [5,12]. This is amplified by numerous private-sector smart card based eIDs. Thus, smart cards are the predominating technology for the realization of e-signature solutions that fulfil the requirements of the eIDAS Regulation. In most cases, the same smart cards are also used to provide citizens with adequate eID functionality, i.e. citizens can use this token to authenticate at e-services.

While smart cards have turned out to be an appropriate technology for the realization of eID and e-signature solutions at a high assurance level, their use raises various technical challenges. In this context, especially accessing smart cards, connected to citizens' client systems, turned out to be challenging. Although strategies to accomplish this task differ in technical details, all smart card based eID and e-signature solutions basically require two components: a smart card reading device to physically connect the client system with the smart card and a component that runs on the client system and acts as middleware between the smart card and the software requiring smart card access. In the CEN workshop agreement CWA 14170 this middleware is denoted as Signature Creation Application (SCA) [3]. Nearly all current smart card based eID and e-signature solutions implement the SCA in the form of a software running on the citizen's client system. This software acts as intermediary between the locally connected smart card and e-services requiring access to credentials on it. Furthermore, the software interacts with the citizen by reading required credentials such as smart card PINs and displaying relevant data.

The software-based nature of the SCA is a serious problem. Evidently, the citizen's client system must not be assumed secure. Recent statistics show that more than 32 % of end-user devices are infected by malware [20]. If such malware targets software-based SCA implementations on the client system, it could intercept entered credentials or modify the data-to-be-signed (DTBS) during signature creation processes. Today, software-based SCA implementation represent a weak link in smart card based eID and e-signature solutions and, thus, somewhat limit the security benefits gained by the use of secure hardware tokens.

In this paper we propose a solution to this emerging problem. We identify the execution of software-based SCA implementations on the client platform as root of the problem and propose a more secure, dedicated-hardware based alternative to it. For this purpose, we propose and introduce the concept of a *personal security device*, which encapsulates critical SCA functionality in a secure environment. We discuss relevant concepts behind our proposal and evaluate its feasibility and applicability by means of a concrete implementation that relies on state-of-the-art technology.

2   Related Work

The work presented in this paper targets weaknesses of current smart card based eID and e-signature solutions. These weaknesses are caused by the software-based realization of client components that are required for smart card access and user interaction, discussed, e.g., by Langweg et al. [21]. Interestingly, most existing smart card based eID and e-signature solutions that are deployed in European countries rely on similar smart cards but differ in the realization of required software components. In this section, a brief overview of current realizations is given. This way, the current state of the art is sketched and limitations of existing solutions are identified.

2.1   The Classical Approach: Smart Card and Software

Belgium was one of the first European countries that deployed a smart card based eID and e-signature solution on national scale. Details of the Belgian eID have been introduced and discussed by De Cock et al. [4]. To use the Belgian eID, citizens need to install a software, i.e. an implementation of SCA functionality, on their client computer. The software is provided for all common operating systems [13]. Once installed, the software acts as middleware between the web browser and locally connected eID cards.

The Belgian eID implementation is a prime example of a typical smart card based solution. It requires the citizen to possess a smart card reading device and to install specific software. As this software is required to communicate with the card, it is obviously an attractive target for attacks. By compromising this software, the DTBS processed by the software could, for instance, be modified before being sent to the card. In the worst case, even a secure PIN can get disclosed, if it is entered at the client system and forwarded to the card by a compromised SCA software.

Despite its disadvantages, the approach implemented by the Belgian eID is also followed by smart card based eID solutions in other European countries. For instance, also the Estonian eID card requires citizens to install client software on their local system [15]. Similarly, also the Austrian eID card, which has been introduced by Leitold et al. [17] in more detail, can be accessed using software running on the citizen's client system. Due to the open specifications, Austrian citizens can choose between different software vendors [1].

The Belgium, Estonian, and Austrian solutions are just three out of many comparable solutions that are in productive operation in Europe. This underpins the fact that the combination of smart card technology and local software is still predominating in European eID and e-signature solutions.

2.2   Breaking New Ground: MOCCA

Limitations of smart card based solutions relying on client software have been identified early. However, in most cases the main concerns were about usability rather than about security. A prime example for that is the situation in Austria. As mentioned above, Austria has supplied citizens with a combination of smart cards and client software for accessing these smart cards from the beginning. As user acceptance remained below expectations, more usable alternatives to locally installed software have been investigated. The main outcome of these efforts was MOCCA—the Modular Open Citizen Card Architecture [2].

In contrast to classical SCA implementations, MOCCA relies on a server based architecture. Requests to access a locally connected smart card are not directed to a locally installed software, but to a server component. This server component then deploys a Java Applet in the citizens web browser. The Java Applet uses Java's Smart Card I/O library to access the smart card [22].

When MOCCA was introduced in 2010 [2], it showed several advantages compared to classical solutions relying on local software. Most advantages concerned usability aspects, as MOCCA rendered the installation and maintenance of local middleware software by users unnecessary. In the meantime, however, web-browser support for Java Applets has decreased for security reasons, rendering the application of MOCCA increasingly difficult in practice.

2.3   Heading Towards the Future: The FutureID Client

The previously discussed implementations were tailored to the specific requirements of national eIDs. Each SCA implementation has, thus, supported only one, or a very limited number of smart cards. A different approach has been taken with the FutureID client. The FutureID client is a generic middleware solution. Based on the Open eCard client [6] and extended as part of the EU project FutureID, this client provides a standardized interface to access arbitrary secure tokens. By implementing ISO 24727 [16], new smart cards can be integrated by providing a so-called *CardInfo* file, a XML structure that describes the card layout and supported functionality. Thus, this middleware not only supports a single token, protocol, or use case, but provides an extensible framework, which can integrate arbitrary credentials while offering a consistent look and feel. During FutureID, several European governmental and private-sector eIDs have been integrated.

In addition, the FutureID client also provides electronic signature capabilities. For that, the client can be accessed via the OASIS-DSS [18] protocol to issue electronic signatures using the advanced electronic signature formats PAdES, CAdES or XAdES [7–9]. A basic user interface was integrated into the client. However, the full potential can be accessed by specifying OASIS-DSS signature-creation requests, which can be done by arbitrary third-party applications. Due to the flexible design, it was also possible to integrate eID solutions that are based on remote signatures, like the Austrian Mobile Phone Signature [19].

3   Problem Analysis

The overview of current middleware implementations in Europe has emphasized the relevance of eID and e-signature for European e-government solutions. It has also revealed that existing implementations suffer from several limitations that threaten to compromise security. In this section, we analyze problems of existing implementations. For this purpose, we first develop implementation-independent models of middleware-based eID and e-signature solutions. From these models, shortcomings are then identified on conceptual level. This way, findings of the conducted problem analysis are universally valid and not restricted to certain types of implementations.

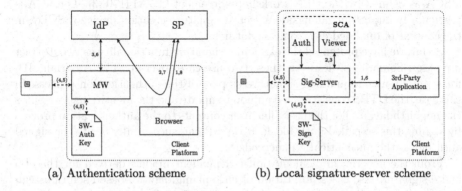

(a) Authentication scheme   (b) Local signature-server scheme

Fig. 1. Block diagrams of the basic use cases

The first use case is the basic authentication scheme, shown in Fig. 1a. A user wants to access some resource at the service provider (SP) that requires authentication (Step 1). In Step 2, the SP redirects the user to an identity provider (IdP). In more elaborate schemes this might be an intermediary, sometimes called broker, which is capable to handle multiple IdPs or even additional intermediaries. The IdP uses some form of middleware (MW) on the client platform to access a credential, like a certificate and private-key pair stored on a smart card or software key store (Step 3). At Step 4, the middleware either connects to a hardware token or key store to perform the actual authentication. This is illustrated in the graphic by the alternative, dashed paths of the Steps 4 and 5. At this step, the user will also be required to enter some secret like a password or PIN. The result of the authentication is returned to the IdP, via the Steps 5 and 6. The IdP creates some form of assertion about the user and redirects back to the SP (Step 7). Finally, the SP grants access to the requested resource, in Step 8, after verifying this assertion.

The second use case is an electronic signature service, shown in Fig. 1b. In this case, the middleware operates as local signature server. First, in Step 1, an external application sends a signature creation request to the middleware, which corresponds to the Sig-Server component in Fig. 1b. Prior to issuing the signature, the user can inspect the DTBS (Viewer in Fig. 1b) and proceed with the signature creation (Steps 2 and 3). The user has to be authenticated to authorize the signature creation. In case of smart card credentials this is done by entering the PIN, for software-based certificates by entering the key-store password. This happens in Step 4, while accessing the hardware token or software key store. If supported by the smart card reader, the PIN might be entered directly on the reader, else a PIN/password-entry dialog has to be provided (Auth component) by the SCA. If the user can be authenticated, the signature is issued using the smart card or other signing credentials (Step 5) and returned to the requesting application (Step 6). The viewer of the DTBS and the user authentication together with the core of the signature service are the main building blocks of a SCA as defined by the CEN workshop agreement CWA14170 [3]. The SCA is particularly important, alongside a secure signature creation device (SSCD), in the context of qualified electronic signatures.

So far, we have presented the eID and e-signature functionality as two distinct use cases. Sometimes, however, these two use cases overlap. The Austrian eID, for example, uses a qualified signature as part of the authentication process. In this case, the DTBS consists of a common template and the identifying attributes (name, birthday, ...) of the user. The user consents to the authentication process by signing this so-called auth block. If the SP can successfully verify the signed auth block, the authentication succeeds.

From the generic, implementation independent models derived for the eID and e-signature use cases, limitation of current middleware-based solutions can be defined. In particular, current solutions show the following shortcomings that we address in this work:

- The middleware and SCA do process security-critical data on the client platform. If the client platform is compromised by malware, an attacker may intercept the user authentication and learn the smart card PIN or key-store password. Thus, an attacker might be able to issue legally binding signatures or access protected resources. The attacker might, additionally, be able to compromise the viewer component and present a document that differs from the one that is actually going to be signed.
- Some eID systems rely on software-based credentials. A malicious software might upload the key stores of these credentials into the domain of an attacker to perform a brute-force attack. Once the password is known, either by compromising the user authentication module or by brute-force, unlimited signatures or authentications can be performed, since there is obviously no equivalent to simply removing a smart card from the reader.
- Smart card readers are very uncommon for mobile devices like smartphones or tablet computers. Smart card access on mobile devices is also possible via the NFC protocol. However, the NFC device is not accessible on all phones by third-party software and the number of IdPs that issue NFC-enabled smart cards is very limited. Consequently, many smart card based eID systems are not available on these platforms.

– Finally, many eID systems lack broad user acceptance and uptake. The reason often lies in the complexity of these systems. Users need to install the middleware, sometimes also a Java VM and the smart card reader drivers; and they have to keep their systems up-to-date, which sometimes can break one of the components. An example here is the Java Applet based solution MOCCA, used in Austria. It was specifically developed to reduce the burden on the citizens to install and maintain the middleware software. Yet, it still suffers from the ceased support of Java Applets in general by modern web browsers, which is a result of updated security policies by the browser vendors.

4 Proposed Solution

To overcome the problems identified in the previous section, we propose a basic *personal security device*, a low power, low cost, single purpose device that handles security-critical code in the context of eID and e-signature tasks. Our solution, splits the application that typically runs on the client platform. On the insecure client system, only a thin proxy-layer remains. This proxy layer ensures that our changes are transparent to external applications and IdPs.

The main part of the client software, however, is executed on a dedicated security device. The benefit of a dedicated platform is its single purpose and the general isolation from the rest of the world. At hardware level, this secure platform consists, at least, of the main processing unit, a display, a basic input device (touch screen) and the facilities to access secure tokens, that are required for the different use cases. This minimal hardware configuration ensures that the user can process the authentication or signature creation solely on the secure device.

The secure platform, obviously, also needs a connection to the proxy layer. This connection between the proxy and the secure part of the middleware is the only interface that is provided by the personal security device. From an architectural perspective it is irrelevant how the low-level connection between secure device and client platform is established. Examples are connections via a serial

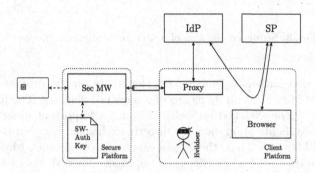

Fig. 2. Authentication scheme using a secure platform

cable or ethernet, or wireless connection, like Wi-Fi or Bluetooth. Regarding the degree of isolation that can be achieved, point-to-point connections are preferable to connections that are shared between multiple parties. However, the low-level connection will in the end most likely be a compromise between security and usability.

On the application layer, the connection must be further protected by an encrypted channel. This ensures, on the one hand, confidentiality of the data transmitted between the proxy and the secure platform; on the other hand, this guarantees that only previously paired devices may interact with each other. The key exchange to establish this channel must, therefore, be part of the pairing-process between client platform and security device.

The resulting architecture of our two use cases is shown in Figs. 2 and 4. Figure 2 shows the proxy layer that runs on the client platform. Towards the IdP, the interfaces are unchanged, hence, our changes are completely transparent.

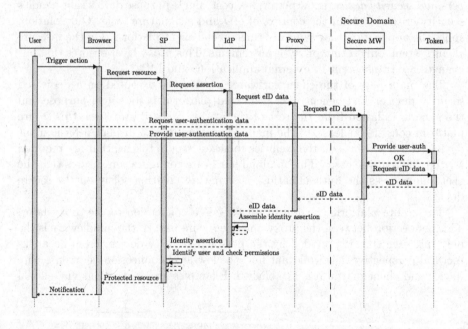

Fig. 3. Sequence diagram of a user-authentication process

A typical user-authentication process that relies on the proposed architecture is illustrated in Figure 3 by means of a sequence diagram. The process flow is similar to the one sketched in Sect. 3. The most important difference is the fact that user-authentication data are directly exchanged between the user and the secure middleware. Thus, these data cannot be compromised by a compromised middleware on the user's client system. Figure 3 also shows that additional processing steps are required due to the distributed realization of the middleware. However, these processing steps are transparent to the user and hence do not affect usability.

To realize the illustrated process flow, the middleware on the secure platform does not need to be changed considerably compared to common middleware implementations. Many middleware applications provide a so-called local-host binding. That is, they provide an interface that arbitrary applications on the same host can access. This interface must be changed to allow only connections from previously paired proxies. Finally, the user interface (UI) also requires changes. In a traditional approach, the middleware is one of many processes on the client system. It is therefore often implemented as a background process, probably with a tiny icon, which appears in the foreground upon incoming requests only. On the security device, however, the middleware is the primary application. Consequently, it should provide a full-screen main window that is visible per default. This window must provide access to all settings that are available to the user. These settings should be extensive enough that the user does not need access to the underlying operating system, and other tools and applications on the secure platform. When considering small and portable secure devices, constrained display resolutions and touch input devices may require further changes to the UI.

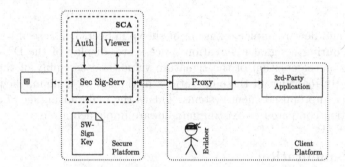

Fig. 4. Electronic-signature scheme using a secure platform

For the adapted signature use case, shown in Fig. 4, basically the same rules apply. The proxy layer on the client platform acts as signature server, which provides identical interfaces to external applications. An encrypted channel protects the connection between proxy and secure signature server. The SCA on the secure platform has to be adapted to accept connections only from previously paired proxies. Finally, the UI has to be aligned to meet the constraints of the platform and fit the requirements of a single-purpose device. Based on the proposed architecture shown in Fig. 4, a typical signature-creation process can be sketched. This process flow is illustrated by the sequence diagram shown in Fig. 5. From the sequence diagram it becomes apparent that, again, all security-critical operations are performed within the secure domain. This distinguishes the signature-creation process of the proposed solution from respective processes

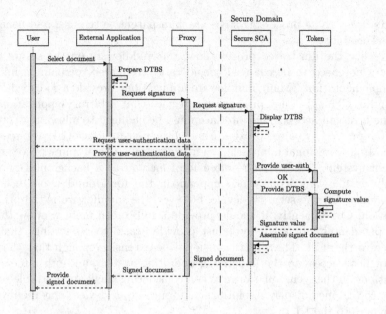

Fig. 5. Sequence diagram of an electronic signature creation process

of existing middleware implementations as shown in Sect. 3. The security-critical operations during a signature-creation process are: display of the DTBS, user authentication, calculation of the signature value, and assembly of the signed document. By realizing all these operations in the secure domain, they remain immune to compromised client systems. This is the main advantage of our proposed solution compared to existing middleware implementations.

5   Implementation

The feasibility of the proposed solution has been demonstrated by means of a concrete implementation. Our implementation is based on the FutureID client as middleware and a RaspberryPI as dedicated platform. The RaspberryPI is an ARM-based, smart card sized, single-board computer. It has been extended by a four-inch touch screen, a Bluetooth adapter and a simple class 1 smart card reader.

The FutureID client has been chosen for its generic approach. It is an open-source project and the flexible architecture greatly supported our development. For the low-level connection between the client platform and the secure device, we have chosen Bluetooth. It offers a point-to-point connection and many users should be familiar with the Bluetooth pairing process, which improves the usability, acceptance and consequently uptake. Furthermore, Bluetooth is available on mobile devices. Smart card based eID and e-signature solutions can, thus, be easily made accessible on smartphones or tablet computers. We are aware

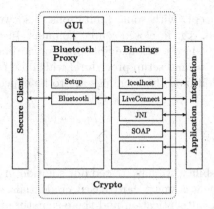

Fig. 6. FutureID-client proxy layer

that Bluetooth transmissions may be intercepted by so-called Bluetooth sniffers. If already the pairing process was captured, it is easy to break the low-level encryption. To circumvent this problem, our solution requires an additional TLS channel on the application layer.

The architecture of the proxy layer can be seen in Fig. 6. It consists only of the bindings layer, i.e. the interfaces to external applications, and a Bluetooth proxy. Additionally, the proxy layer has a user interface to start the pairing process.

The FutureID client on the secure platform, shown in Fig. 7, is similar to the original FutureID client. However, the only binding that is available is a new Bluetooth binding, which connects only to a previously paired proxy. In addition, also the GUI was modified to fit the small display of the device.

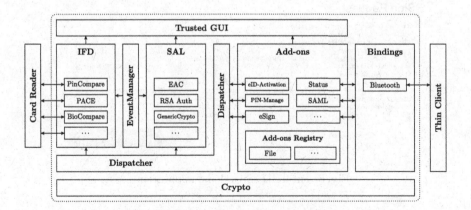

Fig. 7. FutureID client on the secure platform

Note that our concept, with some limitations, also works for unmodified middleware application, e.g. in closed-source domains. In this case, the proxy has to be built with standard tools, like SSH port forwarding. This also requires a different pairing process and setup procedure, which might not be suitable for a broad user base. Additional shortcomings are to be expected with regards to the UI in that case.

6   Evaluation

To evaluate its applicability, we have tested our solution in real-world scenarios with existing governmental smart card based credentials. We have conducted tests for both the user-authentication and the e-signature use case. In general, the procedures of these use cases are very similar. Since the e-signature case also includes the trusted viewer, and can hence be regarded more complex, we focus on this use case here. We tested the e-signature use case using an e-sign demo HTML/Javascript app, which has been developed during the FutureID project. A screenshot of this app is presented in Fig. 8. On the first page the user has to select the DTBS. The user can either select an existing file and choose the signature format (XAdES, CAdES or, if applicable PAdES), or dynamically create simple PDF documents. The corresponding OASIS-DSS sign request can be inspected and, for debugging purposes, modified before it is sent to the localhost binding of the FutureID proxy layer. The proxy layer forwards the request via the established Bluetooth connection to the FutureID instance on the personal security device.

Fig. 8. FutureID eSign demo application

The screenshots of the procedure on the security device can be seen in Fig. 9. On the personal security device, the document is evaluated and presented (Fig. 9a). The user then must provide a signature token, like a smart

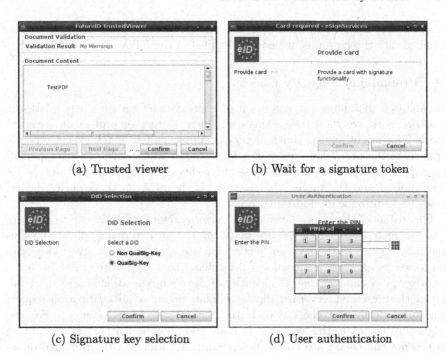

(a) Trusted viewer   (b) Wait for a signature token

(c) Signature key selection   (d) User authentication

Fig. 9. Screenshots of a signature creation process on the secure platform

card (Fig. 9b), and select a signing certificate (Fig. 9c). Finally, the user must enter a PIN for authentication (Fig. 9d) and authorize the signature creation.

Apart from the successful functional test, we also evaluated the applicability as portable device. For this, we used an external battery for smartphones. The powerbank was rated at 5000 mAh and had approximately the size of a modern smartphone. Since the RaspberryPI is very efficient and the load created by the FutureID client is only little, the whole device, including display and smart card reader, could be operated for several hours.

All conducted test have successfully evaluated our proposed solution and its implementation. Concretely, it has been shown that our solution works with existing eID-based and e-signature-based applications. Still, several lessons have been learned during the implementation and evaluation process. These lessons, which will serve as basis for future work, are discussed in the following section.

7   Lessons Learned

The primary goal of the conducted implementation was to demonstrate the feasibility of our proposed solution. As a consequence, the present implementation is rather a solid prototype than a production-ready solution. From the remaining limitations of our implementation, and also from the evaluation conducted, several useful findings can however be derived. Most relevant findings can be classified into three groups, which are detailed in the following subsections.

7.1   Preliminary Security Checks

Our solution mandates the execution of a proxy layer on the client platform. In future work, we want to use this component to further protect our security device. This might appear contradictory at a first glance, as the execution environment of the proxy layer must not be assumed secure. Still, this component can implement logic for preliminary security checks. If the client platform is not compromised and the target of the attack is the SCA on the security device, these checks provide an additional firewall.

For instance, the proxy layer could perform rigorous sanity checks on data it has to relay between the secure platform and an external application. This especially applies to the user-authentication use case, in which involved parties and messages exchanged are known beforehand to a high degree. For instance, the proxy layer can establish the identity of the communication endpoint by validating the presented server certificate, validate potential authentication-request signatures, or inspect the payloads to identify unexpected content. For the e-signature use case, the situation is more complex, as neither the requesting entities nor the DTBS are known beforehand. Additionally, the provided documents are supposed to be opened, processed and presented by the trusted viewer. A maliciously crafted document, thus, could try to exploit known vulnerabilities of the viewer component. Consequently, the checks on the client platform, in this case, can only be of general nature.

In summary, capabilities of the proxy layer to improve security are limited. Nevertheless, we believe that selected measures can be useful to improve the overall security of the solution. We hence regard the realization of such measures as future work.

7.2   Protection of DTBS

The proposed solution has shown to be advantageous in terms of protecting authentication data entered by the user and DTBS presented to the user. As all user interaction is implemented on the secure device, this information is not prone to be disclosed via the potentially compromised client platform. Unfortunately, this does not apply to the DTBS in the e-signature use case, as these data have to be routed through the proxy layer. Hence, additional measures to protect these data should be implemented. For instance, the external application that defines the DTBS and the personal security device could establish a secure channel before exchanging security-critical data. While this would preserve the privacy of the DTBS, it increases complexity in terms of implementation and deployment. Nevertheless, investigating measures to adequately protect the DTBS is also regarded as future work.

We are aware that the encryption of the DTBS contradicts the previous subsection as we now cannot inspect incoming data before it is processed on the security device. However, the situation is still not worse than the current state-of-the-art, plus we deem it more important to protect against a malicious attacker on the client platform than a malicious SP.

7.3 Usability and Acceptance

Although smart card based solutions are wide spread, their usability and acceptance is often hampered by the need for additional hardware in the form of a card-reading device and software maintenance. We are aware that our proposed solution, which necessitates an additional device, does not obviously relieve this situation. However, we believe that integrated hardware solutions and coordinated deployment strategies can lead to efficient and usable roll-out scenarios. By providing fully configured and maintained personal security devices that are accessed via Bluetooth, a widespread, state-of-the-art and simple to use technology, our solution can increase the acceptance and uptake of strong authentication and e-signature solutions for users of personal computers. Additionally, we address also the large and ever growing number of users of smartphones and tablet computers, which can now access their smart card credentials via Bluetooth and a personal security device. We acknowledge that our solution will impose additional costs on its users. However, we believe that the increased security and additional functionalities will justify this investment. For instance, we are currently working on a password store that is usable across multiple devices without the need to share the container via the cloud.

8 Conclusion

In Europe, smart cards are still a popular enabling technology for implementations of eID and e-signature solutions. Although more usable mobile solutions are slowly emerging, smart card based solutions are still most wide-spread in European countries. Security concepts of these solutions rely on the smart cards' capabilities to securely store data and to carry out cryptographic operations. Unfortunately, these concepts often neglect the fact that a smart card must be connected to and accessed from a potentially insecure end-user device.

We have addressed this issue by proposing the concept of a personal security device, to which security-critical tasks are outsourced. An implementation of the proposed solution has shown its feasibility with state-of-the-art technology. Furthermore, evaluation results obtained show that the proposed and implemented solution works with existing eID and e-signature solutions.

Thus, we can conclude that our solution has the potential to enhance the security of smart card based eID and e-signature solutions, which are central building blocks of transactional e-government services. This way, the proposed solution represents a considerable step towards secure smart card based e-government solutions, which can gain broad acceptance by the citizens.

References

1. A-SIT: Mobile Phone Signature & Citizen Card. http://www.buergerkarte.at
2. Centner, M., Orthacker, C., Bauer, W.: Minimal-Footprint Middleware for theCreation of Qualified Signatures. In: Institute for Systems and Technologies of Information, Control and Communication (ed.) Proceedings of the 6th International Conference onWeb Information Systems and Technologies, pp. 64–69. INSTICC - Institute for Systems and Technologies of Information, Control and Communication, Portugal (2010)
3. CWA 14170: Security requirements for signature creation applications (2004)
4. Cock, D., Wouters, K., Preneel, B.: Introduction to the Belgian EID card. In: Katsikas, S.K., Gritzalis, S., López, J. (eds.) EuroPKI 2004. LNCS, vol. 3093, pp. 1–13. Springer, Heidelberg (2004). doi:10.1007/978-3-540-25980-0_1
5. Ducastel, N.: International Comparison eID Means. Technical report PBLQ (2015)
6. ecsec: Open eCard App. https://www.openecard.org. Accessed 11 April 2016
7. ETSI: Electronic Signatures and Infrastructures (ESI); PDF Advanced Electronic Signatures (PAdES); TS 102 778. Technical report, European Telecommunication Standards Institute (2009)
8. ETSI: Electronic Signatures and Infrastructures (ESI); XML Advanced Electronic Signatures (XAdES); TS 101 903. Technical report, European Telecommunication Standards Institute (2010)
9. ETSI: Electronic Signatures and Infrastructures (ESI); CMS Advanced Electronic Signatures (CAdES); TS 101 733. Technical report, European Telecommunication Standards Institute (2013)
10. European Parliament: Directive 95/46/EC. In: Official Journal of the European Communities, vol. 38, pp. 31–50. European Commision (1995)
11. European Parliament: eIDAS - Regulation (EU) No 910/2014. In: Official Journal of the European Union, vol. 57, pp. 73–114. European Commision (2014)
12. Eurosmart: Landscape of eID in Europe in 2013. Technical report, Eurosmart (2014)
13. FEDICT: eID Belgium
14. IDABC: Study on eID Interoperability for PEGS: Update of Country Profiles (2009)
15. ID.ee: ID Card (2016)
16. ISO, IEC 24727: Identification cards - Integrated circuit card programming interfaces, Part 1–6
17. Leitold, H., Hollosi, A., Posch, R.: Security architecture of the Austrian citizen card concept. In: 18th Annual Computer Security Applications Conference, Proceedings, pp. 391–400 (2002)
18. OASIS: Digital signature services core protocols, elements, and bindings (2007)
19. Orthacker, C., Centner, M., Kittl, C.: Qualified mobile server signature. In: IFIP Advances in Information and Communication Technology. vol. 330, pp. 103–111 (2010)
20. Panda Security: Pandalabs' Annual Report 2015
21. Spalka, A., Cremers, A.B., Langweg, H.: Trojan horse attacks on software for electronic signatures. Informatica (Slovenia) 26(2) (2002)
22. Sun Microsystems Inc.: JSR 268: Java Smart Card I/O API (2006)
23. Zefferer, T., Teufl, P.: Leveraging the adoption of mobile eID and e-Signature solutions in Europe. In: Kő, A., Francesconi, E. (eds.) EGOVIS 2015. LNCS, vol. 9265, pp. 86–100. Springer, Heidelberg (2015). doi:10.1007/978-3-319-22389-6_7

Retrofitting Mutual Authentication to GSM Using RAND Hijacking

Mohammed Shafiul Alam Khan$^{(\boxtimes)}$ and Chris J. Mitchell

Information Security Group, Royal Holloway,
University of London, Egham, Surrey TW20 0EX, UK
shafiulalam@gmail.com, me@chrismitchell.net

Abstract. As has been widely discussed, the GSM mobile telephony system only offers unilateral authentication of the mobile phone to the network; this limitation permits a range of attacks. While adding support for mutual authentication would be highly beneficial, changing the way GSM serving networks operate is not practical. This paper proposes a novel modification to the relationship between a Subscriber Identity Module (SIM) and its home network which allows mutual authentication without changing any of the existing mobile infrastructure, including the phones; the only necessary changes are to the authentication centres and the SIMs. This enhancement, which could be deployed piecemeal in a completely transparent way, not only addresses a number of serious vulnerabilities in GSM but is also the first proposal explicitly designed to enhance GSM authentication that could be deployed without modifying any of the existing network infrastructure.

Keywords: GSM · Mutual authentication · SIM application toolkit · RAND

1 Introduction

This paper proposes a way of adding network-to-phone authentication to the GSM mobile phone system, in a way that is completely transparent to the existing network infrastructure. Currently, GSM only supports authentication of the phone to the network, leaving the system open to a wide range of threats (see, for example, [21]). Despite the introduction and deployment of 3G (UMTS) and 4G (LTE) mobile phone systems, which rectify the GSM problem by providing mutual authentication between phone and network, GSM remains of huge practical importance worldwide and is not likely to be replaced for many decades to come. As a result, finding ways of improving the security offered by GSM, without the need for changes to the deployed phones and access networks, is clearly of great practical significance. This observation motivates the work described in this paper.

M.S.A. Khan is a Commonwealth Scholar, funded by the UK government.

© Springer International Publishing AG 2016
G. Barthe et al. (Eds.): STM 2016, LNCS 9871, pp. 17–31, 2016.
DOI: 10.1007/978-3-319-46598-2_2

It is somewhat counterintuitive to propose that authentication of the network to the phone can be achieved without modifying the way in which the existing network and phones operate. This apparently paradoxical result is achieved by using a technique we refer to as *RAND hijacking*. This involves using the *RAND* value, which serves as a nonce in the existing unilateral authentication protocol and is sent from the network to the phone, to contain data which enables the recipient SIM to verify its origin and freshness. That is, the *RAND* is hijacked to act as a communications channel between a home network and a SIM.

The remainder of the paper is structured as follows. Key facts about the GSM network, including details of the operation of the GSM authentication and key establishment (AKA) protocol, are given in Sect. 2. This is followed in Sect. 3 by an introduction to the notion of *RAND hijacking*. In Sect. 4, the novel enhanced version of the GSM authentication scheme is described, and Sect. 5 describes how the SIM can use the results of the network authentication to affect UE behaviour. An analysis of the novel system is provided in Sect. 6. The relationship of the proposed scheme to the prior art is discussed in Sect. 7, and the paper concludes in Sect. 8.

2   GSM

2.1   Terminology

We start by providing a brief overview of key terminology for mobile systems. We focus in particular on the GSM network, but much of the description applies in slightly modified form to 3G and 4G networks. A more detailed description of GSM security features can, for example, be found in Pagliusi [22].

A complete mobile phone is referred to as a *user equipment (UE)*, where the term encapsulates not only the *mobile equipment (ME)*, i.e. the phone, but also the *subscriber identity module (SIM)* within it, where the SIM takes the form of a cut-down smart card. The SIM embodies the relationship between the human user and the issuing *home network*, including the *International Mobile Subscriber Identity (IMSI)*, the telephone number of the UE, and other user (subscriber) data, together with a secret key shared with the issuing network which forms the basis for all the air interface security features.

To attach to a mobile network, a UE connects via its radio interface to a radio tower. Several radio towers are controlled by a single *radio network controller (RNC)* which is connected to one *mobile switching center/visitor location register (MSC/VLR)*. The MSC/VLR is responsible for controlling call setup and routing. Each MSC/VLR is also connected to the carrier network's *home location register (HLR)* where corresponding subscriber details can be found. The HLR is associated with an *authentication center (AuC)* that stores cryptographic credentials required for communicating with the SIM; specifically, the AuC shares a unique secret key K_i with each SIM issued by the network to which it belongs. The RNC and the MSC/VLR are part of the *visiting/serving network* whereas the HLR and the AuC are the *home network* component.

2.2 GSM Authentication Protocol

To prevent unauthorised mobile devices gaining access to network service, GSM incorporates an authentication procedure which enables the network to verify that the SIM in a UE is genuine. The authentication procedure operates as follows. Further details can be found in technical specifications GSM 03.20 [10] and GSM 04.08 [12].

1. The UE visits a network, and is initially identified using its IMSI.
2. The visited network identifies the UE's home network from the supplied IMSI, and contacts the home network for authentication information.
3. The home network's AuC generates one or more *authentication triples* ($RAND$, $XRES$, K_c), and sends them to the visited network, where $RAND$ is a 128-bit random 'challenge' value, $XRES$ is the 64-bit 'expected response', and K_c is a 64-bit short-term session key to be used to encrypt data sent across the air interface between the UE and the network.
4. The visited network sends $RAND$ to the UE as an authentication challenge.
5. The ME receives the $RAND$, and passes it to the SIM.
6. The SIM computes $SRES = \mathrm{A3}_{K_i}(RAND)$ and $K_c = \mathrm{A8}_{K_i}(RAND)$, where A3 and A8 are network-specific cryptographic functions; A3 is a MAC function and A8 is a key derivation function. Note that precisely the same computation was performed by the AuC in step 3 to generate $XRES$ and K_c.
7. The SIM passes $SRES$ and K_c to the ME.
8. The ME keeps the session key K_c for use in data encryption, and forwards $SRES$ to the serving network.
9. The serving network compares $SRES$ with $XRES$; if they are the same the UE is deemed authenticated, and K_c can now be used for traffic encryption using any of the standardised algorithms (i.e. one of A5/1, A5/2 and A5/3), as selected by the serving network.

2.3 Vulnerabilities

The GSM AKA protocol clearly only provides one-way authentication. As widely documented (see, for example, [21]), this permits a 'false' base station to impersonate a genuine network and interact with a UE. This in turn gives rise to a range of security weaknesses. We are particularly interested in attacks of the following types.

– Because the network always decides whether or not to enable encryption, it is possible for a malicious party to act as an intermediary between a UE and a genuine network, impersonating the network to the UE and using a genuine SIM of its own to talk to the network. All traffic sent via the man-in-the-middle is simply relayed. The false network does not enable encryption on the link to the UE, so the fact that it does not know the encryption key does not matter. If the genuine network chooses to enable encryption, then the man-in-the-middle can communicate with it successfully since it is using its own

SIM for this leg of the communications. As a result, the man-in-the-middle can seamlessly listen to all the voice traffic sent to and from the victim UE, at the cost of paying for the call.

- The fact that the network decides whether or not to enable data encryption also enables the well known Barkan-Biham-Keller attack, [2]. This attack is designed to recover the encryption key K_c, and hence enable unlimited interception of phone calls. The attack takes advantage of three key facts: A5/2 is very weak, the network decides which algorithm to use, and the same key K_c is used with all three encryption algorithms. One possible scenario for the attack is as follows.

Suppose an eavesdropper intercepts the AKA exchange between the network and a UE (notably including the $RAND$), and also some of the subsequent encrypted voice exchanges involving that UE. Suppose also that the UE is subsequently switched on within the range of a fake network operated by the attacker. The fake network inaugurates the AKA protocol with the UE, and sends the previously intercepted $RAND$, causing the SIM in the UE to generate the same K_c as was used to encrypt the intercepted data. The UE responds with $SRES$ (which the fake network ignores) and the fake network now enables encryption using A5/2. The UE will now send data to the network encrypted using A5/2 with the key K_c; because of certain details of the GSM protocol, the plaintext data will contain predictable redundancy. The fake network now takes advantage of the weakness of A5/2 to recover K_c from the combination of the ciphertext and known redundancy in the corresponding plaintext. The key K_c can now be used to decrypt all the previously intercepted data, which may have been encrypted using a strong algorithm such as A5/3.

The lack of mutual authentication has been addressed in 3G and later networks. As a result it is tempting to suggest that trying to fix GSM is no longer of relevance. However, GSM continues to be very widely used worldwide and will continue to be for many years to come; so finding ways of upgrading GSM post-deployment appears to be worthwhile. However, any such solution must work with the existing infrastructure, i.e. the existing serving network systems. We are therefore interested in a solution which only requires SIMs and the home network to be upgraded. Such a solution can be rolled out piecemeal with no impact on the existing global infrastructure, and this is the focus of the remainder of this paper.

2.4 Proactive SIM

Before proceeding we need to briefly review a key piece of GSM technology which enables the SIM to send an instruction to the ME. *Proactive SIM* is a service operating across the SIM-ME interface that provides a mechanism for a SIM to initiate an action to be taken by the ME. It forms part of the *SIM application toolkit (STK)*, which was introduced in the GSM 11.14 technical specification [11]. Communications between an ME and a SIM are command/response based, and STK provides a set of commands which allow the SIM to interact and operate with any ME which supports them.

The GSM technical specification [13] states that the ME must communicate with the SIM using either the T = 0 or T = 1 protocol, specified in ISO/IEC 7816-3 [16]. In both cases the ME is always the *master* and thus initiates commands to the SIM; as a result there is no mechanism for the SIM to initiate communications with the ME. This limits the possibility of introducing new SIM features requiring the support of the ME, as the ME needs to know in advance what actions it should take. The proactive SIM service provides a mechanism that allows the SIM to indicate to the ME, using a response to an ME-issued command, that it has some information to send. The SIM achieves this by including a special status byte ('91' followed by the length of the instruction to send) in the response application protocol data unit. The ME is then required to issue the *FETCH* command to find out what the information is [14]. The ME must now execute the SIM-initiated command and return the result in the *TERMINAL RESPONSE* command. To avoid cross-phase compatibility problems, this service is only permitted to be used between a SIM and an ME that support the STK commands. The fact that an ME supports specific STK commands is revealed when it sends the *TERMINAL PROFILE* command during SIM initialisation.

The SIM can make a variety of requests using the proactive SIM service. Examples include: requesting the ME to display SIM-provided text, initiating the establishment of on demand channels, and providing local information from the ME to the SIM. The commands of interest here are *GET CHANNEL STATUS*, which requests the ME to return the current status of all available data channel(s), and *CLOSE CHANNEL*, which requests the ME to close the specified data channel. Both of these STK commands are marked as 'class e', which means that an ME that supports 'class e' STK commands is capable of executing both commands of interest [9]. Although support of STK is optional for an ME, if an ME claims compliance with a specific GSM release then it is mandatory for the ME to support all functions of that release. Since 1998 almost all of the mobile phones produced have been STK enabled, and today every phone on the market supports STK [1].

3   RAND Hijacking

We use the term *RAND hijacking* to refer to the idea of using the *RAND*, sent from the network to the UE during AKA, as a way of conveying information from the AuC to the SIM. That is, instead of generating the *RAND* at random, it is generated to contain certain information; this information is typically sent in encrypted form so that to an eavesdropper it is indistinguishable from a random value.

This idea was apparently first described in a patent due to Dupré [6]. However, the use Dupré makes of the idea is rather different to that proposed here. Later, Vodafone introduced the concept of a *special RAND* [23] in 3GPP TSG document S3-030463. As for Dupré, the purpose of the *special RAND* was completely different to that proposed here. The other published references to the notion appear in papers [4,5,18] that independently propose the use of *RAND hijacking* for improving the privacy properties of GSM, 3G and 4G networks. As far as the authors are aware, no previous authors have proposed the use of this technique with the explicit goal of providing mutual authentication in GSM networks.

4   Server-to-SIM Authentication

We now propose a way of using *RAND hijacking* to enable authentication of the network to the SIM. For this to operate the SIM must be programmed to support the scheme, as well as possess certain (modest) additional data, as detailed below. The AuC of the network issuing the 'special' SIM must also store certain additional data items for each such SIM, and must generate its *RAND* values in a special way for such SIMs. No other changes to existing systems are required. It is important to note that the system could be deployed gradually, e.g. by including the additional functionality in all newly issued SIMs, whilst existing SIMs continue to function as at present.

4.1   Prerequisites

In addition to sharing K_i, A3 and A8 (as required for executing the standard GSM AKA protocol), the SIM and AuC must both be equipped with the following information and functions:

- functions $f1$ and $f5$, where $f1$ is a MAC function and $f5$ is a cipher mask generation function, both capable of generating a 64-bit output;
- a secret key K_a to be used with functions $f1$ and $f5$ which should be distinct from K_i—to minimise memory requirements, K_a and K_i could, for example, both be derived from a single SIM-specific master key;
- a 48-bit counter to be used to generate and verify sequence numbers[1].

The functions could be precisely the same as their counterparts used in 3G (UMTS). Indeed, the function names and string lengths have deliberately been made identical to those used in 3G systems to make implementation and migration as simple as possible.

4.2   Protocol Operation

The novel AKA protocol only differs from the 'standard' GSM AKA protocol (as described in Sect. 2.2 above) in steps 3 and 6. Thus, since these steps only involve the AuC and SIM, it should be clear that the scheme is inherently transparent to the serving network and the ME. We describe below how these steps are changed.

---

[1] As in 3G, an AuC might choose to manage a single counter shared by all user accounts (see, for example, [20]).

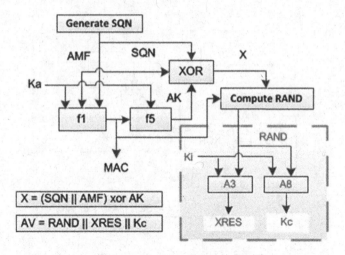

Fig. 1. Modifications at the AuC

4.3   Revised Steps

Step 3 is changed to the following step 3*. To generate a new authentication triple, the AuC proceeds as follows (see Fig. 1, in which the dotted block represents the usual operation of the AuC).

3.1 The AuC uses its counter value to generate a 48-bit sequence number SQN, which must be greater than any previously generated value for this user account.

3.2 A 16-bit value AMF is also generated, which could be set to all zeros, or could be used for purposes analogous to the AMF value for 3G networks.

3.3 A 64-bit tag value MAC is generated using function $f1$, where

$$MAC = f1_{K_a}(AMF\|SQN),$$

and, as throughout, $\|$ denotes concatenation of data items.

3.4 A 64-bit encrypting mask AK is generated using function $f5$, where

$$AK = f5_{K_a}(MAC).$$

3.5 The 128-bit $RAND$ is computed as

$$RAND = ((AMF\|SQN) \oplus AK)\|MAC,$$

where, as throughout, $\oplus$ denotes the bitwise exclusive or operation.

3.6 The $XRES$ and K_c values are computed in the standard way, that is $XRES = A3_{K_i}(RAND)$ and $K_c = A8_{K_i}(RAND)$.

Step 6 is changed to step 6*, as follows (see Fig. 2, in which the dotted block represents the usual operation of the SIM).

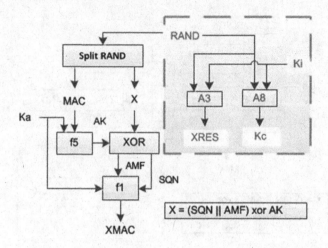

Fig. 2. Modifications at the SIM

6.1 On receipt of the 128-bit *RAND* value, the SIM first splits it into two 64-bit strings X and MAC^*, where $X \| MAC^* = RAND$.

6.2 A 64-bit decrypting mask AK^* is generated using function $f5$, where

$$AK^* = f5_{K_a}(MAC^*).$$

6.3 A 16-bit string AMF^* and a 48-bit string SQN^* are computed as:

$$AMF^* \| SQN^* = X \oplus AK^*.$$

6.4 A 64-bit tag $XMAC$ is computed as:

$$XMAC = f1_{K_a}(AMF^* \| SQN^*).$$

6.5 The recovered sequence number SQN^* is compared with the SIM's stored counter value and $XMAC$ is compared with MAC^*:
   - if SQN^* is greater than the current counter value **and** $XMAC = MAC^*$, then:
     - the network is deemed to be successfully authenticated;
     - the SIM's counter value is updated to equal SQN^*; and
     - $SRES$ and K_c are computed as specified in the current step 6;
   - if either of the above checks fail then:
     - network authentication is deemed to have failed;
     - the SIM's counter value is unchanged; and
     - $SRES$ and K_c are set to random values.

   It should be clear that, in step 6*, AK^*, AMF^*, MAC^* and SQN^* should respectively equal the AK, AMF, MAC and SQN values originally computed by the AuC in step 3*.

4.4 Design Rationale

The composition of the $RAND$ value in the above scheme has been made as similar as possible to the 128-bit value $AUTN$ used to provide server-to-UE authentication in the 3G AKA protocol. This is for two main reasons. Firstly, as stated above, by adopting this approach it is hoped that implementation of, and migration to, this new scheme will be made as simple as possible for network operators. Secondly, the 3G AKA protocol is widely trusted to provide authentication, and it is hoped that trust in the novel scheme will be maximised by adopting the same approach.

The only differences between the 3G $AUTN$ and the above construction of $RAND$ are relatively minor, and are as follows.

– In 3G, the AK value is computed as a function of the $RAND$, whereas here it is necessarily only computed as a function of the last 64 bits of $RAND$. However, these last 64 bits are computed as a function of data which changes for every authentication triple, and hence the AK should still do an effective job of concealing the content it is used to mask.
– In 3G the AK is only 48 bits long, and is only used to encrypt (mask) the SQN. Here we use it to mask the SQN and the AMF, to ensure that a 'new style' $RAND$ is indistinguishable from an 'old style' randomly generated $RAND$ to any party without the key K_a.
– In 3G, the MAC is computed as a function of the $RAND$, SQN and AMF, whereas in the above scheme it is computed only as a function of SQN and AMF, again for obvious reasons. This is the only significant difference from the perspective of authenticating the network to a UE, but we argue below in Sect. 6.2 that this change does not affect the security of the protocol.

The $AUTN$ checking process proposed here and that used in 3G are essentially the same.

One other issue that merits mention is the fact that it is proposed that the SIM outputs random values if authentication fails. It is necessary for the SIM to output values of some kind, since this is part of the existing SIM-ME protocol. That is, placeholder values are required. It is important for reasons discussed below that the SIM should *not* output the correct session key K_c. The only other 'obvious' placeholder values would be to use fixed strings, but the use of random values seems less likely to be obvious if these values are sent across the network (in the case of the $SRES$ value) or used for encryption purposes (for K_c). There may be advantages in not revealing to a casual eavesdropper the fact that authentication has failed.

5 Using the Authentication Results

In the previous section we showed how the SIM can authenticate the network; that is, as a result of step 6*, the SIM will know whether or not the $RAND$ genuinely originates from the AuC and is fresh. However, we did not describe any way for the ME to know whether authentication has failed or succeeded—indeed, the ME will not understand the concept, as we are assuming it is a 'standard' GSM device.

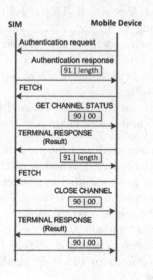

Fig. 3. SIM-ME interactions to drop the established connection

We propose that the proactive SIM feature described in Sect. 2.4 be used to achieve the desired objective. That is, in the event of a network authentication failure, when sending the $SRES$ and K_c (in this case random) values back to the ME, the SIM should signal to the phone that it has information to send. When, as a result, the ME sends the $FETCH$ command to the SIM, the SIM should respond with the $GET\ CHANNEL\ STATUS$ command to learn about the established channels in the present connection. Upon receiving the channel information in the $TERMINAL\ RESPONSE$ command, the SIM uses the response status byte in its response to request the ME to send a further $FETCH$ command. Once it receives the $FETCH$ command, the SIM responds with a $CLOSE\ CHANNEL$ command, specifying the channel information it received from the ME in response to its previous $CHANNEL\ STATUS$ command. The interactions between a SIM and an ME are summarised in Fig. 3. The STK commands issued by the SIM should cause the phone to drop the connection, and (hopefully) prevent any attempted use of the $SRES$ or key K_c. The values 90 and 91, shown in Fig. 3, represent the value of the *status byte* sent by the SIM in response to the previous command, where the value 90 means OK, and the value 91 instructs the ME to issue a $FETCH$ command to retrieve data from the SIM. The 'length' with the status byte 91 indicates the length of the data in bytes which the SIM wants to send.

6   Analysis

6.1   Deployment Issues

We next consider certain practical issues that may arise when using the scheme proposed in Sect. 4.3.

It seems that at least some GSM networks issue authentication triples in batches (see Sect. 3.3.1.1 of GSM 03.20 [10]), thereby reducing the inter-network communications overhead. Currently, the order in which GSM authentication triples are used does not matter. However, under the scheme described above, triples must be used in ascending order of SQN. This may seem problematic; however, since the requirement to use authentication datasets in the correct order already applies to the corresponding 5-tuples used in 3G, serving networks will almost certainly already be equipped to do this.

In existing GSM networks it is possible, although prohibited by the technical specifications [10], for serving networks to 're-use' authentication triples, i.e. to send the same $RAND$ value to a UE on multiple occasions. This will no longer work with the new scheme, since the SIM will detect re-use of a $RAND$ value. Arguably this is good, since re-use of $RAND$ values is highly insecure: such behaviour would allow the interceptor of a $RAND/SRES$ pair to impersonate a valid UE and perhaps steal service at that UE's expense, an attack that would be particularly effective in networks not enabling encryption.

Finally note that, in order to fully implement the scheme as described in Sect. 4, MEs need to support 'class e' STK commands, although, as discussed above, this proportion seems likely to be very high. It is not clear what proportion of mobile phones in current use support those STK commands.

6.2   Security

We divide our security discussion into three parts: confidentiality and privacy issues, authentication of network to SIM, and authentication of SIM to network.

Confidentiality and Privacy Issues. In 'standard' GSM the $RAND$ value is randomly selected, and so does not reveal anything about the identity of the phone to which it is sent. In the scheme proposed in Sect. 4.3, the $RAND$ is a function of a SIM-specific key as well as a potentially SIM-specific SQN value. However, the SQN is sent encrypted, and, assuming the functions $f1$ and $f5$ are well-designed, an interceptor will not be able to distinguish an intercepted $RAND$ computed according to the new scheme from a random value. Thus the scheme does not introduce a new threat to identity confidentiality.

The new scheme does not change the way the data confidentiality key K_c is generated, so the strength of data confidentiality is not affected.

Network-to-SIM Authentication. The novel protocol for network-to-SIM authentication bears strong similarities to the corresponding protocol for 3G.

It also conforms to the one-pass unilateral authentication mechanism specified in clause 5.1.1 of 9798-4 [15,17]. All the protocols in this standard have been formally analysed (and shown to be secure) by Basin et al. [3]. Whilst these arguments do not provide a completely watertight argument for the protocol's security, it is clearly a significant improvement over no authentication at all.

An interesting side observation deriving from the novel scheme is that the 3G and 4G AKA protocols appear to be overly complex. The randomly generated $RAND$ value sent from the network to the SIM, which is used to authenticate the response from the SIM to the network, is actually unnecessary, and the $AUTN$ value could be used in exactly the same way as the $RAND$ is currently. Whilst such a change is not possible in practice, it would have avoided the need for the AuC to generate random values and saved the need to send 16 bytes in the AKA protocol.

It is interesting to speculate why this design redundancy is present. It seems possible that the network-to-SIM authentication was added as a completely separate protocol to complement the GSM-type SIM-to-network authentication mechanism, and no-one thought how the two mechanisms could be combined and simplified (as in the mechanism we propose).

SIM-to-Network Authentication. The novel scheme does not affect how the existing SIM-to-network authentication protocol operates, except that a random $RAND$ is replaced by one which is a cryptographic function of a sequence number. The new-style $RAND$ remains unpredictable to anyone not equipped with the key K_a, and is deterministically guaranteed to be non-repeating (a property that only holds in a probabilistic way for a random $RAND$). To see why the $RAND$ is non-repeating, suppose two separate $RAND$ values sent to the same USIM incorporate the same MAC values (as necessary if they are to be the same). It follows that the AK values used to mask the $SQNs$ embedded in the $RAND$ values will also be the same and thus, since the SQN values themselves will be different, the two $RAND$ values will also differ. That is, it possesses precisely the qualities required by the existing protocol, and hence the security of SIM-to-network authentication is unaffected.

6.3   Impact on Known Attacks

We conclude our analysis of the protocol by considering how it affects possible attacks on GSM networks.

Fake Network Attacks. As discussed in Sect. 2.3, if a phone joins a fake GSM serving network, then this fake network can send any $RAND$ value it likes as part of the AKA protocol, and the UE will complete the process successfully. If the network does not enable encryption, then communications between the UE and the network will work correctly, which could enable the network to act as an eavesdropping man-in-the-middle by routing calls from the captured UE via a genuine network. This will no longer be true if the new scheme is implemented, since the SIM will instruct the ME to drop the connection when supplied with a non-genuine *RAND* value.

Of course, it may be possible for a fake network to avoid the AKA protocol altogether, and simply start communication with a newly attached UE. Whether MEs will accept unauthenticated communication is currently not clear to the authors.

Barkan-Biham-Keller Attacks. We next consider a particular type of fake network attack, namely the Barkan-Biham-Keller attack outlined in Sect. 2.3. As described there, the attack requires the re-sending of an 'old' *RAND* to a UE. The new scheme will clearly prevent such an attack, i.e. the Barkan-Biham-Keller attack will be prevented, at least in most practical scenarios.

7 Relationship to the Prior Art

This is by no means the first practical proposal for enhancing GSM to incorporate mutual authentication. Indeed, the 3G AKA protocol, discussed widely in this paper, can be regarded as doing exactly that. Although several 3GPP TSG documents [7,8] proposed the introduction of network authentication into the GSM network, none were adopted, presumably because of cost/feasibility issues. The Ericsson proposal [8] suggested transferring authentication responsibility to the terminal by implementing the core of the UMTS AKA protocol entirely in software, which in turn raised other security threats. Other proposals have been made, including by Kumar et al., [19]. However, all previous proposals are completely impractical in that they would require replacing all the GSM infrastructure. Such a major change to an existing very widely deployed scheme is simply not going to happen.

The most similar proposals to that given here are some of the other schemes using *RAND hijacking*, summarised in Sect. 3. In particular, van den Broek et al. [4] propose a similar structure for a hijacked GSM *RAND*, in their case including a sequence number, a new temporary identity for the SIM, and a MAC, all encrypted in an unspecified way. However, their objective is not to provide authentication of the network to the SIM, but to provide a way to reliably transport new identities from the AuC to the SIM.

8 Concluding Remarks

We have proposed a method for enhancing the GSM AKA protocol to provide authentication of the network to the UE, complementing the UE-to-network authentication already provided. This provides protection against some of the most serious threats to the security of GSM networks. This is achieved in a way which leaves the existing serving network infrastructure unchanged, and also does not require any changes to existing MEs (mobile phones). That is, unlike previous proposals of this general type, it is practically realisable.

A number of practical questions remain to be answered, including the proportion of MEs supporting 'class e' STK commands, the behaviour of MEs in networks which never perform the AKA protocol, and whether serving networks can be relied upon to use GSM authentication triples in the intended order. Discovering answers to these questions remains as future work.

Acknowledgements. We thank Fabian van den Broek and the anonymous reviewers for their thoughtful feedback and suggestions which have improved the paper.

References

1. SIM Toolkit http://www.bladox.cz/devel-docs/gen_stk.html. Accessed 31 May 2016
2. Barkan, E., Biham, E., Keller, N.: Instant ciphertext-only cryptanalysis of GSM encrypted communication. In: Boneh, D. (ed.) CRYPTO 2003. LNCS, vol. 2729, pp. 600–616. Springer, Heidelberg (2003). doi:10.1007/978-3-540-45146-4_35
3. Basin, D., Cremers, C., Meier, S.: Provably repairing the ISO/IEC 9798 standard for entity authentication. In: Degano, P., Guttman, J.D. (eds.) POST 2012. LNCS, vol. 7215, pp. 129–148. Springer, Heidelberg (2012). doi:10.1007/978-3-642-28641-4_8
4. van den Broek, F., Verdult, R., de Ruiter, J.: Defeating IMSI catchers. In: Ray, I., Li, N., Kruegel, C. (eds.) Proceedings of the 22nd ACM SIGSAC Conference on Computer and Communications Security, Denver, CO, USA, 12–16 October 2015, pp. 340–351. ACM (2015)
5. Choudhury, H., Choudhury, B.R., Saikia, D.K.: Enhancing user identity privacy in LTE. In: IEEE 11th International Conference on Trust, Security and Privacy in Computing and Communications (TrustCom), pp. 949–957. IEEE (2012)
6. Dupré, M.: Process to control a Subscriber Identity Module (SIM) inmobile phone system. US Patent Office (February 2004), US Patent 6,690,930, 25 May 1999
7. Ericsson: Enhancements to GSM/UMTS AKA. 3GPP TSG SA WG3 Security, S3-030542, Povoa de Varzim, Portugal, 6–10 October 2003
8. Ericsson: On the introduction and use of UMTS AKA in GSM. 3GPP TSG SA WG3Security, S3-040534, Acapulco, Mexico, 6–9 July 2004
9. European Telecommunications Standards Institute (ETSI): ETSI TS 101 267V8.18.0 (2007-06): Technical Specification; Digital cellular telecommunications system (Phase 2+); Specification of the SIM Application Toolkit (SAT) for the Subscriber Identity Module–Mobile Equipment (SIM–ME)interface (3GPP TS 11.14 version 8.18.0 Release 1999)
10. European Telecommunications Standards Institute (ETSI): ETSI-GSM Technical Specification; European digital cellular telecommunication system (phase 1); Security-related network functions (GSM 03.20), February 1992
11. European Telecommunications Standards Institute (ETSI): GSM 11.14: Technical-Specification; Digital cellular telecommunications system (Phase 2+); Specification of the SIM Application Toolkit for the Subscriber IdentityModule–Mobile Equipment (SIM–ME) interface, December 1996
12. European Telecommunications Standards Institute (ETSI): GSM TechnicalSpecification; Digital cellular telecommunication system (phase 2+); Mobile radio interface layer 3 specification (GSM 04.08), July 1996

13. European Telecommunications Standards Institute (ETSI): GSM TechnicalSpecification; Digital cellular telecommunications system (Phase 2+); Specification of the Subscriber Identity Module–Mobile Equipment (SIM–ME)interface; (GSM 11.11), July 1996

14. European Telecommunications Standards Institute (ETSI): ETSI TS 102 223 Version11.1.0; Smart Cards; Card Application Toolkit (CAT) (2012)

15. International Organization for Standardization, Genève, Switzerland:ISO/IEC 9798–4: 1999, Information technology — Security techniques— Entity authentication — Part 4: Mechanisms using a cryptographiccheck function 2nd (edn.) (1999)

16. International Organization for Standardization: ISO/IEC 7816–3; Identificationcards—Integrated circuit cards; Part 3: Cards with contacts—Electricalinterface and transmission protocols, November 2006

17. International Organization for Standardization, Genève, Switzerland:ISO/IEC 9798–4: 1999/Cor 1:2009, Technical Corrigendum 1 (2009)

18. Khan, M.S.A., Mitchell, C.: Improving air interface user privacy in mobile telephony. In: Chen, L., Matsuo, S. (eds.) SSR 2015. LNCS, vol. 9497, pp. 165–184. Springer, Heidelberg (2015). doi:10.1007/978-3-319-27152-1_9

19. Kumar, K.P., Shailaja, G., Kavitha, A., Saxena, A.: Mutual authentication and key agreement for GSM. In: 2006 International Conference on Mobile Business (ICMB 2006), Copenhagen, Denmark, 26–27 June 2006, p. 25. IEEE ComputerSociety (2006)

20. Mitchell, C.J.: Making serial number based authentication robust against loss of state. ACM Operating Syst. Rev. **34**(3), 56–59 (2000)

21. Mitchell, C.J.: The security of the GSM air interface protocol. Technical report RHUL-MA-2001-3, Mathematics Department, Royal Holloway, University of London, Egham, Surrey TW20 0EX, UK, August 2001. http://www.ma.rhul.ac.uk/techreports

22. Pagliusi, P.S.: A contemporary foreword on GSM security. In: Davida, G., Frankel, Y., Rees, O. (eds.) InfraSec 2002. LNCS, vol. 2437, pp. 129–144. Springer, Heidelberg (2002). doi:10.1007/3-540-45831-X_10

23. Vodafone: Cipher key separation for A/Gb security enhancements. 3GPP TSG SAWG3 Security, S3-030463, San Francisco, USA, 15–18 July 2003

DAPA: Degradation-Aware Privacy Analysis of Android Apps

Gianluca Barbon[1], Agostino Cortesi[2(✉)],
Pietro Ferrara[3], and Enrico Steffinlongo[2]

[1] Université Grenoble Alpes - Inria - LIG, Grenoble, France
gianluca.barbon@inria.fr
[2] Università Ca' Foscari, Venice, Italy
{cortesi,enrico.steffinlongo}@unive.it
[3] Julia Srl, Verona, Italy
pietro.ferrara@juliasoft.com

Abstract. When installing or executing an app on a smartphone, we grant it access to part of our (possibly confidential) data stored in the device. Traditional information-flow analyses aim to detect whether such information is leaked by the app to the external (untrusted) environment. The static analyser we present in this paper goes one step further. Its aim is to trace not only if information is possibly leaked (as this is almost always the case), but also how relevant such a leakage might become, as an under- and over-approximation of the actual degree of values degradation. The analysis captures both explicit dependences and implicit dependences, in an integrated approach. The analyser is built within the Abstract Interpretation framework on top of our previous work on data-centric semantics for verification of privacy policy compliance by mobile applications. Results of the experimental analysis on significant samples of the DroidBench library are also discussed.

1 Introduction

Mobile applications have access to a large variety of confidential information like geographical data, and user identifiers (e.g., IMEI and phone number). Often the access to this sensitive data is essential for the functionality of the mobile app: a navigation system needs access to the current position of the user, while a photo editor accesses the picture gallery of the user. In addition, the business model might exploit this confidential information for contextual advertisement. On the other hand, a malicious app might exploit confidential information to capture sensitive data. For instance, the user might be tracked by recording and leaking the location and identifier of the mobile device.

The current Android model guards the access to sensitive data through permissions. For instance, an app should obtain the `ACCESS_FINE_LOCATION` permission in order to access precise geographical information. Therefore, each Android app has to list the permissions it needs in the manifest. The user is then asked to accept this list before installing the app or during the first execution of the app.

© Springer International Publishing AG 2016
G. Barthe et al. (Eds.): STM 2016, LNCS 9871, pp. 32–46, 2016.
DOI: 10.1007/978-3-319-46598-2_3

However, this model allows an app to get only full or no access to a resource, and it does not take into account how the resource is accessed, and the information manipulated. In particular, the application might *degrade* the confidential information before leaking it. For instance, an app performing contextual advertisement exposing to the advertisement engine only the zip code of the user (instead of the full location) together with the user identifier. Degradation-unaware analysis would conservatively consider that the full location could be leaked, and the user could be precisely tracked.

Therefore, degradation-awareness is crucial to precisely infer what kind of and how much sensitive information is accessed, manipulated, and possibly leaked in a mobile app. In this scenario, we introduce a novel degradation-aware static analysis based on the abstract interpretation framework. Our approach tracks both explicit and implicit flows of information as well as the degradation levels of operators applied to the confidential data. We implemented our system in a prototype and applied to some representative examples taken from the Droid-Bench test suite [19]. Our experimental results show the practical interest of our solution.

The rest of the paper is structured as follows. In the rest of this Section, we introduce two motivating examples. Section 2 discusses the related work, while Sect. 3 formalizes the language, and the concrete and abstract semantics of our approach. The architecture of our tool is then described in Sects. 4 and 5 presents the experimental results. Finally, Sect. 6 concludes.

1.1   Motivating Examples

Consider the motivating example in Fig. 1, a simplified version of the ImplicitFlow1 test case from the DroidBench application set [19], an open source standard benchmark suite for information flow analyses of Android apps. This set has been created and maintained by the Secure Software Engineering Group of the Technische Universität Darmstadt. This program reads the device identifier (IMEI), and leaks it after some obfuscation steps. Obfuscation is performed by applying functions obfuscateIMEI and copyIMEI. Both the functions contain loops that are using the data derived from the IMEI as condition. This generates implicit flows which partially reveal confidential information about the original IMEI. Furthermore, it is interesting to notice that the functions and operators applied to the IMEI in the two methods are obfuscating it in different way, thus releasing implicitly different quantities of information.

In Fig. 2 another motivating example is shown. The program reads the IMEI and a user password. Then it hashes the password and it uses it as key for the encryption of the IMEI. Finally, the encrypted IMEI is explicitly released. In this example we can notice that, even if the program is leaking the password and the IMEI, it would not be possible to extract any sensitive information from the released values. Indeed the obfuscation steps performed through the hash and the encrypt operators make the reconstruction of the original values from the leaked ones hardly feasible.

```
1  class ImplicitFlow1 extends Activity {
2    static String obfuscateIMEI(String imei){
3      String result, tmp;
4      int idx;
5      String [] array;
6      result = "";
7      idx = 0;
8
9      array = toCharArray(imei);
10     while (idx < stdlib.length(imei)) {
11       tmp = array[idx];
12       if (tmp == "0")
13         result = result ++ "a";
14       elif (tmp == "1")
15         result = result ++ "b";
16       elif (tmp == "2")
17         result = result ++ "c";
18       elif (tmp == "3")
19         result = result ++ "d";
20       elif (tmp == "4")
21         result = result ++ "e";
22       elif (tmp == "5")
23         result = result ++ "f";
24       elif (tmp == "6")
25         result = result ++ "g";
26       elif (tmp == "7")
27         result = result ++ "h";
28       elif (tmp == "8")
29         result = result ++ "i";
30       elif (tmp == "9")
31         result = result ++ "j";
32       else
33         skip;
34       idx = idx + 1;
35     }
36     return result;
37   }
38
39   static String copyIMEI(String imei){
40     //ASCII values for integer: 48−57
41
42     String [] imeiAsChar, newOldIMEI;
43     String res;
44     int [] numbers;
45     int idx;
46     idx = 0;
47     numbers = new int[58];
48     while (idx < 58) {
49       numbers[idx] = idx;
50       idx = idx + 1;
51     }
52
53     imeiAsChar = toCharArray(imei);
54     newOldIMEI = new String[18];
55     idx = 0;
56     while (idx < len(imeiAsChar)) {
57       int tmp;
58       tmp = numbers[stdlib.strToInt(imeiAsChar[idx])];
59       newOldIMEI[idx] = stdlib.intToString(tmp);
60       idx = idx + 1;
61     }
62     res = "";
63     idx = 0;
64     while (idx < len(newOldIMEI)) {
65       res = res ++ newOldIMEI[idx];
66       idx = idx + 1;
67     }
68     return res;
69   }
70
71   static void writeToLog(String message){
72     Log.i("INFO", message); //sink
73   }
74
75   // @Override
76   static void onCreate(Bundle savedInstanceState) {
77     String imei;
78     String obfuscatedIMEI;
79     imei = TelephonyManager.getDeviceId(); //source
80     obfuscatedIMEI = obfuscateIMEI(imei);
81     writeToLog(obfuscatedIMEI);
82
83     obfuscatedIMEI = copyIMEI(imei);
84     writeToLog(obfuscatedIMEI);
85   }
86 }
```

Fig. 1. ImplicitFlow1

```
1  class ObfuscatedFlow extends Activity {
2
3    static void onCreate() {
4      String imei;
5      String pwd;
6
7      imei = TelephonyManager.getDeviceId();
8      pwd = stdlib.hash(readlib.readUsrPwd("5v6QewblOIMh"));
9      log( stdlib.encrypt(imei, pwd));
10   }
11 }
```

Fig. 2. ObfuscatedFlow

Both examples show the need of a sound and precise analysis able to track (i) implicit flows and (ii) how the confidential information is obfuscated, by collecting the operators and functions that are applied to the confidential datum.

2   Related Works

Static [5,21] and dynamic [12] taint analyses have been deeply investigated to enforce integrity and confidentiality properties. The main idea of this approach is to check if information coming from a source (e.g., the input of the user or the method providing the IMEI of the device) flows into a sink (e.g., the execution of a SQL query or an internet connection) without being sanitized (e.g., removing or modifying special characters or encrypting it). Taint analysis has been widely applied to Android app as well. Flowdroid [1] models precisely the Android app lifecycle, and it performs a precise static taint analysis to discover leakages of information. Taintdroid [12] is instead a precise dynamic taint analysis with a low overhead. Amandroid [24] builds up a precise interprocedural call graph and data dependence graph, and it provides a framework to develop security analyses for Android apps. However, it can detect only explicit flows, and therefore it is not expressive enough to support our approach. Similarly, DroidSafe [14] proposes an accurate static information flow analysis, and HornDroid [6] introduces a fast and precise java bytecode analysis, but they do not track implicit flows. Taint analysis can track both implicit and explicit information flows, but it propagates only one bit of information (tainted or not). Instead, our approach tracks semantic information on how confidential data is processed and degraded. Implicit flows have been treated in [2,7,15,23], but all these works are related to browsers vulnerabilities and focus on Java Script, while we apply the implicit flow notion to the Android environment. Instead, [26] tracks implicit flows on Java programs, but it does not consider degradation operators.

Various approaches have extended standard taint analysis to track more precise information for mobile software. MorphDroid [13] formalizes and implements a precise semantic analysis that infers what specific parts of confidential information are leaked (e.g., the zip code of the current location). However, it requires to manually define the semantics of degradation methods as well as tailored representation of each information of interest (e.g., IMEIs and locations), while our approach is agnostic on the type of information we deal with. BayesDroid [22] dynamically detects information leaks through Bayesian reasoning, that is, by comparing confidential data with leaked values. If the similarity among these values is above a given threshold, then BayesDroid infers that confidential data is leaked. While this approach is quite more efficient than existing taint tracking, it does not track how confidential information is degraded. Another dynamic approach is represented by AppIntent [25], a tool that records all GUI events and asks a security analyst if the data computed through a sequence of GUI events can be leaked.

A different approach was studied by Quantitative Information Flow [17]. Instead of tracking taints, this approach is aimed at inferring the quantity of information leaked by a program. On the one hand, we share with this field of research the belief that is crucial, especially for mobile applications, to track precisely the amount of information that is leaked. On the other hand, our approach targets the sequence of degradation operations applied to confidential data rather than an estimation of the quantity carried on by a value.

An orthogonal field of research has been the development of security oriented specification languages [20] to cover a large variety of aspects (e.g., access control). Some of these languages like [11] were focused on confidentiality properties. However, these languages do not take into account how values are transformed and degraded, while this is the main focus of our work.

In our previous work [3], we introduced an information flow analysis that tracked the bit (i.e., quantity) of confidential information contained by each variable in a program. Instead, in this work we take a rather different approach by collecting the degradation operators (rather than a precise quantity) applied to the information stored in each variable. In this way, we overcome several limits of our previous solution, and in particular we track the implicit flow of strict equalities comparisons.

3   Concrete and Abstract Semantics

3.1   Syntax

As said in the Introduction, the target of our analyser are Android applications. For the sake of clarity, we will introduce our approach by restricting the view on a basic imperative language, supporting arithmetic, boolean and textual expressions, and arrays. Following [8], the formalization is focused on three types of data: strings ($s \in \mathbb{S}$), integers ($n \in \mathbb{Z}$) and Booleans ($b \in \mathbb{B}$). String, integer, and Boolean expressions are respectively denoted by $sexp$, $nexp$, and $bexp$. ℓ is used to represent (possibly sensitive) data-store entries, and $lexp$ denotes label expressions. For instance, string expressions are defined by: $sexp ::= s \mid sexp_1 \circ sexp_2 \mid enc(sexp, k) \mid pre(sexp, k) \mid hash(sexp) \mid read(lexp)$, where $\circ$ represents concatenation, enc the encryption of a string with a key k, pre the prefix substring of $sexp$ of length k, $hash$ the computation of the hash value, and $read$ the function that returns the value in the data-store that corresponds to the given label.

3.2   Domain

By $adexp$ we denote an atomic data expression that tracks the explicit and implicit data sources of a specific expression. Formally, an atomic data expression $adexp$ is a set of elements $\langle \ell, L_{dir}, D_{dir}, L_{imp}, D_{imp} \rangle$ where:

- Lab is the (finite) set of labels corresponding to possibly sensitive information sources stored in the device;
- $\ell \in$ Lab;

- $L_{dir} = \{(op_j, \ell'_j) : j \in J\}$, says that the datum corresponding to label ℓ has been combined with data corresponding to labels ℓ'_j through operators op_j to get the actual value of the expression.
- $D_{dir} = \{(op_j, v_j) : j \in J\}$ says that the actual value of the expression is obtained from the datum corresponding to label ℓ by applying the operator op_j with values belonging to the set v_j.
- $L_{imp} = \{(op_j, \ell'_j) : j \in J\}$, says that the actual value of the expression implicitly depends on the datum corresponding to label ℓ combined with data corresponding to labels ℓ'_j through the operator op_j.
- $D_{imp} = \{(op_j, v_j) : j \in J\}$ says that the actual value of the expression implicitly depends on the datum corresponding to label ℓ by applying the operator op_j with values belonging to the set v_j.

The set of atomic data expressions is defined by: $\mathbb{D} = \{\langle \ell_i, L^i_{dir}, D^i_{dir}, L^i_{imp}, D^i_{imp} \rangle : i \in I \subseteq \mathbb{N}, \ell_i \in \mathsf{Lab}, L^i_k \subseteq \wp(\mathsf{Op} \times \mathsf{Lab}), D^i_k \subseteq \wp(\mathsf{Op} \times \mathsf{V})\}$, where Lab is the set of labels, and Op is the set of operators, and V contains sets of uniform values (integer intervals, sets of string, etc.). For $\ell \in \mathsf{Lab}$, we denote by $\hat{\ell}$ the (constant) value stored in ℓ.

An environment relates variables to their values as well as to the set of atomic data expressions. Formally, $\Sigma = \Phi \times \Psi$, where (i) $\Phi : \mathbf{Var} \longrightarrow (\mathbb{Z} \cup \mathbb{S} \cup \{\text{true, false}\})$ is the usual environment that tracks value information, and (ii) $\Psi : \mathbf{Var} \longrightarrow \wp(\mathbb{D})$ maps local variables in $\mathbf{Var}$ to a set $\{\langle \ell_i, L^i_{dir}, D^i_{dir}, L^i_{imp}, D^i_{imp} \rangle : i \in I\}$. The special symbol $\star$ represents data coming from the user input and from the constants of the program.

Observe that the definition above refines [3], by introducing the explicit and implicit degradation sets that allow to keep track of the values the operators combine with the labels in Lab.

3.3   Concrete Semantics

We denote by $S_N : Nexp \times \Sigma \rightarrow \mathbb{Z}$, $S_S : Sexp \times \Sigma \rightarrow \mathbb{S}$, and $S_B : Bexp \times \Sigma \rightarrow \{\text{true, false}\}$ the standard concrete evaluations of numerical, string, and Boolean expressions. In addition, $S_L : Lexp \times \Sigma \rightarrow \mathsf{Lab}$ returns a data label given a label expression. An array c of length n is represented by $n+1$ variables: $c_{length}, c[0], \ldots c[n-1]$ where c_{length} stores the value of the length of the array c.

The semantics of expressions on atomic data $S_A : sexp \times \Sigma \rightarrow \mathbb{S} \times \wp(\mathbb{D})$ is described in Table 1, for some basic unary and binary operators (like array selection, encryption enc and string prefix pre operators). Similar rules for numerical and boolean expressions are omitted here for the sake of space. Observe that the only new implicit flow is introduced when evaluating an array element, as the expression yielding the index may carry information that implicitly flows when accessing the corresponding array element.

The operator $\uplus$ is defined on the degradation elements as follows: $D_1 \uplus D_2 = \{(op, S_1 \cup S_2) : (op, S_1) \in D_1, (op, S_2) \in D_2\}$.

The operator $\diamond$ allows to inherit implicit dependences. Let $A = (a, \{\langle \ell^1_i, L^{1i}_{dir}, D^{1i}_{dir}, L^{1i}_{imp}, D^{1i}_{imp} : i \in I\}\rangle)$ and $B = (b, \{\langle \ell^2_j, L^{2j}_{dir}, D^{2j}_{dir}, L^{2j}_{imp}, D^{2j}_{imp} \rangle :$

$j \in J\}$). $A \diamond B$ captures the fact that the expression represented by A implicitly reveals data contained in the expression represented by B. Formally, $A \diamond B = (a, \{\langle \ell_i^1, L_{dir}^{1i}, D_{dir}^{1i}, \bigcup_{j \in J}(L_{dir}^{2j} \cup L_{imp}^{2j}) \cup L_{imp}^{1i}, \biguplus_{j \in J}(D_{dir}^{2j} \uplus D_{imp}^{2j}) \uplus D_{imp}^{1i}\rangle : i \in I\}$.

Given a statement c, we denote by $\mathtt{Def}(c)$ the set of variable that are assigned in the statement c.

The (concrete) semantics of statements is depicted in (Fig. 3). Observe that implicit flows are introduced in correspondence of *if* and *while* statements and arrays (Fig. 3).

Table 1. Semantics of textual expressions on atomic data

$$
\begin{aligned}
S_A[\![s]\!](v,a) &= (S_S[\![s]\!](v), \{\langle \star, \emptyset, \emptyset, \emptyset, \emptyset \rangle\}) \\
S_A[\![n]\!](v,a) &= (S_N[\![n]\!](v), \{\langle \star, \emptyset, \emptyset, \emptyset, \emptyset \rangle\}) \\
S_A[\![x]\!](v,a) &= (v(x), a(x)) \\
S_A[\![read(lexp)]\!](v,a) &= \text{let } \ell = S_L[\![lexp]\!](v,a) \text{ in } (\hat{\ell}, \{\langle \ell, \emptyset, \emptyset, \emptyset, \emptyset \rangle\}) \\
S_A[\![c[nexp]]\!](v,a) &= \text{let } (n,d) = S_A[\![nexp]\!](v,a) \text{ in } (v(c[n]), a(c[n]) \diamond d) \\
S_A[\![enc(sexp, n)]\!](v,a) &= \text{let } (t, \{\langle \ell_i, L_{dir}^i, D_{dir}^i, L_{imp}^i, D_{imp}^i \rangle : i \in I\}) = S_A[\![sexp]\!](v,a) \text{ in } \\
&\quad (enc(t,n), \\
&\quad \{\langle \ell_i, L_{dir}^i \cup \{(enc, \ell_i)\}, D_{dir}^i \uplus \{(enc, \{n\})\}, L_{imp}^i, D_{imp}^i \rangle : i \in I\}) \\
S_A[\![sexp_1 \circ sexp_2]\!](v,a) &= \text{let } (t_1, \{\langle \ell_i^1, L_{dir}^{1i}, D_{dir}^{1i}, L_{imp}^{1i}, D_{imp}^{1i} \rangle) : i \in I\}) = S_A[\![sexp_1]\!](v,a) \text{ and } \\
&\quad \text{let } (t_2, \{\langle \ell_j^2, L_{dir}^{2j}, D_{dir}^{2j}, L_{imp}^{2j}, D_{imp}^{2j} \rangle) : j \in J\}) = S_A[\![sexp_2]\!](v,a) \text{ in } \\
&\quad (t_1 \circ t_2, \\
&\quad \bigcup_{i \in I, j \in J}(\{\langle \ell_i^1, L_{dir}^{1i} \cup \{(\circ, \ell_j^2)\}, D_{dir}^{1i} \uplus \{(\circ, \{t_2\})\}, L_{imp}^{1i}, D_{imp}^{1i} \rangle)\} \cup \\
&\quad \{\langle \ell_j^2, L_{dir}^{2j} \cup \{(\circ, \ell_i^1)\}, D_{dir}^{2j} \uplus \{(\circ, \{t_1\})\}, L_{imp}^{2j}, D_{imp}^{2j} \rangle)\}) \\
S_A[\![pre(sexp, n)]\!](v,a) &= \text{let } (t, \{\langle \ell_i, L_{dir}^i, D_{dir}^i, L_{imp}^i, D_{imp}^i \rangle : i \in I\}) = S_A[\![sexp]\!](v,a) \text{ in } \\
&\quad (pre(t,n), \\
&\quad \{\langle \ell_i, L_{dir}^i \cup \{(pre, \ell_i)\}, D_{dir}^i \uplus \{(pre, \{n\})\}, L_{imp}^i, D_{imp}^i \rangle : i \in I\})
\end{aligned}
$$

$$
\begin{aligned}
S[\![x := sexp]\!](v,a) &= \text{let } (t,d) = S_A[\![sexp]\!](v,a) \text{ in } \\
&\quad (v[x \mapsto t], a[x \mapsto d]) \\
S[\![c[nexp] := sexp]\!](v,a) &= \text{let } (t, d_1) = S_A[\![sexp]\!](v,a) \text{ and let } (n, d_2) = S_A[\![nexp]\!](v,a) \text{ in } \\
&\quad (v[c[n] \mapsto t], a[c[n] \mapsto d_1 \diamond d_2]) \\
S[\![input(x)]\!](v,a) &= \text{let } v_{read} \text{ be the input value in } \\
&\quad (v[x \mapsto v_{read}], a[x \mapsto \{\langle \star, \emptyset, \emptyset, \emptyset, \emptyset \rangle\}]) \\
S[\![skip]\!](v,a) &= (v,a) \\
S[\![send(sexp)]\!](v,a) &= (v,a) \\
S[\![c_1; c_2]\!](v,a) &= S[\![c_2]\!](S[\![c_1]\!](v,a)) \\
S[\![if\ b\ then\ c_1\ else\ c_2]\!](v,a) &= \text{let } (v_1, a_1) = S[\![c_1]\!](v,a) \text{ and let } (v_2, a_2) = S[\![c_2]\!](v,a) \text{ in } \\
&\quad \begin{cases} (v_1, a_1') & \text{if } S_A[\![b]\!](v,a) = (\text{true}, d) \\ (v_2, a_2') & \text{if } S_A[\![b]\!](v,a) = (\text{false}, d) \end{cases} \\
&\quad \text{where } \begin{cases} a_1'(x) = a_1(x) \diamond d & \text{if } x \in \mathtt{Def}(c_1) \\ a_1'(x) = a_1(x) & \text{otherwise} \end{cases} \\
&\quad \text{and } \begin{cases} a_2'(x) = a_2(x) \diamond d & \text{if } x \in \mathtt{Def}(c_2) \\ a_2'(x) = a_2(x) & \text{otherwise} \end{cases} \\
S[\![while\ c_1\ do\ c_2]\!](v,a) &= S[\![if\ (c_1)\ then\ (c_2; while\ c_1\ do\ c_2)\ else\ skip]\!](v,a)
\end{aligned}
$$

Fig. 3. Concrete semantics of statements

Example 1. Consider the following program:

(1) $x = read(\ell)$;
(2) $input(y)$;
(3) if $(x < y)\{$
(4) $x = x + y$; $\}$
(5) $z = x + 1$;

By applying the rules above, assuming that $\hat{\ell} = 3$ and that the input value assigned to y is 4, we get:

$$
\begin{aligned}
x_{(1)} &\mapsto (3, \{\langle \ell, \emptyset, \emptyset, \emptyset, \emptyset \rangle\}) \\
y_{(2)} &\mapsto (4, \{\langle \star, \emptyset, \emptyset, \emptyset, \emptyset \rangle\}) \\
(x < y)_{(3)} &\mapsto (\text{true}, \{\langle \ell, \{(<, \star)\}, \{(<, \{4\})\}, \emptyset, \emptyset \rangle, \langle \star, \{(<, \ell)\}, \{(<, \{3\})\}, \emptyset, \emptyset \rangle\}) \\
(x + y)_{(4)} &\mapsto (7, \{\langle \ell, \{(+, \star)\}, \{(+, \{4\})\}, \emptyset, \emptyset \}, \{\langle \star, \{(+, \ell)\}, \{(+, \{3\})\}, \emptyset, \emptyset \}\}) \\
z_{(5)} &\mapsto (8, \{\langle \ell, \{(+, \star)\}, \{(+, \{1, 4\})\}, \{(<, \star), (<, \ell)\}, \{(<, \{3, 4\})\}\}, \\
&\qquad\quad \langle \star, \{(+, \ell)\}, \{(+, \{1, 3\})\}, \{(<, \star), (<, \ell)\}, \{(<, \{3, 4\})\}\})
\end{aligned}
$$

3.4 Abstract Semantics

By following the Abstract Interpretation framework, in order to lift the concrete semantics to an abstract semantics, suitable abstractions of the domains of concrete values should be given, as well as operators on such abstractions that safely over-approximate the effects of the corresponding concrete ones. In our actual implementation, numerical values are abstracted in the lattice of `Intervals` [18], while textual values are abstracted by the `Prefix` domain [9,10]. The abstract semantics of expressions and statements strictly follows the concrete one, with the usual exceptions: (1) in the evaluation of the conditional and iterative statements the least upper bound operator is applied when the truth value of the conditional expression cannot be inferred, and (2) a threshold widening operator is applied on intervals when evaluating while loops to guarantee termination of the analysis, as the domain of intervals does not satisfy the ascending chain condition.

The least upper bound operator of abstract atomic data is $\sqcup$ [8]. Abstraction and concretization functions are inherited from [8]. The *join* operator is used to define the least upper bound of abstract values (numerical, boolean and string). The abstract semantics of statements are depicted in (Fig. 4). For simplicity, the abstract semantics of expressions are not explicitly described, since they corresponds to the concrete ones lifted to the abstract environment. Only the abstract semantic for the array *get* is defined here:

$$
\begin{aligned}
S_A^a[\![c[nexp]]\!](v^a, a^a) = \text{let } (n^a, d^a) = S_A[\![nexp]\!](v^a, a^a) \text{ in} \\
\left(\bigsqcup_i v^a(c[i]), \left(\bigsqcup_i a^a(c[i]) \right) \diamond d^a \right) \mid i \in \gamma(n^a) \wedge i \in [0, \ldots, c_{length}]
\end{aligned}
$$

Given an abstract element $(\tilde{a}, \{\langle \ell_i, \tilde{L}_{dir}^i, \tilde{D}_{dir}^i, \tilde{L}_{imp}^i, \tilde{D}_{imp}^i \rangle : i \in I\})$, it represents concrete expressions whose value is represented by $\tilde{a}$, and that may contain fingerprints of values stored in ℓ_i. An over-approximation of the operations and values under which such (direct or implicit) fingerprints may be hidden in that value are collected in the last four components.

Example 2. Consider again the program of Example 1. Assume that the value of ℓ is bounded in the interval $[2, 4]$, and that the input value assigned to y is

$$S^a [\![x := sexp]\!](v^a, a^a) = \text{let } (t^a, d^a) = S_A^a [\![sexp]\!](v^a, a^a) \text{ in}$$
$$(v^a[x \mapsto t^a], a^a[x \mapsto d^a])$$
$$S^a [\![c[nexp] := sexp]\!](v^a, a^a) = \text{let } (t^a, d_1^a) = S_A^a [\![sexp]\!](v^a, a^a) \text{ and}$$
$$\text{let } (n^a, d_2^a) = S_A^a [\![nexp]\!](v^a, a^a) \text{ in}$$
$$(\textstyle\bigsqcup_i v(c[i] \mapsto t^a), \textstyle\bigsqcup_i a(c[i] \mapsto (d_1^a \diamond d_2^a)))$$
$$\mid i \in \gamma(n^a) \wedge i \in [0, \dots, c_{length}]$$
$$S^a [\![input(x)]\!](v^a, a^a) = \text{let } v_{read}^a \text{ be an abstract input value in}$$
$$(v^a[x \mapsto v_{read}^a], a^a[x \mapsto \{\langle \star, \emptyset, \emptyset, \emptyset, \emptyset \rangle\}])$$
$$S^a [\![skip]\!](v^a, a^a) = (v^a, a^a)$$
$$S^a [\![send(sexp)]\!](v^a, a^a) = (v^a, a^a)$$
$$S^a [\![c_1; c_2]\!](v^a, a^a) = S[\![c_2]\!](S[\![c_1]\!](v^a, a^a))$$
$$S^a [\![\text{if } b \text{ then } c_1 \text{ else } c_2]\!](v^a, a^a) = \text{let } (v_1^a, a_1^a) = S^a [\![c_1]\!](v^a, a^a) \text{ and let } (v_2^a, a_2^a) = S^a [\![c_2]\!](v^a, a^a)$$
$$\text{in } (join(v_1^a, v_2^a), a')$$
$$\text{where } S_A^a [\![b]\!](v^a, a^a) = (t, d^a)$$
$$\text{and } \begin{cases} a'(x) = \{(a_1^a(x) \diamond d^a) \sqcup a_2^a(x)\} & \text{if } x \in \text{Def}(c_1) \\ a'(x) = \{a_1^a(x) \sqcup (a_2^a(x) \diamond d^a)\} & \text{if } x \in \text{Def}(c_2) \\ a'(x) = \{(a_1^a(x) \diamond d^a) \sqcup (a_2^a(x) \diamond d^a)\} \\ \quad \text{if } x \in \text{Def}(c_1) \wedge x \in \text{Def}(c_2) \\ a'(x) = \{a_1^a(x) \sqcup a_2^a(x)\} & \text{otherwise} \end{cases}$$
$$S^a [\![\text{while } c_1 \text{ do } c_2]\!](v, a) = fix(S[\![\text{if } (c_1) \text{ then } (c_2; \text{while } c_1 \text{ do } c_2) \text{ else } skip]\!](v, a))$$

Fig. 4. Abstract semantics of statements

bounded by the interval $[3, 5]$. By applying the abstract semantics rules we get:

$$x_{(1)} \mapsto ([2, 4], \{\langle \ell, \emptyset, \emptyset, \emptyset, \emptyset \rangle\})$$
$$y_{(2)} \mapsto ([3, 5], \{\langle \star, \emptyset, \emptyset, \emptyset, \emptyset \rangle\})$$
$$(x < y)_{(3)} \mapsto (\top, \{\langle \ell, \{(<, \star)\}, \{(<, [3, 5])\}, \emptyset, \emptyset\rangle, \langle \star, \{(<, \ell)\}, \{(<, [2, 4])\}, \emptyset, \emptyset\rangle\})$$
$$(x + y)_{(4)} \mapsto ([5, 9], \{\langle \ell, \{(+, \star)\}, \{(+, [3, 5])\}, \emptyset, \emptyset\rangle, \{\langle \star, \{(+, \ell)\}, \{(+, [2, 4])\}, \emptyset, \emptyset\rangle\})$$
$$z_{(5)} \mapsto ([3, 10], \{\langle \ell, \{(+, \star)\}, \{+, [1, 5]\})\}, \{(<, \star), (<, \ell)\}, \{(<, [3, 5])\}\rangle\},$$
$$\langle \star, \{(+, \ell)\}, \{(+, [1, 4])\}, \{(<, \star), (<, \ell)\}, \{(<, [3, 5])\}\rangle\}).$$

Observe that the value of the expression $(x < y)_{(3)}$ is the top element of the boolean lattice $\{\bot, \text{true}, \text{false}, \top\}$ representing the fact that the abstraction does not allow to predict the truth value of such expression. Therefore, while computing $z_{(5)}$ both the branches of the conditional statement will be considered.

If we look at the abstract evaluation of $z_{(5)}$, we can say that under the mentioned initial conditions:

- the value of z at point (5) will definitely belong to the interval $[3, 10]$;
- the value of z may depend on either the value stored in ℓ, or from program constants, or from input values, but no other confidential information stored in $\ell_j \neq \ell$ may have affected the value of z, neither directly nor by implicit information flow;
- the only operator that might have been used to get the value of z out of ℓ is the numerical addition, with arguments that were never out of the interval $[1, 5]$;
- the possible implicit information flow from ℓ to the value of z can be only due to a strict ordering comparison with values in the interval $[3, 5]$.

4 The DAPA Tool

We developed DAPA, a static analysis tool based on the abstract interpretation framework. We adopted the Scala language for the development of the tool. Our tool is able to analyse both explicit and implicit flows and obtain a set of Degradation Elements from an Android app source code (translated in our language). It also computes results of functions and expressions in the form of abstract values, in order to collect them through the Degradation Elements. One of the main strength of the analyser is the capability to collect conditions of *If* and *While* constructs as implicit statements. This allows to propagate the implicit information flow throughout the analysis and to check whether confidential labels are present in the form of implicit information in sink points.

The analyser is conceived in such a way to be modular and easily extensible in case of future improvements. We adopted Scala traits to mask the underlying implementation of the atomic data expression and lattices. This means that it is possible to modify the used abstraction by just providing an alternative implementation of the abstract types to the analyser, ensuring the modularity of the whole project. Standard join, meet and widening methods from the abstract interpretation framework are provided. In addition to these methods, a *union* function for atomic data expression is introduced, which allows to collect different behaviours for the over and under approximation. It performs the meet for the under approximation and the join for the over approximation of the elements of the atomic data expression. Operators present in statements are collected through an update function, which ensures the insertion of the operator in the atomic data expressions of all the involved labels. This method implements the ⊎ operator defined in Sect. 3. The ◇ operator is also implemented in order to produce implicit flows.

Three types of basic abstract values are implemented: boolean, numerical and string, following the ones defined in the theory and adopting solutions described in [4,16,18]. Also abstract values implementation is hidden through the use of common interface, ensuring modularity.

The output of DAPA consists in a list of *adexp* as defined in Sect. 3. This list of *adexp* highlights the degradation applied to every confidential label in the analysed app, by listing all the functions and operators applied to it, along with other labels involved as parameters. Specific information about the implicit flows will also appear in the output. A detailed explanation of the output is provided in Sect. 5.

Multiplicity of the Degradation Element. In the tool the *Degradation Element* is extended with a multiplicity notion, in order to associate the times it appears in a loop, allowing to track the number of repetitions of the element. These ones are tracked through an abstract interval, allowing proper handling during loop widening. This will contain the abstract number of times that such operator has been evaluated, giving a useful information to be associated to the degradation of the current label. This allows to abstract the operators present inside the scope of the loop. We also introduce information regarding position in the code of the statement in order to have an unambiguous element. The tool is thus more precise with respect to the semantics.

Widening of While Loops. While loops are analysed through the use of widening from the abstract interpretation framework. A threshold (or guard) can be modified by the user in order to stop loop iterations and start widening of the remaining ones. The under approximation in the resulting expressions will contain the smallest possible number of iterations (possibly, no iterations at all). Instead, the over approximation will be the set of all the possible iterations (the maximum possible number of iterations) of the loop.

5   Results

In this Section we present a qualitative analysis of the DAPA tool. Quantitative evaluation has also been made, in order to evaluate performances.

5.1   Motivating Examples

Results of the analysis of the motivating example ImplicitFlow1, introduced in Sect. 1, are here described. A special *star* label is used to collect every degradation that does not belong to any labels. The IMEI_0 label is the only confidential label used in this example. It contains the IMEI value associated to a device.

Figure 5 contains the output of the analysis of ImplicitFlow1. The upper part of the figure corresponds to the first release of the IMEI with method `writeToLog`, while the lower one corresponds to the second release. The two calls to this methods correspond to two different obfuscation methods usage, the `obfuscateIMEI` and the `copyIMEI` respectively. These two methods have different obfuscation powers. Our tool was able to track these differences by reporting the usage of different operators.

```
Explicit: []
Implicit: [IMEI_0 ->
    S: [{(length_1, IMEI_0), (<_1, star), (toCharArray_1, IMEI_0), (==_2, star)}:
        {(length_1, IMEI_0), (<_1, star), (toCharArray_1, IMEI_0), (==_2, star)}]
    D: [[(length_1, ImplicitFlow1.java@10.22) -> ({"*"}, [1,1]),
        (<_1, ImplicitFlow1.java@10.20) -> ([0,+oo], [1,1]),
        (toCharArray_1, ImplicitFlow1.java@9.17) -> ({"*"}, [1,1]),
        (==_2, ImplicitFlow1.java@12.21) -> ({"0"}, [1,1]):
        [(toCharArray_1, ImplicitFlow1.java@9.17) -> ({"*"}, [1,1]),
        (==_2, ImplicitFlow1.java@12.21) -> ({"0"}, [1,1]),
        (<_1, ImplicitFlow1.java@10.20) -> ([0,+oo], [1,1]),
        (length_1, ImplicitFlow1.java@10.22) -> ({"*"}, [1,1]),
        (==_2, ImplicitFlow1.java@22.23) -> ({"5"}, [1,1])]]]]

Explicit: []
Implicit: [IMEI_0 ->
    S: [{(toCharArray_1, IMEI_0), (strToInt_1, IMEI_0), (<_1, star)}:
        {(toCharArray_1, IMEI_0), (strToInt_1, IMEI_0), (<_1, star)}]
    D: [[(toCharArray_1, ImplicitFlow1.java@53.22) -> ({"*"}, [1,1]),
        (strToInt_1, ImplicitFlow1.java@58.27) -> ({"*"}, [1,1]),
        (<_1, ImplicitFlow1.java@56.20) -> ([0,+oo], [1,1]):
        [(toCharArray_1, ImplicitFlow1.java@53.22) -> ({"*"}, [1,1]),
        (strToInt_1, ImplicitFlow1.java@58.27) -> ({"*"}, [1,1]),
        (<_1, ImplicitFlow1.java@56.20) -> ([0,+oo], [1,1])]]]]
```

Fig. 5. ImplicitFlow1 results

Results are split into two sections, S and D, which in turn are divided into two parts by a colon, for under and over approximation respectively. The S part contains the atomic data expression composed by couples (*operator, label*), as defined in [3]. This allows to know which are the label that were combined through the related operator. The D part contains the degradation elements. It shows the operator, the position in the code, the abstract content and the number of iterations. Operators are annotated with an index. For instance, in the line 56 of the motivating example, the condition

idx < len(imeiAsChar)

will degradate IMEI by < _1 of idx, that is in position 1 of the arguments of <. While idx will be degraded by < _2 of imeiAsChar, but this is not listed in Fig. 5 since it belongs to the *star* label. The same holds for the S part. This allows to obtain an accurate explanation of the obfuscation. The position is composed of the name of the file, the number of row and the column in the code. Abstract values are related to the type of the label: numerical values are described through intervals, contained in square brackets, while strings are contained in braces. In this example, iterations are interval [1,1], because there were no loops, thus no repeated elements. The user can in this way know which were the applied methods and operators used to obfuscate the IMEI.

Please notice that the only existing explicit flow is related to the special label *star* (not reported in the figure for the sake of space). This is because the value returned by the obfuscating methods does not explicitly contains the IMEI label. On the other hand, this value contains implicit information about the IMEI label. This is correctly tracked by the DAPA analyser.

```
Explicit:
[IMEI_0 -> S: [{(encrypt_2, pwd_0)}:
              {(encrypt_2, pwd_0)}]
          D: [[(encrypt_2, main/resources/StmDegr.java@12.13) -> ({"*"}, [1,1])]:
              [(encrypt_2, main/resources/StmDegr.java@12.13) -> ({"*"}, [1,1])]],

  pwd_0 -> S: [{(hash_1, pwd_0), (encrypt_1, IMEI_0)}:
              {(hash_1, pwd_0), (encrypt_1, IMEI_0)}]
          D: [[(hash_1, main/resources/StmDegr.java@10.15) -> ({"*"}, [1,1]),
              (encrypt_1, main/resources/StmDegr.java@12.13) -> ({"*"}, [1,1])]:
              [(hash_1, main/resources/StmDegr.java@10.15) -> ({"*"}, [1,1]),
              (encrypt_1, main/resources/StmDegr.java@12.13) -> ({"*"}, [1,1])]]]
```

Fig. 6. ObfuscatedFlow results

In a similar way, in Fig. 6 the analysis results for the example in Fig. 2 are presented. Since no implicit flow is produced, only the explicit one is reported. The atomic data expression part S shows that an hash operator is applied to the password label. Then this hashed password is used by the encrypt operator as key to obfuscate the IMEI label.

These examples show that our analysis is able to track every degradation operation applied to confidential data.

5.2 Quantitative Evaluation: The DroidBench Test Set

The DAPA analyser has been tested using a set of simple Android-like apps from the DroidBench application set [19]. Where needed, the original Java code has been modified in order to be recognised by the analyser, since it still lacks support for actual libraries and some typical Java elements. Similar considerations must be taken into account for the Android libraries. The table in Fig. 7 describes analyser results in terms of time performances and detected leakage (explicit and implicit). The computer used for tests execution was equipped with an Intel i5 450M processor and 8 GB of DDR2 RAM.

file name	time	explicit leakage	implicit leakage
ArrayAccess1	151ms	no	no
ArrayAccess2	212ms	no	no
ArrayCopy1*	200ms	yes	no
ArrayToString1	237ms	yes	no
DirectLeak1	166ms	yes	no
ImplicitFlow1	1838ms	no	yes
ImplicitFlow2*	300ms	no	yes
LoopExample1	488ms	yes	yes
LoopExample2	682ms	yes	yes
SourceCodeSpecific1	392ms	yes	no
StringToCharArray1	424ms	yes	yes
UnreachableCode	33ms	no	no

Fig. 7. DroidBench results

Even if the code in test cases contains some small differences with the original ones (with the exceptions of ArrayCopy1 and ImplicitFLow2, that were heavily modified), the DAPA tool was able to discover correctly explicit or implicit leaks when present.

5.3 Results Discussion

A quantitative test comparison with other existing tools, such as FlowDroid, DroidSafe, BayesDroid, was not possible. This is because the testing step has been made on simple basic applications. Nevertheless, the results obtained by DAPA are richer from a qualitative point of view when comparing to other tools. This is because we are performing a privacy degradation aware analysis, while common tools are more focused on pure taint analysis. This means that DAPA collects all the operations applied to sensible data, when such data are released. Moreover, when no degradations are applied to the confidential data, DAPA returns in any case richer results, since it is also capable to track implicit flows.

6   Conclusions

We introduced a new static analyser for information flow analysis of Android apps, that captures both explicit and implicit leakage and support degradation awareness. Our preliminary experimental results show the effectiveness of this approach, and the modularity of the analyser allows to tune the accuracy and efficiency of the analysis by plugging in more or less sophisticated abstract domains.

Future improvements will consist in implementing objects in our language. A complete move to Java will be considered too, since it will introduce the possibility to analyse real Android app, without the need of conversions. Moreover, the evaluation of policies based on confidentiality and obfuscation notions [8], already captured by the current analyser, should be considered in the future.

Finally, we would also consider to reuse the bit quantity introduced in [3] in order to define a function able to compute the final exported explicit and implicit quantity as a result of the degradation. Since the definition of this function would have required a considerable research effort about operators information release, it was outside the scope of this work, and we planned it only as possible future improvement.

References

1. Arzt, S., Rasthofer, S., Fritz, C., Bodden, E., Bartel, A., Klein, J., Traon, Y.L., Octeau, D., McDaniel, P.: FlowDroid: precise context, flow, field, object-sensitive and lifecycle-aware taint analysis for android apps. In: PLDI. ACM (2014)
2. Bandhakavi, S., King, S.T., Madhusudan, P., Winslett, M.: Vex: vetting browser extensions for security vulnerabilities. In: USENIX Security. USENIX Association (2010)
3. Barbon, G., Cortesi, A., Ferrara, P., Pistoia, M., Tripp, O.: Privacy analysis of android apps: implicit flows and quantitative analysis. In: Saeed, K., Homenda, W. (eds.) CISIM 2015. LNCS, vol. 9339, pp. 3–23. Springer, Heidelberg (2015). doi:10.1007/978-3-319-24369-6_1
4. Bohlender, G., Kulisch, U.W.: Definition of the arithmetic operations and comparison relations for an interval arithmetic. Reliable Comput. 15(1), 36–42 (2011)
5. Braghin, C., Cortesi, A., Focardi, R.: Control flow analysis of mobile ambients with security boundaries. In: Jacobs, B., Rensink, A. (eds.) FMOODS 2002. ITIFIP, vol. 81, pp. 197–212. Springer, Heidelberg (2002). doi:10.1007/978-0-387-35496-5_14
6. Calzavara, S., Grishchenko, I., Maffei, M.: Horndroid: practical and sound static analysis of android applications by SMT solving. In: EuroS&P. IEEE (2016)
7. Chugh, R., Meister, J.A., Jhala, R., Lerner, S.: Staged information flow for javascript. SIGPLAN Not. 44(6), 50–62 (2009)
8. Cortesi, A., Ferrara, P., Pistoia, M., Tripp, O.: Datacentric semantics for verification of privacy policy compliance by mobile applications. In: Jobstmann, B., Leino, K.R.M. (eds.) VMCAI 2016. LNCS, vol. 9583, pp. 61–79. Springer, Heidelberg (2015). doi:10.1007/978-3-662-46081-8_4
9. Costantini, G., Ferrara, P., Cortesi, A.: Static analysis of string values. In: Butler, M., Conchon, S., Zaïdi, F. (eds.) ICFEM 2015. LNCS, vol. 9407, pp. 505–521. Springer, Heidelberg (2011). doi:10.1007/978-3-642-24559-6_34

10. Costantini, G., Ferrara, P., Cortesi, A.: A suite of abstract domains for static analysis of string values. Softw. Pract. Exper. **45**(2), 245–287 (2015)
11. Cuppens, F., Demolombe, R.: A deontic logic for reasoning about confidentiality. In: DEON. ACM (1996)
12. Enck, W., Gilbert, P., Chun, B.-G., Cox, L.P., Jung, J., McDaniel, P., Sheth, A.: TaintDroid: an information-flow tracking system for realtime privacy monitoring on smartphones. In: OSDI (2010)
13. Ferrara, P., Tripp, O., Pistoia, M.: Morphdroid: fine-grained privacy verification. In: ACSAC (2015)
14. Gordon, M.I., Kim, D., Perkins, J., Gilham, L., Nguyen, N., Rinard, M.: Information-flow analysis of android applications in droidsafe. In: NDSS. ACM (2015)
15. Just, S., Cleary, A., Shirley, B., Hammer, C.: Information flow analysis for javascript. In: PLASTIC. ACM (2011)
16. Kulisch, U.W.: Complete interval arithmetic and its implementation on the computer. In: Cuyt, A., Krämer, W., Luther, W., Markstein, P. (eds.) Numerical Validation in Current Hardware Architectures. LNCS, vol. 5492, pp. 7–26. Springer, Heidelberg (2009)
17. McCamant, S., Ernst, M.D.: Quantitative information flow as network flow capacity. In: PLDI. ACM (2008)
18. Miné, A.: Weakly relational numerical abstract domains. Ph.D. thesis, École Polytechnique, December 2004. http://www-apr.lip6.fr/~mine/these/these-color.pdf
19. Secure software engineering group - Ec Spride. DroidBench. http://sseblog.ec-spride.de/tools/droidbench/
20. Swamy, N., Corcoran, B.J., Hicks, M.: Fable: a language for enforcing user-defined security policies. In: S&P. IEEE (2009)
21. Tripp, O., Pistoia, M., Fink, S.J., Sridharan, M., Weisman, O.: TAJ: effective taint analysis of web applications. In: PLDI (2009)
22. Tripp, O., Rubin, J.: A Bayesian approach to privacy enforcement in smartphones. In: USENIX Security (2014)
23. Vogt, P., Nentwich, F., Jovanovic, N., Kirda, E., Krügel, C., Vigna, G.: Cross site scripting prevention with dynamic data tainting and static analysis. In: NDSS. The Internet Society (2007)
24. Wei, F., Roy, S., Ou, X., Robby.: Amandroid: a precise and general inter-component data flow analysis framework for security vetting of android apps. In: CCS. ACM (2014)
25. Yang, Z., Yang, M., Zhang, Y., Gu, G., Ning, P., Wang, X.S.: AppIntent: analyzing sensitive data transmission in android for privacy leakage detection. In: CCS. ACM (2013)
26. Zanioli, M., Ferrara, P., Cortesi, A.: SAILS: static analysis of information leakage with sample. In: SAC. ACM (2012)

Access Control Enforcement
for Selective Disclosure of Linked Data

Tarek Sayah, Emmanuel Coquery, Romuald Thion[✉], and Mohand-Saïd Hacid

Université de Lyon, CNRS, Université Lyon 1,
LIRIS, UMR5205, 69622 Lyon, France
{tarek.sayah,emmanuel.coquery,
romuald.thion,mohand-said.hacid}@liris.cnrs.fr

Abstract. The Semantic Web technologies enable Web-scaled data linking between large RDF repositories. However, it happens that organizations cannot publish their whole datasets but only some subsets of them, due to ethical, legal or confidentiality considerations. Different user profiles may have access to different authorized subsets. In this case, selective disclosure appears as a promising incentive for linked data. In this paper, we show that modular, fine-grained and efficient selective disclosure can be achieved on top of existing RDF stores. We use a data-annotation approach to enforce access control policies. Our results are grounded on previously established formal results proposed in [14]. We present an implementation of our ideas and we show that our solution for selective disclosure scales, is independent of the user query language, and incurs reasonable overhead at runtime.

Keywords: RDF · Authorization · Enforcement · Linked Data

1 Introduction

The Linked Data movement [5] (aka Web of Data) is about using the Web to create typed links between data from different sources. Technically, Linked Data refers to a set of best practices for publishing and connecting structured data on the Web in such a way that it is machine-readable, its meaning is explicitly defined, it is linked to other external data sets, and can in turn be linked to from external data sets [4]. Linking data distributed across the Web requires a standard mechanism for specifying the existence and meaning of connections between items described in this data. This mechanism is provided by the Resource Description Framework (RDF). Multiple datastores that belong to different thematic domains (government, publications, life sciences, etc.) publish

This work is supported by Thomson Reuters in the framework of the Partner University Fund project: "Cybersecurity Collaboratory: Cyberspace Threat Identification, Analysis and Proactive Response". The Partner University Fund is a program of the French Embassy in the United States and the FACE Foundation and is supported by American donors and the French government.

© Springer International Publishing AG 2016
G. Barthe et al. (Eds.): STM 2016, LNCS 9871, pp. 47–63, 2016.
DOI: 10.1007/978-3-319-46598-2_4

their RDF data on the web[1]. The size of the Web of Data is estimated to about 85 billions of RDF triples (statements) from more than 3400 open data sets[2]. One of the challenges of the Linked Data is to encourage businesses and organizations worldwide to publish their RDF data into the linked data global space. Indeed, the published data may be sensitive, and consequently, data providers may avoid to release their sensitive information, unless they are certain that the desired access rights of different accessing entities are enforced properly. Hence the issue of securing RDF content and ensuring the selective exposure of information to different classes of users is becoming all the more important. Several works have been proposed for controlling access to RDF data [1,6,7,9–11,13]. In [14], we proposed a fine-grained access control model with a declarative language for defining authorization policies (we call this model AC4RDF in the rest of this paper).

Our enforcement framework allows to define multi-subject policies with a global set of authorizations $\mathscr{A}$. A subset $\mathscr{A}_s \subseteq \mathscr{A}$ of authorizations is associated to each subject S who executes a (SPARQL) query. The subject's policy is then enforced by AC4RDF which computes the subgraph corresponding to the triples accessible by the authenticated subject. We use an annotation based approach to enforce multi-subject policies: the idea is to materialize every triple's applicable authorizations of the global policy, into a bitset which is used to annotate the triple. The base graph G is transformed into a graph $G^{\mathscr{A}}$ by annotating every triple $t \in G$ with a bitset representing its set of applicable authorizations $ar(G, \mathscr{A})(t) \subseteq \mathscr{A}$. The subjects are similarly assigned to a bitset which represents the set of authorizations assigned to them. When a subject sends a query, the system evaluates it over the her/his positive subgraph. In Sect. 3 we give an overview about RDF data model and SPARQL query language. In Sect. 4 we give the semantics of AC4RDF model which are defined using positive subgraph from the base graph. In Sect. 5 we propose an enforcement approach of AC4RDF model in multiple-subject context. We present and prove the correctness of our encoding approach. In Sect. 6 we give details about the implementation and experimental results.

2   Related Work

The enforcement techniques can be categorized into three approaches: *pre-processing*, *post-processing* and *annotation based*.

- The *pre-processing* approaches enforce the policy before evaluating the query. For instance, the query rewriting technique consists of reformulating the user query using the access control policy. The new reformulated query is then evaluated over the original data source returning the accessible data only. This technique was used by Costabello et al. [6] and Abel et al. [1].

---

[1] http://lod-cloud.net/.
[2] http://stats.lod2.eu.

- In the *post-processing* approaches, the query is evaluated over the original data source. The result of the query is then filtered using the access control policy to return the accessible data. Reddivari et *al.* [13] use a post-processing approach to enforce their models.
- In the *annotation based* approaches, every triple is annotated with the access control information. During query evaluation, only the triples annotated with a permit access are returned to the user. This technique is used by Papakonstantinou et *al.* [11], Jain et *al.* [9], Lopes et *al.* [10] and Flouris et *al.* [7].

The advantage of the pre-processing approaches such as query rewriting, is that the policy enforcer is independent from RDF data. In other words, any updates on data would not affect the policy enforcement. On the other hand, this technique fully depends on the query language. Moreover, the query evaluation time may depend on the policy. The experiments in [1] showed that the query evaluation overhead grows when the number of authorizations grows, in contrast to our solution which does not depend on the number of authorizations. In the post-processing approaches, the query response time may be considerably longer since policies are enforced after all data (allowed and not allowed) have been processed. The data-annotation approach gives a fast query answering, since the triples are already annotated with the access information and only the triples with a grant access can be used to answer the query. On the other hand, any updates in the data would require the re-computation of annotations.

Some works [11] support incremental re-computation of the annotated triples after data updates. In this paper, we do not handle data updates and we leave the incremental re-computation as future work.

In the data-annotation based approaches that hard-code the conflict resolution strategy [7], annotations are fully dependent on the used strategy so they need to be recomputed in case of change of the strategy. Our encoding is independent of the conflict resolution strategy function which is evaluated at query time, which means that changing the strategy does not impact the annotations.

As the semantics of an RDF graph are given by its closure, it is important for an access control model to take into account the implicit knowledge held by this graph. In the Semantic Web context, the policy authorizations deny or allow access to triples whether they are implicit or not. In [13] the implicit triples are checked at query time. Inference is computed during every query evaluation, and if one of the triples in the query result could be inferred from a denied triple, then it is not added to the result. Hence the query evaluation may be costly since there is a need to use the reasoner for every query to compute inferences. To protect implicit triples, [9,10] and [11] proposed a propagation technique where the implicit triples are automatically labeled on the basis of the labels assigned to the triples used for inference. Hence if one of the triples used for inference is denied, then the inferred triple is also denied. This introduces a new form of inference anomalies where if a triple is explicit (stored) then it is allowed, however, if the triple is inferred then it is denied. We illustrate with the following example.

Example 1. Let us consider the graph G_0 of Fig. 1. Suppose we want to protect G_0 by applying the policy $P = \{$*deny access to triples with type : Cancerous, allow access to all resources which are instance of : Patient*$\}$. The triple t_9 is inferred from t_2 and t_7 using the RDFS subClassOf inheritance rule. With the propagation approaches which consider inference [9–11], the triple $t_9 = $ (: *alice* ; *rdf* : *type* ;: *Patient*)$\}$ will be denied since it is inferred from denied triples (t_7). Hence the fact that alice is a patient will not be returned in the result even though the policy clearly allows access to it. Moreover, such a triple could also have been part of the explicit triples and this could change its accessibility to the subject even though the graph semantics do not change.

In our model, explicit and implicit triples are handled homogeneously to avoid this kind of inference anomalies.

3   RDF Data Model

"Graph database models can be defined as those in which data structures for the schema and instances are modeled as graphs or generalizations of them, and data manipulation is expressed by graph-oriented operations and type constructors" [2]. The graph data model used in the semantic web is RDF (*Resource Description Framework*) [8]. RDF allows decomposition of knowledge in small portions called *triples*. A triple has the form "(*subject* ; *predicate* ; *object*)" built from pairwise disjoint countably infinite sets I, B, and L for IRIs (*Internationalized Resource Identifiers*), blank nodes, and literals respectively. The subject represents the resource for which information is stored and is identified by an IRI. The predicate is a property or a characteristic of the subject and is identified by an IRI. The object is the value of the property and is represented by an IRI of another resource or a literal. In RDF, a resource which does not have an IRI can be identified using a blank node. Blank nodes are used to represent these unknown resources, and also used when the relationship between a subject node and an object node is n-ary (as is the case with collections). For ease of notation, in RDF, one may define a *prefix* to represent a namespace, such as rdf : type where rdf represents the namespace http://www.w3.org/1999/02/22-rdf-syntax-ns.

Note 1. In this paper, we explicitly write rdf and rdfs when the term is from the RDF or the RDFS standard vocabulary. However, we do not prefix the other terms for the sake of simplicity.

For instance the triple (: *alice* ;: *hasTumor* ;: *breastTumor*) states that alice has a breast tumor. A collection of RDF triples is called an *RDF Graph* and can be intuitively understood as a directed labeled graph where resources represent the nodes and the predicates the arcs as shown by the example RDF graph G_0 in Fig. 1.

Definition 1 *(RDF graph). An RDF graph (or simply "graph", where unambiguous) is a finite set of RDF triples.*

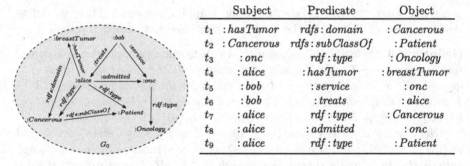

	Subject	Predicate	Object
t_1	: hasTumor	rdfs : domain	: Cancerous
t_2	: Cancerous	rdfs : subClassOf	: Patient
t_3	: onc	rdf : type	: Oncology
t_4	: alice	: hasTumor	: breastTumor
t_5	: bob	: service	: onc
t_6	: bob	: treats	: alice
t_7	: alice	rdf : type	: Cancerous
t_8	: alice	: admitted	: onc
t_9	: alice	rdf : type	: Patient

Fig. 1. An example of an RDF graph G_0

Example 2. Figure 1 depicts a graph G_0 constituted by triples t_1 to t_9, both pictorially and textually.

We reuse the formal definitions and notation used by Pérez et al. [12]. Throughout this paper, $\mathscr{P}(\mathsf{E})$ denotes the *finite powerset* of a set E and $\mathsf{F} \subseteq \mathsf{E}$ denotes a *finite subset* F of a set E.

3.1 SPARQL

An RDF query language is a formal language used for querying RDF triples from an *RDF store* also called *triple store*. An RDF store is a database specially designed for storing and retrieving RDF triples. SPARQL (*SPARQL Protocol and RDF Query Language*) is a W3C recommendation which has established itself as the *de facto* language for querying RDF data. SPARQL borrowed part of its syntax from the popular and widely adopted SQL (*Structured Query Language*). The main mechanism for computing query results in SPARQL is sub-graph matching: RDF triples in both the queried RDF data and the query patterns are interpreted as nodes and edges of directed graphs, and the resulting query graph is matched to the data graph using variables.

Definition 2 *(Triple Pattern, Graph Pattern). A* term t *is either an IRI, a variable or a literal. Formally* $t \in \mathsf{T} = \mathsf{I} \cup \mathsf{V} \cup \mathsf{L}$. *A tuple* $t \in \mathsf{TP} = \mathsf{T} \times \mathsf{T} \times \mathsf{T}$ *is called a* Triple Pattern (TP). *A* Basic Graph Pattern (BGP), *or simply a* graph, *is a finite set of triple patterns. Formally, the set of all BGPs is* $\mathsf{BGP} = \mathscr{P}(\mathsf{TP})$.

Given a triple pattern $tp \in \mathsf{TP}$, $\mathsf{var}(tp)$ *is the set of variables occurring in tp. Similarly, given a basic graph pattern* $B \in \mathsf{BGP}$, $\mathsf{var}(B)$ *is the set of variables occurring in the BGP defined by* $\mathsf{var}(B) = \{v \mid \exists tp \in B \land v \in \mathsf{var}(tp)\}$.

In this paper, we do not make any formal difference between a basic graph pattern and a graph. When graph patterns are considered as instances stored in an RDF store, we simply call them *graphs*.

The evaluation of a graph pattern B on another graph pattern G is given by mapping the variables of B to the terms of G such that the structure of B is preserved. First, we define the substitution mappings as usual. Then, we define the evaluation of B on G as the set of substitutions that embed B into G.

Definition 3 *(Substitution Mappings).* *A* substitution (mapping) η *is a partial function* $\eta : V \rightarrow T$. *The domain of* η, $\mathsf{dom}(\eta)$, *is the subset of* V *where* η *is defined. We overload notation and also write* η *for the partial function* $\eta^* : T \rightarrow T$ *that extends* η *with the identity on terms. Given two substitutions* η_1 *and* η_2, *we write* $\eta = \eta_1\eta_2$ *for the substitution* $\eta : ?v \mapsto \eta_2(\eta_1(?v))$ *when defined.*

Given a triple pattern $tp = (s \,; p \,; o) \in \mathsf{TP}$ *and a substitution* η *such that* $\mathsf{var}(tp) \subseteq \mathsf{dom}(\eta)$, $(tp)\eta$ *is defined as* $(\eta(s)\,; \eta(p)\,; \eta(o))$. *Similarly, given a graph pattern* $B \in \mathsf{BGP}$ *and a substitution* η *such that* $\mathsf{var}(B) \subseteq \mathsf{dom}(\eta)$, *we extend* η *to graph pattern by defining* $(B)\eta = \{(tp)\eta \mid tp \in B\}$.

Definition 4 *(BGP Evaluation).* *Let* $G \in \mathsf{BGP}$ *be a graph, and* $B \in \mathsf{BGP}$ *a graph pattern. The evaluation of* B *over* G *denoted by* $[\![B]\!]_G$ *is defined as the following set of substitution mappings:*

$$[\![B]\!]_G = \{\eta : V \rightarrow T \mid \mathsf{dom}(\eta) = \mathsf{var}(B) \wedge (B)\eta \subseteq G\}$$

Example 3. Let B be defined as $B = \{(?d \,;: service \,; ?s), (?d \,;: treats \,; ?p)\}$. B returns the doctors, their services and the patients they treat. The evaluation of B on the example graph G_0 of Fig. 1 is $[\![B]\!]_{G_0} = \{\eta\}$, where η is defined as $\eta : ?d \mapsto : bob, ?s \mapsto : onc$ and $?p \mapsto : alice$.

Formally, the definition of BGP evaluation captures the semantics of SPARQL restricted to the conjunctive fragment of SELECT queries that do not use FILTER, OPT and UNION operators (see [12] for further details).

Another key concept of the Semantic Web is *named graphs* in which a set of RDF triples is identified using an IRI forming a *quad*. This allows to represent meta-information about RDF data such as provenance information and context. In order to handle named graphs, SPARQL defines the concept of *dataset*. A dataset is a set composed of a distinguished graph called the *default graph* and pairs comprising an IRI and an RDF graph constituting named graphs.

Definition 5 *(RDF dataset).* *An RDF dataset is a set:*

$$\mathcal{D} = \{G_0, \langle u_1, G_1 \rangle, \dots, \langle u_n, G_n \rangle\}$$

where $G_i \in \mathsf{BGP}$, $u_i \in \mathsf{I}$, *and* $n \geq 0$. *In the dataset,* G_0 *is the default graph, and the pairs* $\langle u_i, G_i \rangle$ *are named graphs, with* u_i *the name of* G_i.

4 Access Control Semantics

AC4RDF semantics is defined using *authorization policies*. An authorization policy P is defined as a pair $P = (\mathcal{A}, \mathsf{ch})$ where $\mathcal{A}$ is a set of authorizations and $\mathsf{ch} : \mathscr{P}(\mathcal{A}) \rightarrow \mathcal{A}$ is a so called (abstract) *conflict resolution function* that picks out a unique authorization when several ones are applicable. The semantics of the access control model are given by means of the positive (authorized) subgraph G^+ obtained by evaluating P on a base RDF graph G.

4.1   Authorization Semantics

Authorizations are defined using basic SPARQL constructions, namely basic graph patterns, in order to facilitate the administration of access control and to include homogeneously authorizations into concrete RDF stores without additional query mechanisms. In the following definition, effect + (resp. −) stands for access to be granted (resp. denied).

Definition 6 *(Authorization). Let* Eff = $\{+, -\}$ *be the set of applicable effects. Formally, an* authorization $a = (e, h, b)$ *is a element of* Auth = Eff × TP × BGP. *The component e is called the* effect *of the authorization a, h and b are called its* head *and* body *respectively. The function* effect : Auth → Eff *(resp.,* head : Auth → TP, body : Auth → BGP*) is used to denote the first (resp., second, third) projection function. The set* hb(a) = $\{$head(a)$\}$ ∪ body(a) *is called the* underlying graph pattern *of the authorization a.*

The concrete syntax "GRANT/DENY h WHERE b" is used to represent an authorization $a = (e, h, b)$. The GRANT keyword is used when $e = +$ and the DENY keyword when $e = -$. Condition WHERE $\emptyset$ is elided when b is empty.

Example 4. Consider the set of authorizations shown in Table 1. Authorization a_1 grants access to triples with predicate : *hasTumor*. Authorization a_2 states that all triples of type : *Cancerous* are denied. Authorizations a_3 and a_4 state that triples with predicate : *service* and : *treats* respectively are permitted. Authorization a_5 states that triples about admission to the oncology service are specifically denied, whereas the authorization a_6 states that such information are allowed in the general case. a_7 grants access to predicates' domains and a_8 denies access to any triple which object is : *Cancerous*. Finally, authorization a_9 denies access to any triple, it is meant to be a default authorization.

Table 1. Example of authorizations

$$a_1 = \text{GRANT}(?p \; ;: hasTumor \; ; ?t)$$
$$a_2 = \text{DENY} \quad (?p \; ; rdf : type \; ;: Cancerous)$$
$$a_3 = \text{GRANT}(?d \; ;: service \; ; ?s)$$
$$a_4 = \text{GRANT}(?d \; ;: treats \; ; ?p)$$
$$a_5 = \text{DENY} \quad (?p \; ;: admitted \; ; ?s)$$
$$\qquad \text{WHERE} \; \{(?s \; ; rdf : type \; ;: Oncology)\}$$
$$a_6 = \text{GRANT}(?p \; ;: admitted \; ; ?s)$$
$$a_7 = \text{GRANT}(?p \; ; rdfs : domain \; ; ?s)$$
$$a_8 = \text{DENY} \quad (?s \; ; ?p \; ;: Cancerous)$$
$$a_9 = \text{DENY} \quad (?s \; ; ?p \; ; ?o)$$

Given an authorization $a \in$ Auth and a graph G, we say that a is *applicable* to a triple $t \in G$ if there exists a substitution θ such that the head of a is mapped to t and all the conditions expressed in the body of a are satisfied as well. In other words, we evaluate the underlying graph pattern $\mathsf{hb}(a) = \{\mathsf{head}(a)\} \cup \mathsf{body}(a)$ against G and we apply all the answers of $[\![\mathsf{hb}(a)]\!]_G$ to $\mathsf{head}(a)$ in order to know which $t \in G$ the authorization a applies to. In the concrete system we implemented, this evaluation step is computed using the mechanisms used to evaluate SPARQL queries. In fact, given an authorization a, the latter is translated to a SPARQL CONSTRUCT query which is evaluated over G. The result represents the triples over which a is applicable.

Definition 7 *(Applicable Authorizations). Given a finite set of authorizations $\mathscr{A} \in \mathscr{P}(\mathsf{Auth})$ and a graph $G \in \mathsf{BGP}$, the function ar assigns to each triple $t \in G$, the subset of* applicable authorizations *from $\mathscr{A}$:*

$$\mathsf{ar}(G, \mathscr{A})(t) = \{a \in \mathscr{A} \mid \exists \theta \in [\![\mathsf{hb}(a)]\!]_G, t = (\mathsf{head}(a))\theta\}$$

Example 5. Consider the graph G_0 shown in Fig. 1 and the set of authorizations $\mathscr{A}$ shown in Table 1. The applicable authorizations on triple t_8 are computed to $\mathsf{ar}(G_0, \mathscr{A})(t_8) = \{a_5, a_6, a_9\}$.

The set of triples in a given graph G to which an authorization a is applicable, is called the *scope* of a in G.

Definition 8 *(Authorization scope). Given a graph $G \in \mathsf{BGP}$ and an authorization $a \in \mathsf{Auth}$, the scope of a in G is defined by the following function $\mathsf{scope} \in \mathsf{BGP} \times \mathsf{Auth} \rightarrow \mathsf{BGP}$:*

$$\mathsf{scope}(G)(a) = \{t \in G \mid \exists \theta \in [\![\mathsf{hb}(a)]\!]_G, t = (\mathsf{head}(a))\theta\}$$

Example 6. Consider authorization a_8 in Table 1, and the graph G_0 in Fig. 1. The scope of a_8 is computed as follows: $\mathsf{scope}(G_0)(a_8) = \{t_1, t_7\}$.

4.2   Policy and Conflict Resolution Function

In the context of access control with both positive (grant) and negative (deny) authorizations, policies must deal with two issues: *inconsistency* and *incompleteness*. Inconsistency occurs when multiple authorizations with different effects are applicable to the same triple. Incompleteness occurs when triples have no applicable authorizations. Inconsistency is resolved using a *conflict resolution strategy* which selects one authorizations when more than one applies. Incompleteness is resolved using a *default strategy* which is an effect that is applied to the triples with no applicable authorizations. In [14], we abstracted from the details of the concrete resolution strategies by assuming that there exists a choice function that, given a finite set of possibly conflicting authorizations, picks a unique one out.

Definition 9 *(Authorization Policy). An (authorization) policy P is a pair $P = (\mathscr{A}, \mathsf{ch})$, where $\mathscr{A}$ is a finite set of authorizations and $\mathsf{ch} : \mathscr{P}(\mathscr{A}) \rightarrow \mathscr{A}$ is a conflict resolution function.*

Example 7. An example policy is $P = (\mathscr{A}, \text{ch})$ where $\mathscr{A}$ is the set of authorizations in Table 1 and ch is defined as follows. For all non-empty subset $\mathscr{B}$ of $\mathscr{A}$, $\text{ch}(\mathscr{B})$ is the first authorization (using syntactical order of Table 1) of $\mathscr{A}$ that appears in $\mathscr{B}$. For $\mathscr{B} = \emptyset$, $\text{ch}(\emptyset) = a_9$.

The semantics of policies are given by composing the functions ar, ch and then effect in order to compute the authorized subgraph of a given graph.

Definition 10 *(Policy Evaluation, Positive Subgraph). Given a policy $P = (\mathscr{A}, \text{ch}) \in \text{Pol}$ and a graph $G \in \text{BGP}$, the set of authorized triples that constitutes the* positive subgraph *of G according to P is defined as follows, writing G^+ when P is clear from the context:*

$$G_P^+ = \{t \in G \mid (\text{effect} \circ \text{ch})(\text{ar}(G, \mathscr{A})(t)) = +\}$$

Example 8. Let us consider the policy $P = (\mathscr{A}, \text{ch})$ defined in Example 7 and the graph G_0 of Fig. 1. Regarding the triple $t_8 = (\text{: } alice \text{ ;: } admitted \text{ ;: } onc)$, $\text{ar}(G_0, \mathscr{A})(t_8) = \{a_5, a_6, a_9\}$. Since a_5 is the first among authorizations in Table 1 and its effect is $-$, we deduce that $t_8 \notin G_{0P}^+$. By applying a similar reasoning on all triples in G_0, we obtain $G_{0P}^+ = \{t_1, t_4, t_5, t_6\}$.

5   Policy Enforcement

To enforce AC4RDF model, we use an annotation approach which materializes the applicable authorizations in an annotated graph denoted by $G^{\mathscr{A}}$. The latter is computed once and for all at design time. The subjects' queries are evaluated over the annotated graph with respect to their assigned authorizations. In the following, we show how the base graph triples are annotated and how the subjects queries are evaluated.

5.1   Graph Annotation

From a conceptual point of view, an annotated triple can be represented by adding a fourth component to a triple hence obtaining a so called *quad*. From a physical point of view, the annotation can be stored in the graph name of the SPARQL dataset (Definition 5). To annotate the base graph, we use the graph name IRI of the dataset to store a bitset representing the applicable authorizations of each triple. First we need a bijective function authToBs which maps a set of authorizations to an IRI representing its bitset. Authorizations are simply mapped to their position in the syntactical order of authorization definitions. In other words, given an authorization a_i and a set authorizations $\mathscr{A}_S$ to be mapped, the i-th bit is set to 1 in the generated bitset if $a_i \in \mathscr{A}_S$. authToBs^{-1} is the inverse function of authToBs.

Next we define a function graphOfAuth which takes a set of authorizations $\mathscr{A}' \subseteq \mathscr{A}$ and a graph G as parameters, and returns the subgraph of G containing triples which have $\mathscr{A}'$ as applicable authorizations. The function graphOfAuth is formally defined as follows:

$$\mathsf{graphOfAuth}(\mathscr{A}', G) = \{t \in G \mid \mathsf{ar}(G, \mathscr{A})(t) = \mathscr{A}'\}$$

Example 9. Consider the policy $P = (\mathscr{A}, \mathsf{ch})$ defined in Example 7 and the graph G_0 of Fig. 1. authToBs($\{a_1, a_9\}$) = 100000001, graphOfAuth($\{a_1, a_9\}, G_0$) = $\{t_4\}$.

Now we are ready to define the dataset representing the annotated graph.

Definition 11 *(Annotated graph). Given a set of authorizations $\mathscr{A}$ and a graph G, the dataset that represents the annotated graph denoted by $G^{\mathscr{A}}$, is defined by:*

$$G^{\mathscr{A}} = \{\langle \mathsf{authToBs}(\mathscr{A}'), \mathsf{graphOfAuth}(\mathscr{A}', G)\rangle \mid$$
$$\mathscr{A}' \in \mathscr{P}(\mathscr{A}) \wedge \mathsf{graphOfAuth}(\mathscr{A}', G) \neq \emptyset\}$$

Definition 11 defines how to annotate the base graph G given a set of authorization. The following Lemma 1 ensures that $G^{\mathscr{A}}$ forms a partition of the base graph G.

Lemma 1. *Given an annotated graph $G^{\mathscr{A}} = \{\langle u_1, G_1\rangle, \ldots, \langle u_n, G_n\rangle\}$, the following properties hold:*

- $\forall i, j \in 1..n : i \neq j \implies G_i \cap G_j = \emptyset$
- $\bigcup_{i \in 1..n} G_i = G$

5.2 Subject's Query Evaluation

The subject is the entity requesting access to the triple store. The determination of the objects accessible by the subject could be based on the subject identity, role or attributes. Given a global set of authorizations $\mathscr{A}$ we suppose that the subset $\mathscr{A}_s$ assigned to the subject is known in advance. The upstream authentication and determination of the authorizations assigned to the subjects is out of the scope of this paper.

Following Definition 10, given a global policy authorization set $\mathscr{A}$, the positive subgraph of a subject having $\mathscr{A}_s \subseteq \mathscr{A}$ as applicable authorizations, is given by the following: $G_s^+ = \{t \in G \mid (\mathsf{effect} \circ \mathsf{ch})(\mathsf{ar}(G, \mathscr{A}_s)(t)) = +\}$. Since we materialized the set of applicable authorizations in $G^{\mathscr{A}}$, we need to define the subject's positive subgraph from the graph annotation, more precisely from $\mathsf{ar}(G, \mathscr{A})$. The following lemma shows that $\mathsf{ar}(G, \mathscr{A}_s)$ can be computed from $\mathscr{A}_s$ and $\mathsf{ar}(G, \mathscr{A})$.

Lemma 2. *Given a graph G, a set of policy authorizations $\mathscr{A}$ and a subset of subject's authorizations $\mathscr{A}_s$, the following holds for any $t \in G$:*

$$\mathscr{A}_s \cap \mathsf{ar}(G, \mathscr{A})(t) = \mathsf{ar}(G, \mathscr{A}_s)(t)$$

Similarly to the triples, subjects are assigned to bitsets representing authorizations applicable to them. If a subject authorization set is $\mathcal{A}_s$, then she/he is assigned a bitset ubs where the i-th bit is set to 1 if $a_i \in \mathcal{A}_s$.

Example 10. Given the set of authorizations $\mathcal{A}$ in Table 1. Eve is a nurse who can see information about patients having tumors (a_1) and which service they are admitted to (a_6). She is denied anything else (a_9). Her assigned bitset is the bitset 100001001 of Table 2. Dave belongs to the administrative staff, he can access doctors services assignment (a_3) and the patients they treat (a_4). He is denied anything else (a_9). His assigned bitset is the bitset 001100001 of Table 2.

Once the graph is annotated, it is made available to the subjects with a filter function which prunes out the inaccessible triples given the subjects's authorization set. In other words, the filter function returns the subjects's positive subgraph by applying the ch function on the subject's assigned authorizations $ar(G, \mathcal{A}_s)(t)$. We showed in Lemma 2 that this subset can be obtained from the applicable authorizations in $G^{\mathcal{A}}$ by computing a bitwise logical *and* (denoted by &) between the subject's and triples' bitsets.

Definition 12 *(Filter function). Given a subject's bitset ubs and an annotated graph $G^{\mathcal{A}}$, filter is defined as follows:*

$$\mathsf{filter}(G^{\mathcal{A}})(ubs) = \bigcup \{G_i \mid \langle u_i, G_i \rangle \in G^{\mathcal{A}} \wedge$$
$$(\mathsf{effect} \circ \mathsf{ch})(\mathsf{authToBs}^{-1}(u_i \mathrel{\&} ubs)) = +\}$$

Once the subject's positive subgraph is computed with filter, the subject's query Q is then evaluated over it returning $[\![Q]\!]_{\mathsf{filter}(G^{\mathcal{A}})(ubs)}$ to the subject. The following theorem shows that filter function applied to the annotated graph returns the subject's positive subgraph[3].

Theorem 1. *Let $\mathcal{A}$ be a set of authorizations, $P = (\mathcal{A}_s, \mathsf{ch})$ be the policy of subject s and ubs her/his associated bitset. If G is a graph and $G^{\mathcal{A}}$ its annotated version, then $\mathsf{filter}(G^{\mathcal{A}})(ubs) = G_s^+$.*

Example 11. Let us consider the policy $P = (\mathcal{A}, \mathsf{ch})$ of Example 7. Table 2 illustrates the annotated graph obtained from G_0 shown in Fig. 1, as well as the two users of Example 10 with their assigned authorizations. The filter function will compute the positive subgraph of Eve as follows: $\mathsf{filter}(G_0^{\mathcal{A}})(100001001) = \{t_4, t_8\}$. Similarly, Dave's positive subgraph equals $\{t_5, t_6\}$.

6   Implementation

Our system is implemented using the JENA JAVA API on top of the JENA TDB[4] (quad) store. APACHE JENA is an open source JAVA framework which provides

---

[3] Proofs are provided at http://liris.cnrs.fr/~tsayah/STM2016/.

[4] https://jena.apache.org/documentation/tdb/.

Table 2. Example of annotated graph and users bitsets

$G_0^{\mathscr{A}}$		$ubs\ \&u$	
u	G	Eve	Dave
		100001001	001100001
000000111	$\{t_1\}$	000000001	000000001
000000001	$\{t_2, t_3, t_9\}$	000000001	000000001
100000001	$\{t_4\}$	100000001	000000001
001000001	$\{t_5\}$	000000001	001000001
000100001	$\{t_6\}$	000000001	000100001
010000011	$\{t_7\}$	000000001	000000001
000011001	$\{t_8\}$	000001001	000000001

an API to manage RDF data. ARQ[5] is a SPARQL query engine for JENA which allows querying and updating RDF models through the SPARQL standards. ARQ supports custom aggregation and GROUP BY, FILTER functions and path queries. Jena TDB is a native RDF store which allows to store and query RDF quads.

To generate $G^{\mathscr{A}}$, the dataset of annotated triples, we use SPARQL CONSTRUCT queries to obtain authorizations scopes (see Definition 8). An authorization a is transformed into $Q_a = $ CONSTRUCT head(a) WHERE hb(a). We use an in-memory hash map in which we store the ids of the triples and the correspondent bitset. For every authorization a_i, a CONSTRUCT query Q_{a_i} is run over the raw dataset, and the result triples are added/updated to the hash map with the bit i set to 1. Once the hash map is computed, it is written into a dataset which represents $G^{\mathscr{A}}$. Note that we could have used the dataset directly instead of a hash map, but this would be time consuming due to the high number of disk accesses. In case of a high number of triples that can't hold in memory, we could use a hybrid approach by loading the triples partially, but this extension is left for future work.

During query evaluation, on the fly filtering is applied to the accessed triples. JENA TDB provides a low level quad filter hook[6] that we use for implementation. For each accessed quad, let u be the quad's graph IRI, t its triple and ubs be the subject's bitset. A bitwise logical *and* is performed between (the bitset represented by) u and ubs. The ch function on the authorizations obtained by authToBs^{-1} is then applied in order to allow or deny access to t. If t is allowed, then it is transmitted to the ARQ engine to be used by query Q. Otherwise, it will be hidden to the ARQ engine. An in-memory cache is used to map quad graph IRIs to grant/deny decisions in order to speedup the filtering process.

---

[5] https://jena.apache.org/documentation/query/.
[6] http://jena.apache.org/documentation/tdb/quadfilter.html.

6.1 Experiments

The key input factors for the benchmarking of our solution are the sizes of the *base graphs*, the sizes of the *access control policies*, the sizes of positive subgraphs, the sizes of subjects' policies and the subjects' queries. The factors are reported in Table 3. The *base graphs* are synthetic graphs generated by the Lehigh University Benchmark (LUBM)[7]. Their sizes ($|G|$) vary from 126 k to 1,591 k triples. The *access control policies* are randomly generated using the LUBM vocabulary (about universities and people therein), with three control parameters. The first control parameter is the number of authorizations ($|\mathscr{A}|$) and varies from 50 to 200 authorizations. The second control parameter is the *scope average* of the policy with respect to the G. In other words, the percentage of triples in G which are under the influence of the policy authorizations. The last control parameter is the size of the body of each (atomic) authorization $a \in \mathscr{A}$. For the sake of brevity, the results we report here are for fixed scope (about 4 % by authorization) and fixed sizes of bodies (set to 2 for each authorization). The size of positive subgraph parameter $|G^+|_{|G|}$ varies from 10 to 100 % of $|G|$ and the number of subject's authorizations $|\mathscr{A}_s|$ from 50 to 200. Regarding the subject query parameter Q_s, we used a subset of LUBM test queries. We analyzed both the static (creation time) and the dynamic (evaluation time) performance of our solution. Each experiment is run 6 times on 2 cores and 4 GB RAM virtual machines running on OpenStack.

Table 3. Summary of notations

in	$|G|$	Size of the LUBM dataset
in	$|\mathscr{A}|$	Number of authorizations
in	$|G^+|_{|G|}$	Positive subgraph size w.r.t. raw dataset size
in	$|\mathscr{A}_s|$	Number of authorizations assigned to the subject
in	Q_s	LUBM test Query
out	t_A	Time to build $G^{\mathscr{A}}$ in memory
out	t_W	Time to write $G^{\mathscr{A}}$ to disk
out	t_{G^+}	Time to evaluate Q on materialized G^+
out	$t_{G^{\mathscr{A}}}$	Time to evaluate Q on $G^{\mathscr{A}}$
out	t_G	Time to evaluate Q on (raw) G

Static Performance. We distinguish the time needed to compute $G^{\mathscr{A}}$ between the time required for its *building* and the time required for its *writing*. The time to *build* the authorization bitset $\mathsf{ar}(G,t)$ associated with each triple $t \in G$ in memory is referred to as t_A in Table 3. The time to *write* the annotated graph

---

[7] http://swat.cse.lehigh.edu/projects/lubm/.

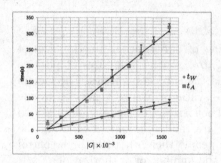

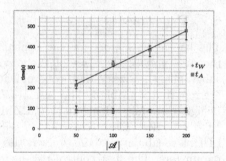

Fig. 2. Annotation and writing times with $|\mathscr{A}| = 100$

Fig. 3. Annotation and writing times with $|G| = 1{,}591\,\mathrm{k}$

$G^{\mathscr{A}}$ from the memory to the quad store is referred to as t_W in Table 3. Figure 2 shows t_A and t_W with $|\mathscr{A}|$ being set to 100 authorizations. Figure 3 shows t_A and t_W with $|G|$ being set to 1,591 k triples. As each $a \in \mathscr{A}$ is mapped to a SPARQL CONSTRUCT query, the results show that t_A grows linearly when $|G|$ or $|\mathscr{A}|$ gets bigger. The annotation time is not negligible but we argue that it is not an issue: $G^{\mathscr{A}}$ is computed once, as long as $\mathscr{A}$ is not modified. The ratio t_A/t_W is about 3.4 on average for fixed value of G in Fig. 2. In other words, for 100 authorizations, our method is amortized if the sum of triples in the positive subgraph for each subject is approximatively 5 times greater then the number of triples in base graph. Figure 3 shows that t_A grows linearly when $|\mathscr{A}|$ grows. However, as expected the results show that t_W is independent of $|\mathscr{A}|$: the overhead incurred by the growing size of the bitsets is negligible for $|\mathscr{A}| \in \{50, 100, 150, 200\}$. On average, the annotated graph $G^{\mathscr{A}}$ requires 50 % more disk space than G.

Dynamic Performance. To evaluate the performance of our solution at runtime, we compare our approach to two extreme methods. Each method computes the positive subgraph G^+ obtained by filtering the result of query Q on a base graph G according to a set $\mathscr{A}$ of authorizations.

The first extreme (naive) method gives an upper bound on the overhead incurred by the filtering process. Indeed, in the post-processing approaches, the access control consists in two steps: (1) compute the full answer $Q(G)$ and (2) filter out the denied triples from $Q(G)$ as a post-processing step. This method avoids duplication of the base graph G at the price of high overhead at runtime. In our experiments, we considered the step (1) only, by computing the full answer $Q(G)$. We refer to this method as t_G in Table 3. The second extreme method gives a lower bound on the overhead incurred by the filtering process. The idea is to materialize G^+ for each user profile and then compute $Q(G^+)$. We refer to this method as t_{G^+} in Table 3. This method avoids the filtering post-process at the price of massive duplication and storage overhead. In contrast, our approach, namely $t_{G^{\mathscr{A}}}$ in Table 3, is a trade-off between the extreme ones: it needs some

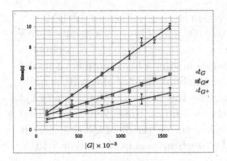

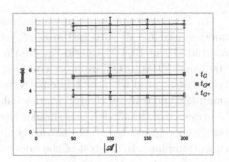

Fig. 4. Query evaluation time with $|\mathscr{A}|$ = 100

Fig. 5. Query evaluation time with $|G|$ = 1,591 k

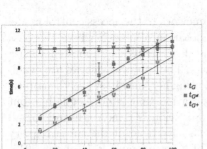

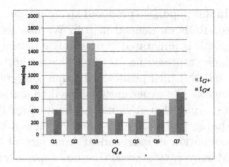

Fig. 6. Query evaluation time with $|\mathscr{A}|$ = 100 and $|G|$ = 1,591 k

Fig. 7. Query evaluation time with $|\mathscr{A}|$ = 100 and $|G|$ = 1,591 k

static computation while offering competitive runtime performance. Our results are shown in Fig. 4 for varying sizes of $|G|$ with $|\mathscr{A}|$ and $|\mathscr{A}_s|$ set to 100, and $|G^+|_{|G|}$ set to 40 %. The subject query Q_s is set to the worst case which is the select all query. The key insight from these experiments is that the overhead *is independent from* $|G|$ and is about 50 %.

Another advantage of our approach is its independence from the number of authorizations of both the policy and those assigned to the subject. In Fig. 5 we vary the number of policy authorizations ($|\mathscr{A}|$) with $|G|$ set to 1,591 k triples and Q_s to the select all query. The experiments show a constant overhead while changing $|\mathscr{A}|$.

Regarding $|G^+|_{|G|}$, the size of the positive subgraph with respect to the size of the annotated graph, the experiments in Fig. 6 show that the query answer time $t_{G^{\mathscr{A}}}$ grows linearly when $|G^+|_{|G|}$ grows, with $|G|$ fixed to 1,591 k and $|\mathscr{A}|$ and $|\mathscr{A}_s|$ fixed to 100. Q_s being the select all query. This shows that the overhead w.r.t. a materialized $Q(G^+)$ does not depend on the size of the positive subgraph. Note that t_G does not vary since we did not consider the filtering step of post-processing approaches, otherwise it would grow linearly when $|G^+|_{|G|}$ grows.

In Fig. 7 we run experiments on our system with a subset of LUBM test queries used by [3] with $|\mathscr{A}|$ and $|\mathscr{A}_s|$ set to 100, and $|G^+|_{|G|}$ set to 40 %. We computed the LUBM queries evaluation times and repeated the experiments 100 times. Q1 and Q3 are more complex queries having a high number of initial triples associated with the triple patterns, but the final number of results is quite small (28 and 0 respectively). Figure 7 shows that the time to evaluate query Q3 in presence of the filter $t_{G^\mathscr{A}}$ is smaller than the evaluation time over materialized positive subgraph t_{G^+}. The reasons could be the empty result of Q3 or different execution plans. In the rest of the queries, the overhead was between 6 and 40 %.

7   Conclusion

In this paper, we proposed an enforcement framework to the access control model for RDF we defined in [14]. We used an annotation approach where the base graph is annotated at the policy design time. Each triple is annotated with a bitset representing its applicable authorizations. The subjects' queries are evaluated over their positive subgraph constructed using her/his bitset and the triples' bitset. The experiments showed that the annotation time is not negligible, but we argue that it is not an issue since this operation is done once and for all during policy design time. We showed that the overhead of the subject query evaluation is independent from size of the base graph, and it is about 50 %. Moreover, we showed that our approach is independent from the number of policy authorizations as well as the used query language in contrast to the query rewriting techniques.

Ongoing work on this platform includes the design of an algorithm for the incremental update of $G^\mathscr{A}$ when G is modified, high-level optimizations for the construction of $G^\mathscr{A}$ using the partial order between authorizations induced by basic graph pattern containment and new empirical evaluations on both synthetic and real-life data.

References

1. Abel, F., Coi, J.L., Henze, N., Koesling, A.W., Krause, D., Olmedilla, D.: Enabling advanced and context-dependent access control in RDF stores. In: Aberer, K., et al. (eds.) ASWC/ISWC -2007. LNCS, vol. 4825, pp. 1–14. Springer, Heidelberg (2007)
2. Angles, R., Gutiérrez, C.: Survey of graph database models. ACM Comput. Surv. **40**(1), 1–39 (2008)
3. Atre, M., Chaoji, V., Zaki, M.J., Hendler, J.A.: Matrix "bit" loaded: a scalable lightweight join query processor for RDF data. In: WWW, pp. 41–50 (2010)
4. Berners-Lee, T.: Linked data-design issues (2006). https://www.w3.org/DesignIssues/LinkedData.html
5. Bizer, C., Heath, T., Berners-Lee, T.: Linked data - the story so far. Int. J. Semantic Web Inf. Syst. **5**(3), 1–22 (2009)
6. Costabello, L., Villata, S., Delaforge, N., et al.: Linked data access goes mobile: context-aware authorization for graph stores. In: LDOW-5th WWW Workshop (2012)

7. Flouris, G., Fundulaki, I., Michou, M., Antoniou, G.: Controlling access to RDF graphs. In: Berre, A.J., Gómez-Pérez, A., Tutschku, K., Fensel, D. (eds.) FIS 2010. LNCS, vol. 6369, pp. 107–117. Springer, Heidelberg (2010). doi:10.1007/978-3-642-15877-3_12

8. Hayes, P.J., Patel-Schneider, P.F.: RDF 1.1 semantics. W3C recommendation (2014). http://www.w3.org/TR/rdf11-mt/

9. Jain, A., Farkas, C.: Secure resource description framework: an access control model. In: SACMAT, pp. 121–129. ACM (2006)

10. Lopes, N., Kirrane, S., Zimmermann, A., Polleres, A., Mileo, A.: A logic programming approach for access control over RDF. In: ICLP, pp. 381–392 (2012)

11. Papakonstantinou, V., Michou, M., Fundulaki, I., Flouris, G., Antoniou, G.: Access control for RDF graphs using abstract models. In: SACMAT, pp. 103–112 (2012)

12. Pérez, J., Arenas, M., Gutierrez, C.: Semantics and complexity of SPARQL. ACM Trans. Database Syst. **34**(3), 1–45 (2009)

13. Reddivari, P., Finin, T., Joshi, A.: Policy-based access control for an RDF store. In: WWW, pp. 78–81 (2005)

14. Sayah, T., Coquery, E., Thion, R., Hacid, M.-S.: Inference leakage detection for authorization policies over RDF data. In: Samarati, P. (ed.) DBSec 2015. LNCS, vol. 9149, pp. 346–361. Springer, Heidelberg (2015). doi:10.1007/978-3-319-20810-7_24

Enforcement of U-XACML History-Based Usage Control Policy

Fabio Martinelli, Ilaria Matteucci, Paolo Mori, and Andrea Saracino[✉]

Istituto di Informatica e Telematica, IIT-CNR, Pisa, Italy
{fabio.martinelli,ilaria.matteucci,
paolo.mori,andrea.saracino}@iit.cnr.it

Abstract. Usage Control policies have been introduced to overcome issues related to the usage of resources. Indeed, a Usage Control policy takes into account attributes of subjects and resources which change over time. Hence, the policy is continuously enforced while an action is performed on a resource, and it is re-evaluated at every context change. This permits to revoke the access to a resource as soon as the new context violates the policy. The Usage Control model is very flexible, and mutable attributes can be exploited also to make a decision based on the actions that have been previously authorized and executed. This paper presents a history-based variant of U-XACML policies composed via process algebra-like operators in order to take trace of past actions made on resources by the subjects. In particular, we present a formalization of our idea through a process algebra and the enhanced logical architecture to enforce such policies.

1 Introduction

Modern IT systems can be very complex, implementing a large set of functionalities, and being composed by several components, which interact each other. Consequently, their security requirements could be complex as well, especially in case the resources to be protected are critical and/or valuable ones. This leads to the adoption of proper authorization systems to regulate the *access* to these resources and their *usage*. Through *access control* it is verified if the subject who wants to access a specific resource (perform an operation on such resource), holds such a right at request time, according to a specific policy. However, in environments where the context dynamically changes overtime, the access control does not re-evaluate the policy when the context changes. Such a necessity brought the adoption of the more flexible *Usage Control* (UCON) model. The UCON model has been defined in [9,13] to extend the capability of traditional access control by introducing the continuous enforcement of the security policy

This work was partially supported by the FP7 EU-funded project *Confidential and Compliant Clouds*, Coco Cloud [GA #610853], the H2020 EU-funded project *European Network for Cyber Security*, NeCS, [GA #675320], the EIT-Digital MCloud-DaaS prject and HII on Trusted Cloud Management project.

© Springer International Publishing AG 2016
G. Barthe et al. (Eds.): STM 2016, LNCS 9871, pp. 64–81, 2016.
DOI: 10.1007/978-3-319-46598-2_5

while the access is in progress and interrupting this access as soon as the policy is not satisfied any more.

To meet the security needs of complex systems, the approach we propose in this paper exploits the capabilities of the Usage Control model by allowing policy makers to define History-based Usage Control policies, *i.e.,* Usage Control policies, which define the allowed behaviour of subjects as a trace of actions which can be executed under some conditions. In fact, the Usage Control model allows policy makers to define policies where the rules that must be enforced change over-time depending on the current system state, and it also allows to define the rules to move from one state to the other. History-based Usage Control policies are necessary in those scenarios where the right of executing an action does not depend on that action only, but also on (a proper subset of) all the actions that have been previously executed on the system. For instance, the *Chinese Wall* policy [4] grants the right to access an object depending on the access operations previously performed by the same subject on the objects of the system.

Starting from the work in [5], where the authors proposed U-XACML, a new policy language which enhances the original XACML with the UCON novelties, we propose to combine the U-XACML language with a process algebra language suitable for writing policies, such as the POLPA language [2]. In this way, we are able to express U-XACML policies defining the trace of actions that can be executed by subjects on objects, and to enforce them. The main advantage of adopting the POLPA language to combine U-XACML policies is that POLPA enables policy makers to define the user's behaviour they want to permit in a very simple way. In fact, POLPA operators are used by a policy maker to define in which order U-XACML polices must be enforced. Actually, this could be even done in U-XACML by properly exploiting mutable attributes, conditions, and obligations, but it would require an additional and not negligible effort from the policy makers. Hence, the main aim of our proposal is to allow policy makers to easily write History-based Usage Control policies relieving them from the burden of: *(i)* explicitly defining the required set of states; *(ii)* expressing in U-XACML the obligations, which define the transitions from each of the previously defined states to another, and insert such obligations in the existing U-XACML policies; *(iii)* expressing in U-XACML the conditions defining which of the U-XACML policies must be enforced in each of the states defined in *(i)*, and insert such conditions in the existing U-XACML policies. This machinery will be helpful in several scenarios. A particular field of growing interest matching this description are the Cyber-Physical Systems (CPS), where IT is used to control and to interact with a physical system in different settings and environments, which might also include critical infrastructures. Misuse of the resources governing these systems might cause serious consequences. Hence, to exemplify the proposed approach, we consider an hydroelectric dam, as a critical infrastructure that needs to be protected against both insider and outsider attackers. In particular we consider a dam where allowed actions for subjects (policies), dynamically change according to the current hazard level (state) reported for the system. In these systems, the transitions between different hazard levels are regulated by specific rules, which are reported in the policies as well.

The paper is structured as follows: next section recalls some basic information about the Usage Control Model and the U-XACML policies. Section 3 presents our approach to enhance U-XACML policies with the possibility of managing execution traces. In particular, we present a formalization of history based policy through process algebra like operators and transition systems. We also present an enriched architecture in which we introduce the possibility of managing the change of state occurring after the execution of each action described into the History-based policy. Section 5 exemplifies our approach on a real scenario of a critical infrastructure: an Hydroelectric dam. Section 6 compares our approach with existing works and Sect. 7 draws the conclusion of the paper and lists some ongoing and future works.

2   Usage Control Model and U-XACML

This section recalls some notions about the Usage Control model (UCON) and the extension of the XACML language able to manage usage control policies, U-XACML.

2.1   Usage Control Model

The Usage Control model (UCON), defined in [9,13], encompasses and extends the existing access control models, by introducing new features in the decision process with respect to traditional Access Control models, such as the *mutability of attributes* and the *continuity of policy enforcement*. These features are meant to guarantee that the right of a subject to use a resource holds not only at access request time, but also while the access is in progress. UCON policies consist of the following core components:

Subjects and Objects. The subjects are the entities who exercise their rights on the objects (resources) by performing actions on them.

Actions. The actions represent the operations performed by the subjects on the objects.

Attributes. Attributes are paired to subjects, objects, actions, and environment to describe their features. An attribute is *immutable* when its value does not change frequently, and can be updated only through an administrative action, *e.g.,* the role of the subject. Instead, an attribute is *mutable* when its value changes over time because of the normal operation of the system. Mutable attributes change their values as consequence of the policy enforcement. In fact, a Usage Control policy includes attribute update statements, i.e., policy rules that include assignments of values to attributes, and it specifies whether this attribute updates must be executed before (*pre-update*), during (*on-update*), or after (*post-update*) the execution of the access action. As an example, let us consider the mutable attribute, which represents the number of concurrent accesses to a resource R. The value of this attribute is incremented by a *pre-update* statement in the policy when a subject is authorized to initiate an access to R, and it is decremented by a *post-update* statement in the policy when a subject terminates an existing access to R. The value of a mutable attribute can change also as a consequence of the execution of actions not regulated by the usage control policy. For instance, the attribute that describes the physical location of a subject changes when the subject moves from one place to another. Finally, other attributes change their value independently of the user behaviour, e.g., the CPU load.

A UCON policy can describe one of the following:

Authorizations are predicates that evaluate subject and object attributes and the requested right to decide whether the subject may access the object or not. The evaluation of the authorization predicates can be performed before executing the access (*pre-authorizations*), or continuously while the access is in progress (*on-authorizations*) to promptly react to mutable attribute changes.

Conditions are environmental or system-oriented decision factors, *i.e.,* dynamic factors that do not depend on subjects or objects. Hence, the evaluation of conditions involves attributes of the environment and of the action, and it can be executed before (*pre-conditions*) or during (*on-conditions*) the execution of the action.

Obligations are decision factors which verify whether a subject has satisfied some mandatory requirements before performing an action (*pre-obligations*), or whether a subject continuously satisfies these requirements while performing the access (*on-obligations*). Obligations can be enforced after the execution of an action as well (*post-obligations*). In this case, they cannot affect the execution of the action, but they can be used, for instance, for auditing or notification purposes.

The continuous evaluation of *on-authorizations*, *on-conditions*, and *on-obligations* could result in a policy violation while an access is in progress. In this case, the action is properly interrupted, and the result of the Usage Control policy enforcement is set to *revokeAccess*. Instead, if the Usage Control policy is always satisfied while the action is executed, and the action finishes normally, the result of the policy enforcement is set to *endAccess*.

2.2   U-XACML

U-XACML [5] is an extension of the XACML language that has been defined to express Usage Control policies. In fact, XACML [1] is a standard developed by the OASIS consortium to express and manage access control policies in a distributed environment, but it does not have specific constructs to express the continuity of policy enforcement.

To represent the continuity of policy enforcement, the U-XACML language allows the policy maker to specify when the evaluation of a condition must be executed by adding a clause, *DecisionTime*, in the `<Condition>` clause. The conditions whose decision time is set to *pre* are usual XACML conditions, which are evaluated at access request time, while the conditions whose decision time is set to *on* must be continuously evaluated while the access is in progress. U-XACML extends `<ObligationExpression>` in the same way. In fact, the *DecisionTime* clause determines when the obligation must be executed. The admitted values for the *DecisionTime* clause are: *pre* (*pre-obligations*, i.e., usual XACML obligations), *on* (*on-obligations*), and *post* (*post-obligations*).

Finally, U-XACML introduces a new element, `<AttrUpdates>`, to define attribute updates. This element includes a number of `<AttrUpdate>` elements to specify each update action. Each `<AttrUpdate>` element also specifies when the update must be performed through the clause *UpdateTime* which can have one of the following values: *pre* (*pre-update*), *on* (*on-update*), and *post* (*post-update*).

3   History-Based Usage Control

This paper proposes History-based Usage Control policies, *i.e.,* it combines Usage Control policies by using process-algebra like operators to obtain a policy on execution trace of actions. The resulting policy is named History-based U-XACML policy.

As previously explained, Usage Control policies extend access control ones because they take into account the duration of the actions. In fact, a Usage Control policy defines predicates, which must be satisfied while the action is in progress, *i.e.,* from the beginning to the end of the action. As soon as one of these ongoing predicates is violated, the Usage Control policy evaluation returns a *revokeAccess*, and the execution of the related action is properly interrupted. On the other hand, *endAccess* is the result of the policy enforcement when the action terminates normally.

Enhancing Usage Control policies with History-based capabilities is meant to enable the policy maker to describe the allowed behaviour of the subjects on the system by defining which is the Usage Control policy that must be enforced in a specific moment. In other words, the policy maker exploits process-algebra like operators to define the set of states of the system, which Usage Control policy must be enforced in each of these states, and which new states result from the enforcement of these Usage Control policies. Each History-based Usage Control policy specifies its scope, which defines to which entity the state refers to. In particular, we define three distinct scopes: SUBJECT, OBJECT, or GLOBAL. If the scope is SUBJECT, each subject of the scenario has his own state, and distinct subjects are paired to distinct states. Hence, when a subject *s* tries to perform an action, the system takes into account the state paired with *s* to select the set of Usage Control policies to be enforced, and updates this state as a consequence of the action. Hence, the current state paired to subject *s* depends on the actions that *s* performed on the objects of the system. Instead, if the policy scope is OBJECT, each object of the scenario has its own state. In this case, when a subject wants to access an object *o*, is the state paired with *o* which determines the set of Usage Control policies that must be enforced. The action performed by any subject on the object o results in an update of the state paired to o. Finally, if the scope is GLOBAL the state is shared, i.e., the actions performed by all the subjects on all the objects affect the same state.

Example 1. Let us suppose that a History-based Usage Control policy HUP_{ABC} with scope SUBJECT states that a subject can execute action C only after actions A and B, executed in any order. Moreover, the policy requires that A is entirely executed, i.e., it is not interrupted before its natural end because of a policy violation, and if A is interrupted no more actions can be executed by that subject. The initial state S_0 enforces the Usage Control policies UP_A and UP_B, thus, allowing to perform (under some authorizations conditions and obligations that are immaterial here) respectively, actions A or B. When the subject s tries to perform action A, the policy UP_A allows the execution of A and, if A is not interrupted because of a policy violation, the current state of s is changed to S_1, otherwise the current state is changed in a fail state S_{fail}. The new state S_1 enforces a Usage Control policy UP_B which allows the execution of the action B. Hence, if s tries to perform the action B, the Usage Control policy UP_B allows the action. UP_B changes the current state of s to S_3 regardless from the result returned by the policy. S_3 enforces a further Usage Control policy, UP_C, which allows s to execute action C. We remark that since UP_A, UP_B, and UP_C are Usage Control policies, the actions A, B, and C could be interrupted by the Usage Control system during their execution because of a policy violation. In our example, the policy HUP_{ABC} does not allow to change the state from S_0 to S_1 if the action A is interrupted. In this case, the action A is revoked and S_0 changes in S_{fail}.

3.1   Formal Specification of a Hystory-Based U-XACML Policy

History-based U-XACML policies are the composition of U-XACML policies through (some of) the behavioural operators of the *PO*licy *L*anguage based on *P*rocess *A*lgebra (*POLPA* [2]). We chose the U-XACML language to express Usage Control policies because it directly supports all the features of the Usage Control model. The POLPA language is instead a policy language able to describe the behaviour of an entity in terms of allowed sequences of security relevant actions. The idea is to use process algebra operators to combine UCON-specific policies instead of processes. Let us assume that each Usage Control policy UP is paired with one action only, α_{UP}, that can be differently executed according to the state in which it starts (similarly to what we said for subject and object above), and may also differently end, according to the result of the enforcement of the usage control policy. Indeed, UP terminates with *endAccess* if the execution of α_{UP} terminates normally, or with *revokeAccess*, if some changes occur in the context and the execution of α_{UP} is revoked by the system. We model these conditions with the predicate $exit(UP, r)$, that holds if the policy UP has been enforced with result r ($r \in \{endAccess, revokeAccess\}$). Hence:

$$\alpha ::= \epsilon \parallel \alpha_{UP} \parallel \alpha_{UP}^{ea} \parallel \alpha_{UP}^{ra}$$

Table 1. Semantics rules for inferring the admissible behaviour of HUP.

Basic Case.

$$\overline{UP \xrightarrow{\alpha_{UP}} 0}$$

endAccess.

$$\frac{\delta(UP) = endAccess}{UP.exit(UP, endAccess) \xrightarrow{\alpha_{UP}^{ea}} 0} \qquad \frac{\delta(UP) = revokeAccess}{UP.exit(UP, endAccess) \xrightarrow{\epsilon} UP.exit(UP, endAccess)}$$

revokeAccess.

$$\frac{\delta(UP) = endAccess}{UP.exit(UP, revokeAccess) \xrightarrow{\epsilon} UP.exit(UP, revokeAccess)}$$

$$\frac{\delta(UP) = revokeAccess}{UP.exit(UP, revokeAccess) \xrightarrow{\alpha_{UP}^{ra}} 0}$$

Prefix.

$$\frac{HUP_1 \xrightarrow{\alpha} HUP_1'}{HUP_1; HUP_2 \xrightarrow{\alpha} HUP_1'; HUP_2} \qquad \frac{HUP_2 \xrightarrow{\alpha} HUP_2'}{0; HUP_2 \xrightarrow{\alpha} HUP_2'}$$

Choice.

$$\frac{HUP_1 \xrightarrow{\alpha} HUP_1'}{HUP_1 or HUP_2 \xrightarrow{\alpha} HUP_1'} \qquad \frac{HUP_2 \xrightarrow{\alpha} HUP_2'}{HUP_1 or HUP_2 \xrightarrow{\alpha} HUP_2'}$$

---

where ϵ denotes no actions, α_{UP} denotes the action α associated to the policy UP, α_{UP}^{ea} is α_{UP} that correctly ends, i.e., no policy violations occur during the α_{UP} execution, and α_{UP}^{ra} denotes what happens when the execution of α_{UP} is interrupted by the system (revoked).

A History-based U-XACML policy, hereafter denoted by HUP, results from the composition of U-XACML policies, shortly UP_i, according to the following grammar:

$$HUP ::= 0 \parallel UP \parallel UP.exit(UP, r) \parallel HUP_1; HUP_2 \parallel HUP_1 or HUP_2$$

Remark 1. We assume that each UP_1, UP_2, ..., UP_n refers to a single action $\alpha_{UP_1}, \alpha_{UP_2}, ..., \alpha_{UP_n}$ respectively. Furthermore, we also assume to compose a finite number of UP_i that are processed one by one. Consequently, we do not consider the interleaving operator (*par*) in the provided syntax. It is worth noting that we are currently working in order to consider also parallelism and message exchange to be able to express both policies referred to more than one action and possible interleaving policies, e.g., multi-session ones.

The informal semantics is the following:

- 0 denotes that there are no more policies to enforce;
- UP denotes the basic U-XACML policy;

- $UP.exit(UP, r)$ is the basic policy followed by the predicate $exit$ stating the result of the enforcement of UP (specified by r, where $r \in \{endAccess, revokeAccess\}$). The evaluation of $exit(UP, r)$ depends on the function δ that works as follows: If UP permits the execution of an action, and this action normally terminates (α_{UP}^{ea}), then $\delta(UP) = endAccess$ Instead, if this action is interrupted because of a policy violation (α_{UP}^{ra}), then $\delta(UP) = revokeAccess$. Note that, when the evaluation UP by δ does not match the policy requirement, e.g., $\delta(UP) = revokeAccess$ and the policy is $UP.exit(UP, endAccess)$, no action is performed (ϵ) and the policy to be enforced does not change.
- $HUP_1; HUP_2$ is the *sequential operator*. It represents the possibility of behaving as HUP_1 and then as HUP_2. Note that, both HUP_1 and HUP_2 are composed by a finite number of UP_i^1 and UP_j^2, where $i, j \in I$ is a finite set of indexes.
- $HUP_1 or HUP_2$ is the *choice operator*. It represents the non deterministic choice between HUP_1 and HUP_2. Hence, $HUP_1 or HUP_2$ choices to behave either as HUP_1 or HUP_2 in a non deterministic way.

Formally, the behaviour of a History-Based Usage Control policy HUP can be modelled by Labelled Transition System, LTS, parametrized by a labelling function δ, named $\delta - LTS$. Such a function permits to evaluate the $exit$ predicate of each UP_i composing HUP in each state of the $\delta - LTS$.

Hence, let HUP be associated to a set of states S, which is composed by an initial state, s_0, and all the sets of states S_{HUP_i} of each of HUP_i, with $i \in I$ and I finite, composing HUP.

Definition 1 ($\delta - LTS$ for a HUP). *Let HUP composed by a finite number of HUP_i. $\mathcal{M} = (S, Act, \mathcal{T}, \delta)$ is a $\delta - LTS$ modelling a HUP, where*

- *$S = \{s | s_0 \cup \bigcup_{i \in I} S_{HUP_i}\}$, s_0 is the initial state;*
- *Act is the set of security relevant actions α of the HUP. We consider for each action α, four labels: ϵ, denoting no action, α_{UP_i} managed by each UP_i, $\alpha_{UP_i}^{ea}$ denotes that the action has been correctly terminated, while $\alpha_{UP_i}^{ra}$ denotes that the action has been revoked;*
- *$\mathcal{T} \subseteq S \times Act \times S$ is the transition relation, driven by the rules in Table 1.*
- *$\delta : S \rightarrow \{endAccess, revokeAccess\}$ is a labelling function that associates the value of the exit condition to the UP_i enforced in that state. In practice, it is the enforcement decision function that, by evaluation of the access request, enforces the usage policy UP_i during the execution of the action in order to evaluate if it terminates correctly or it is revoked.*

Remark 2. As usual for (process) description languages, other derived operators may be defined. By using the constant definition, the sequence and the derived parallel (see Remark 1) operators, the iteration and replication operators, $it(HUP)$ and $rec(HUP)$ resp., can be derived. Informally, $it(HUP)$ behaves as the iteration of HUP zero or more times, while $rec(HUP)$ is the parallel composition of the same process an unbounded number of times.

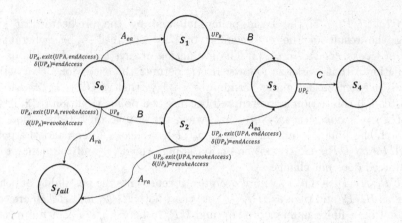

Fig. 1. $\delta - LTS$ of the History-based Usage control Policy in Example 1.

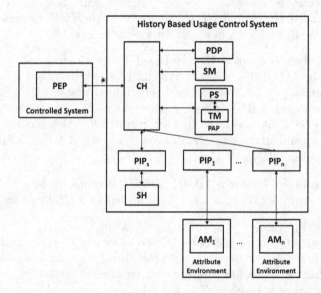

Fig. 2. Logical architecture of the History-based Usage Control framework.

With reference to Example 1, the History-based Usage Control policy HUP_{ABC} (graphically represented in Fig. 1) can be expressed exploiting the POLPA operators previously described as follows:

$$((UP_A.exit(UP_A, endAccess)); UP_B; UP_C) \quad or \quad (UP_A.exit(UP_A, revokeAccess)) \quad or \quad (UP_B; (((UP_A.exit(UP_A, endAccess)); UP_C) \quad or \quad (UP_A.exit(UP_A, revokeAccess)))) \tag{1}$$

The $exit(UP_A, revokeAccess)$ condition launches the A_{ra} action. This specifies the state reached by the system once the A action is revoked. The $exit(UP_A, endAccess)$ condition requires that the enforcement of the policy

UP_A returns *endAccess*, *i.e.*, that A regularly terminates and it is labelled with A_{ea}. Note that, in this example we associate an enforcement result to both the revokeAccess and endAccess conditions. If it is not the case, according to Table 1 the system does not terminate and the policy may be enforced again. On the other hand, because of the absence of the *exit* condition after UP_B, the policy HUP_{ABC} allows the action B to either terminate normally or to be revoked. After each sequence in which A correctly terminated, the policy UP_C is taken into account.

4   Logical Architecture

The UCON model fosters the concept of *Continuity of Policy Enforcement*. In fact, the attribute mutability introduces the necessity to perform the Usage Control policy evaluation process continuously while an access is in progress. This is because the values of the attributes that previously authorized the access could change in such a way that the access right does not hold any longer. In this case, the access is revoked as soon as the policy violation is detected.

The logical architecture of the proposed History-based Usage Control framework is depicted in Fig. 2, and it is an extension of the one defined in [6] which, in turn, is an extension of the XACML reference architecture [1] to enable the policy enforcement continuity. The extension to the UCON architecture proposed in this paper concerns the management of the state of the system, which is required to enable the history-based capability. In Fig. 2, this extension is represented by the components *State Handler (SH)*, *State PIP (PIP$_s$)*, and *Transition Manager (TM)*, which are described in details in Subsects. 4.1 and 4.2. The following of this section, instead, gives a very brief description of the components of the UCON service defined in [6].

Attribute Managers (AMs) manage the attributes of subjects, resources, and environment. An AM could run as a component of the Usage Control service (such as the state one), or could be an external service. *Policy Information Points (PIPs)* are the components implementing the interaction with AMs to retrieve and update attributes. PIPs are required because the attributes for the evaluation of a Usage Control policy could be managed by distinct AMs providing different protocols for interacting with them. Hence, PIPs provide the same interface to the Context Handler, while they implement the specific protocols to interact with the AMs they are paired to. A special AM is the *State Handler (SH)*, which has been introduced to manage the system state and will be described in the next subsections. The *Policy Decision Point (PDP)* is a XACML evaluation engine that takes a policy and an access request as input, evaluates the policy for that request, and returns the decision. The *Session Manager (SM)* is an additional component with respect to the XACML reference architecture, meant to support the continuous enforcement of Usage Control policies while the accesses are in progress. In fact, the SM keeps trace of the current usage sessions (through a Data Base), and determines for which of these sessions the Usage Control policy must be re-evaluated when one attribute (or more) changes its value. The *Context Handler (CH)* is the front-end of the Usage Control service. Its role is to coordinate the other components of the UCON service to (continuously) evaluate the policy. Hence, the CH implements the evaluation of the policy by interacting with the PIPs to collect the updated value of the attributes, with the PDP to request the evaluation of the policy exploiting the collected attribute values, and with the SM to update the status of the usage session. The policy evaluation is triggered by the *Policy Enforcement Point (PEP)* when a new access request is performed by a user. Moreover, a policy re-evaluation for the ongoing accesses is performed by the CH every time an attribute update notification is received from a PIP. If, for a given ongoing access, the policy re-evaluation results in a violation, this access is revoked by the UCON service. To this aim, the CH sends a revoke message to the PEP, which is in charge to properly implement the access revocation. Finally, the *Policy Administration Point (PAP)* stores the Usage Control policies through the *Policy Storage (PS)* component, and includes the *Transition Manager (TM)*, which is required for the system state management, as described in the following.

4.1   State Management

The core of the proposed History-based Usage Control systems is represented by the function defining the state transitions. Each specific History-based Usage Control Policy P defines a different state transition function, called $nextState_P$, because the state transitions are determined by the POLPA operators used to combine the Usage Control Policies, which build P. This function determines the next state of the History-based Usage Control systems, according to the policy scope, by taking as input: *(i)* the current state of the History-based Usage Control systems; *(ii)* the Usage Control policy that has been enforced in that state; and *(iii)* the result of the policy enforcement (*endAccess* or *revokeAccess*). In the proposed model, the current state of the History-based Usage Control systems is represented as a mutable attribute. This attribute is paired to the environment, to the subject or to the object if, respectively, the scope of the History-based Usage Control policy is "GLOBAL", "SUBJECT", or "OBJECT". Hence, when the policy scope is "GLOBAL", one instance only of the state attribute exists, and the actions performed by every subject on every object of the scenario affect this instance. Instead, when the policy scope is "SUBJECT", each subject of the scenario is paired with his own instance of the state attribute. In this case, when a subject performs an action, only his instance of the state attribute is updated by the policy.

In the History-based Usage Control system architecture, the state attribute is managed by a proper Attribute Manager, called *State Handler (SH)*, which is deployed within the Usage Control system itself. The State Handler interacts with the rest of the system through its PIP, called PIP_s, as shown in Fig. 2. As the other PIPs of the system, PIP_s provides an interface which allows to retrieve the value of the current state and to update such value with a new one.

With reference to Example 1, the function $nextState_{HUP_{ABC}}$ applied to the initial state S_0 and to the Usage Control policy UP_A, returns S_1 as new current state for s when the access terminates normally ($endAccess$), while it returns the state S_{fail} when the access is interrupted because of a policy violation ($revokeAccess$). Instead, the new state resulting from $nextState_{HUP_{ABC}}$ applied to the initial state S_0 and to the Usage Control policy UP_B, would be S_2, regardless from the result of the policy enforcement. The state S_1 enforces a Usage Control policy UP_B and, when the action B has been executed, the current state is changed to S_3. Again, the policy of Example 1 states that the new state is the same (S_3) both in case the result of the enforcement of UP_B is $endAccess$ or $revokeAccess$. Summarizing, the output of the function $nextState_{HUP_{ABC}}$ for Example 1 is the following:

$$
\begin{aligned}
nextState_{HUP_{ABC}}(S_0, UP_A, endAccess) &= S_1 \\
nextState_{HUP_{ABC}}(S_0, UP_A, revokeAccess) &= S_{fail} \\
nextState_{HUP_{ABC}}(S_0, UP_B, endAccess) &= S_2 \\
nextState_{HUP_{ABC}}(S_0, UP_B, revokeAccess) &= S_2 \\
nextState_{HUP_{ABC}}(S_1, UP_B, endAccess) &= S_3 \\
nextState_{HUP_{ABC}}(S_1, UP_B, revokeAccess) &= S_3 \\
nextState_{HUP_{ABC}}(S_2, UP_A, endAccess) &= S_3 \\
nextState_{HUP_{ABC}}(S_2, UP_A, revokeAccess) &= S_{fail} \\
nextState_{HUP_{ABC}}(S_3, UP_C, endAccess) &= S_4 \\
nextState_{HUP_{ABC}}(S_3, UP_C, revokeAccess) &= S_4
\end{aligned}
$$

4.2   Implementation

The History Based Usage Control Framework comes as a flexible, adaptable, and portable software designed to be easily integrated in any setting and application environment. To this end, the Java programming language has been chosen to implement it as an application which can run in desktops or servers, being executed as a remote (web)service and easily ported on Android mobile devices. In fact, the framework is also available as an Android app to enforce history based usage control directly on mobile devices. As discussed, the core components of the framework are designed to be application independent, except for PIPs and PEPs, which are implemented for each specific use case, by extending provided interfaces.

The proposed system shows several similarities with a standard usage control framework, like the one described in [6]. The main difference lies in the presence of the *State Handler* (SH) and of the *State PIP* (PIP_s), and on a revised version of the Policy Administration Point (PAP), which includes the *Transition Manager* (TM). The SH and the PIP_s are used to keep the current system state, and to update or query it when needed to handle history-based policies. The PAP, instead, consists of two main components (Fig. 2): the Policy Storage (PS), which stores the U-XACML UPs and the POLPA HUP, and the TM, which translates the HUP and the UPs in a single History-based U-XACML policy, i.e., a U-XACML policy including the constructs required for managing the state. The PS stores all the U-XACML policies (UP) defined for any action which can be performed in the system, independently from the current state. Moreover, the PS stores in a separate file the HUP expressed in POLPA, which connects the UPs, defining the relation between states and allowed actions. The TM merges the POLPA policy and the various UPs in a unique U-XACML policy. The resulting policy is an U-XACML *policy set*, composed by the various UPs, relating them through the usage of the `<Target>` tag to specify the state in which each policy should be considered, and the `<AttrUpdate>` to model the state transition. To this end, the `<UpdateTime>` tag of the `<AttrUpdate>` is exploited to specify in the policy a different value for the next state depending on the reult of the policy enforcement. In particular, we define two different update times: *post-update-endAccess*, and *post-update-revokeAccess*. In the first case, the attribute update is executed if the action controlled by the policy is terminated by the user through an *endAccess*, while in the second case the attribute update is executed if the action is interrupted by our system while in progress. The new state value is determined through the *nextState* function previously defined. A schematic representation of this process is depicted in Fig. 3.

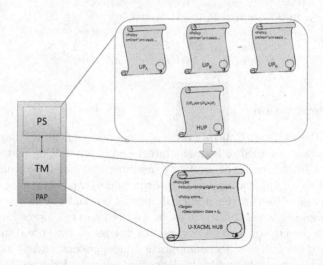

Fig. 3. Generation of U-XACML history-based policy.

As for the example represented in Fig. 1, the TM produces a policy set of three policies. Let us suppose the system to be in the starting state, S_0 for the user s. In this state, only the policies UP_A and UP_B can be enforced. Hence, the TM adds the following clause to UP_A and UP_B in order to make them applicable only when the state of the requesting user is S_0.

```
......
<Target>
  ......
  <AnyOf>
    <AllOf>
      <Match MatchId="urn:oasis:names:tc:xacml:1.0:function:string-equal">
        <AttributeValue DataType="http://www.w3.org/2001/XMLSchema\#string">S0</AttributeValue>
        <AttributeDesignator AttributeId="urn:oasis:names:tc:xacml:3.0:subject:subject-state"
          Category="urn:oasis:names:tc:xacml:1.0:resource-category:access-subject"
          DataType="http://www.w3.org/2001/XMLSchema\#string" MustBePresent="true"></AttributeDesignator>
      </Match>
    </AllOf>
  </AnyOf>
  ......
</Target>
......
```

Let us focus on UP_A. According to the *nextState* function, if the action A terminates naturally, i.e., the result of the policy enforcement is *endAccess*, the <AttrUpdate> tag of UP_A will specify as next state S_1 for the requesting user. This transition will be specified using the <UpdateTime> tag, with a *post-update-endAccess* value. The TM adds the following clause to UP_A to implement this transition.

```
<AttrUpdates>
  ......
  <AttrUpdate UpdateTime="post-update-endAccess">
    <AttributeAssignmentExpression AttributeId="urn:oasis:names:tc:xacml:3.0:subject:subject-state"
      Category="urn:oasis:names:tc:xacml:1.0:resource-category:access-subject">
      <AttributeValue DataType="http://www.w3.org/2001/XMLSchema\#string">S1</AttributeValue>
    </AttributeAssignmentExpression>
  </AttrUpdate>
  ......
<AttrUpdates>
```

For what concerns the management of the current state attribute, it is just another mutable attribute whose value is considered by the PDP to verify request compliance with the policy. Hence, whenever a usage request is issued, the PIP_s enriches the access request by adding the value of the current state and sends the enriched request for evaluation to the PDP. As discussed, the framework exploits the <AttrUpdates> U-XACML construct to express the state transition, which will be practically enforced by the PIP_s by sending the update request with the new value to the SH.

5   An Example: Hydroelectric Dam

An example of critical infrastructure reflecting the aforementioned model can be represented by an automated Hydroelectric Dam, which faces, among the others, the security risks reported in [11]. The automated dam control system considers four hazard levels, namely (i) normal, (ii) alert, (iii) critical and (iv) emergency. The condition to transit from one level to the other is determined by the amount of water passing through the sluices, the number of workers in the structure and the possible presence of mechanical malfunctions. We consider two different set of users: administrators and operators. The considered actions, which should be controlled though usage control, include dangerous operations which might physically endanger the system, or violate privacy constraints of the workers. A list of operations are the following:

– *Open Sluice*: can be performed only when the hazard level is normal.

- *Stream low-res video*: can be performed by administrators at any hazard level and by operators only at alert or higher level. If the video shows the presence of people in dangerous areas, the hazard level is increased by one.
- *Stream high-res video*: can be performed by operators or administrators at critical level, to verify if endangered subjects may need assistance. The hazard level is brought back to alert when the endangered subjects are brought to safety.
- *Verify Sluice*: verifies if the mechanism of a sluice works correctly. It moves the hazard level to alert if the system is not working and to critical if the water flux is above a specific threshold.
- *Close Sluice*: blocks the water flux. The operation requires time and stops the productivity of the hydroelectric system. For this reason this operation can only be triggered by administrators, or by operators only at critical hazard level. If the operation fails and the system is in critical status, the hazard level is moved to emergency. The hazard level transits to normal if the operation is successful.
- *Force Evacuation*: this operation can be triggered by administrators at critical hazard level and also by operators at emergency level.

Let us consider an emergency situation in which an accident has occurred in the dam. Initially the hazard level is set to "normal", thus the sluice is open. When the accident occurs, it is important to verify if there is someone who needs assistance in the dam. Both the administrator and the operator should check this by viewing the stream video of the surveillance cams, in such a way to possibly force the evacuation in order to both manage the alert situation and set again the status to "normal". The idea, is that, whenever a stream video access is performed, the hazard level increases by one. On the other hand, for each recovery action the hazard level decreases by one. To depict this situation through Usage Control Policies, we consider the following policies:

- UP_{SHV}^{Adm} is the policy regulating the possibility of the administrator to view a high resolution video stream, *i.e.*, the action *Stream high-res video*, SHV for short, described above. As a result effect of the application of this policy the hazard level is increased by one.
- UP_{SLV}^{Op} is the policy that regulates the possibility of the operator to view a low resolution video stream, *i.e.*, the action *Stream low-res video*, SLV for short, described above. As a result effect of the application of this policy the hazard level is increased by one.
- $UP_{FE}^{Adm,Op}$ is the policy that allows the Administrator to issue an evacuation alert.
- $UP_{VS}^{Adm,Op}$ is the policy that manages the verification of the sluice conditions.
- UP_{CS}^{Adm} is the policy that manages the closure of the sluice by the Administrator.
- $UP_{OS}^{Adm,Op}$ is the policy that manages the opening of the sluice.

Using our approach, these six policies can be combined in such a way that both the operator and the administrator can: (i) verify if someone endangered is in the building, (ii) call for the rescue team and (iii) try to recover the normal hazard level by forcing the evacuation and closing the sluice. The History-based Usage Control Policy HUP_{Em} has a GLOBAL scope because the state is unique for all the subjects (administrator and operator) and objects (cameras, sluice, and evacuation procedure) involved in the scenario. The History-based Usage Control Policy HUP_{Em} is defined as follows:

$$
\begin{aligned}
HUP_{Em} = \quad & (UP_{SHV}^{Adm}.exit(UP_{SHV}^{Adm}, revokeAccess)) \\
or \quad & ((UP_{SHV}^{Adm}.exit(UP_{SHV}^{Adm}, endAccess)); UP_{SLV}^{Op}; HUP_{RD}) \\
or \quad & (UP_{SLV}^{Op}; (UP_{SHV}^{Adm}.exit(UP_{SHV}^{Adm}, endAccess)); HUP_{RD}) \\
or \quad & (UP_{SLV}^{Op}; (UP_{SHV}^{Adm}.exit(UP_{SHV}^{Adm}, revokeAccess)))
\end{aligned} \tag{2}
$$

where

$$
\begin{aligned}
HUP_{RD} = & (UP_{FE}^{Adm,Op}; (UP_{VS}^{Adm,Op}; UP_{CS}^{Adm}) \\
or & (UP_{VS}^{Adm,Op}; UP_{CS}^{Adm}); UP_{FE}^{Adm,Op}); UP_{OS}^{Adm,Op}
\end{aligned} \tag{3}
$$

HUP_{RD} regulates the "force evacuation" actions as well as the actions related to the sluice. In particular, the policy $UP_{FE}^{Adm,Op}$ and the sequence $(UP_{VS}^{Adm,Op}; UP_{CS}^{Adm})$ may be executed in both the possible orders. Note that, executing one of these actions, the hazard level decreases by one. If, after the recovery actions, the hazard level goes back to "normal" and the sluice can be opened again.

6   Related Work

The usage control is a well known paradigm used to enforce security policies in several setting and environments. The improvement proposed in this work should bring a stronger expressiveness, allowing the definition of more complex policies for different environments. The usage control model has been first define by Sandhu et al. in [10]. The work in [12] proposes the adoption of the UCON in collaborative computing systems, such as the GRID environment based on a centralized Attribute repository (AR) for attribute management. They use the eXtensible Access Control Markup Language (XACML) [1] to specify several aspects of the Usage Control model, exploiting more than one XACML policy for the different policies necessary in the Usage Control model. A first implementation of usage control in GRID systems which does not exploit XACML in [7]. This system uses in fact the POLPA language, to define history-based usage control policies. However, policies in POLPA, though expressive, are difficult to write and do not respect standards. The introduction of history-based policies in XACML proposed in the present work, allows to write expressive policies which can be mapped in the POLPA language, still using an easy, enforceable and standardized language. In [3] Pretschner shows an application of the Usage Control model to preserve people privacy in video surveillance systems. This work is mainly focused on the description of the video surveillance infrastructure and on how policies can be used to preserve user privacy, not allowing camera monitoring when some conditions are not met. Some ideas from this work could be applied to implement some of the security policies described in the dam setting proposed in the current work. However, the work in [3] envisions a system which does not allow the definition of history-based policies, which enables the enforcement of different security policies for different hazard-levels. Another language for security policy specifications is ConSpec, presented in [8]. The ConSpec language can be expressed either as a labeled transition system or in a text form to represent process algebra models, being thus able to define history-based policies. However, the ConSpec language is not compliant with standards, sharing thus the same strength and weaknesses of the POLPA language.

7   Conclusion and Future Work

This paper presents a formal approach to combine Usage Control policy to obtain an History based U-XACML policy that is enforceable at run time. The contribution of the paper is twofold: (i) the definition of the formal model that underpins the specification of History-based Usage Control policy and (ii) the enhancement of U-XACML policy with the definition of the *nextState* function to update the (attribute's) state according to the transition function defined into the formal model. As future work, we plan to test the integration of the *nextState* function implementation on real use cases to evaluate its impact in the enforcement phase. We also aim to enhance the formal model with parallel operator to consider more policies in a concurrent way.

References

1. eXtensible Access Control Markup Language (XACML) Ver. 3.0.http://docs. oasis-open.org/xacml/3.0/xacml-3.0-core-spec-os-en.html
2. Baiardi, F., Martinelli, F., Mori, P., Vaccarelli, A.: Improving grid services security with fine grain policies. In: On the Move to Meaningful Internet Systems 2004: Confederated International Workshops and Posters, GADA, JTRES, MIOS, WORM, WOSE, PhDS, and INTEROP 2004, Agia Napa, Cyprus, October 25–29, pp. 123–134 (2004)
3. Birnstill, P., Pretschner, A.: Enforcing privacy through usage-controlled video surveillance. In: 10th IEEE International Conference on Advanced Video and Signal Based Surveillance, AVSS 2013, Krakow, Poland, August 27–30, pp. 318–323. IEEE (2013)
4. Brewer, D., Nash, M.: The chinese wall security policy. In: Proceedings of the 1989 IEEE Symposium on Security and Privacy, pp. 206–214. IEEE Computer Society Press (1989)
5. Desprez, F., Getov, V., Priol, T., Yahyapour, R.: A proposal on enhancing XACML with continuous usage control features. In: Colombo, M., Lazouski, A., Martinelli, F., Mori, P. (eds.) Grids, P2P and Services Computing, pp. 133–146. Springer, Heidelberg (2010)
6. Lazouski, A., Mancini, G., Martinelli, F., Mori, P.: Usage control in cloud systems. In: Procedings of The 7th International Conference for Internet Technology and Secured Transactions (ICITST-2012), pp. 202–207. Infonomics Society (2012)

7. Martinelli, F., Mori, P.: On usage control for grid systems. Future Gener. Comput. Syst. **26**(7), 1032–1042 (2010)
8. Mauw, S., Massacci, F., Piessens, F., Aktug, I., Naliuka, K.: Special issue on security and trust conspec - a formal language for policy specification. Sci. Comput. Program. **74**(1), 2–12 (2008). http://www.sciencedirect.com/science/article/pii/S0167642308001056
9. Park, J., Sandhu, R.: The uconabc usage control model. ACM Trans. Inf. Syst. Secur. **7**(1), 128–174 (2004). http://doi.acm.org/10.1145/984334.984339
10. Park, J., Sandhu, R.: The $UCON_{ABC}$ usage control model. ACM Trans. Inf. Syst. Secur. **7**, 128–174 (2004)
11. Sarno, C.D., Garofalo, A., Matteucci, I., Vallini, M.: A novel security information and event management system for enhancing cyber security in a hydroelectric dam. IJCIP **13**, 39–51 (2016)
12. Zhang, X., Nakae, M., Covington, M.J., Sandhu, R.: Toward a usage-based security framework for collaborative computing systems. ACM Trans. Inf. Syst. Secur. **11**(1), 3:1–3:36 (2008)
13. Zhang, X., Parisi-Presicce, F., Sandhu, R., Park, J.: Formal model and policy specification of usage control. ACM Trans. Inf. Syst. Secur. **8**(4), 351–387 (2005)

Access Control for Weakly Consistent Replicated Information Systems

Mathias Weber[✉], Annette Bieniusa, and Arnd Poetzsch-Heffter

University of Kaiserslautern, Kaiserslautern, Germany
{m_weber,bieniusa,poetzsch}@cs.uni-kl.de

Abstract. Access control is an important aspect of information systems. It manages and enforces the rules that govern the access of users and applications to the data. In general, both data objects and access rules are subject to change over time, e.g., one might withdraw the right of a user to access a certain data object.

In this paper, we present a new access control model for weakly consistent replicated information systems. Such systems are engineered to be partition-tolerant and higher available than strongly consistent systems – an important aspect in a networked world with mobile devices. In particular, they allow concurrent updates to different replicas and do not enforce serializability of operations. However, this relaxation of consistency threatens access control. If we withdraw the right of a user to access data object o at one replica and then modify o, the user should not be able to see this modification by accessing o on a second replica (information leakage).

Our access control model targets eventually consistent data stores. It avoids information leakage and unauthorized modifications. Furthermore, it guarantees that modifications to the access rules initiated on different replicas eventually converge. Our model allows in particular to implement access-matrix based models such as the read-write-own model employed in file systems. In this paper, we define the model in an abstract way, explain its correctness properties, and describe how it can be efficiently implemented in state-of-the-art weakly consistent data stores.

1 Introduction

Information systems often store sensitive information of customers, clients, and users. To protect the information from unauthorized access, detailed rules are needed that determine who may read and/or modify which data objects. The rules together with the assignment of rights to users are called a *security policy*. An access control system enforces that all executed operations satisfy the current policy. In most systems, the security policy is subject to change. New users or information is entered into the system, users change their roles, and access rights of users have to be modified. Typically, the policy change should be effective instantaneously, that is, for all operations happening afterwards. Since restarting the system for each policy change is often not feasible because of availability

© Springer International Publishing AG 2016
G. Barthe et al. (Eds.): STM 2016, LNCS 9871, pp. 82–97, 2016.
DOI: 10.1007/978-3-319-46598-2_6

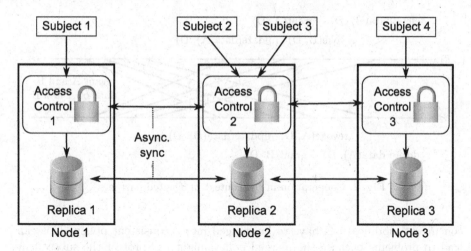

Fig. 1. System setting: Each node has a replica of the data store and the access control system.

requirements, the access control system should support dynamic changes of the policy at runtime.

Figure 1 illustrates our targeted system environment. On each server, a replica of the access control system as well as the data store is hosted. Both the access control system and the data store receive operations from authenticated subjects and exchange these operations asynchronously with the other replicas. The replicas communicate in a peer-to-peer fashion.

For strongly consistent systems, the topic of dynamically adaptable access control is well understood. Several access control models have been proposed [8,12,13,16,17] which implicitly rely on a total ordering of the operations that strongly consistent systems induce on all operations. However, Brewer's conjecture [5,9], also known as the CAP theorem, states that in a network without clock synchronization and with possible message loss, no service can implement strong consistency, high availability and partition tolerance. As partitioning cannot be prevented in computer networks due to network hardware and replicas failing, implementors of data stores have to make some trade-off between high availability and strong consistency. In many systems [1–3,7], consistency is traded for high availability. In such weakly consistent systems, updates are accepted at any replica and propagated asynchronously to the other replicas. These synchronization messages originating from different replicas can arrive in an arbitrary order on a node. To achieve higher throughput, often a connectionless transmission protocol such as UDP is employed, which can even lead to reordering of messages from the same replica during transmission. Though there is usually a well-defined order in which the operations happen on a replica, there is no total global order of all issued operations.

For the access control system, concurrently issued operations can lead to modifications of the same policy in different ways on different replicas. These

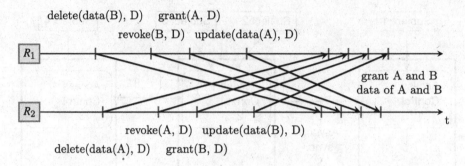

Fig. 2. Cooperation in the context of isolated partners

concurrent modifications have to be merged into a consistent policy. This can lead to problems because the merged policy might not protect the subsequent data operations as the original policies intended.

Consider two organizations A and B with an *isolation policy*: Employees of A are not allowed to access data of B and vice versa. Let us consider a data set D that might include data from A and/or B. If company A should be allowed to work with D, we first have to exclude B's data from D before granting A exclusive access to D. To grant exclusive access for A, we have to explicitly revoke access for B and afterwards grant access for A. We sketch our example in Fig. 2. Independently, company A is given exclusive access to D on replica R_1 and B on replica R_2. Afterwards, the companies update the data in D. When using last-writer-wins [19] as conflict resolution strategy, we end up with a situation that violates the isolation policy by granting access to A and B and possibly having both data visible. As the deletion and updating happen concurrently, the last operation, that is the update, will take precedence, and the data will be present in D. The same is true for the policy modifications. The grant operations win over the revoke operations because the grant operations happen after the revoke operations.

Contributions

We present a model for access control in weakly consistent replicated information systems. Our contributions are as follows:

- We give an abstract model for weakly consistent replicated information systems with access control systems (Sect. 2).
- We provide a notion of correctness for access control in weakly consistent replicated information systems (Sect. 3).
- We discuss the properties of an access control system for the presented setting (Sect. 4) and highlight its applicability and flexibility by instantiating it for a typical application scenario (Sect. 5).
- Finally, we show how to efficiently implementation the access control model using state-of-the-art replicated data stores (Sect. 6).

2   Formal System Model

In this section, we describe a formal system model as a precise foundation for correctness properties of access control systems in weakly consistent replicated information systems.

Abstract executions

As model we take a slight adaptation of the model by Burckhardt et al. [6]: An abstract execution of a weakly consistent data store is defined as a tuple $A_D = (E, \mathsf{repl}, \mathsf{obj}, \mathsf{oper}, \mathsf{ro}, \mathsf{vis})$, where

- $E \subseteq Event_D$ is a set of events from a countable universe $Event_D$;
- an event $e \in E$ captures the execution of an operation $\mathsf{oper}(e) \in Op_{\mathsf{type}(\mathsf{obj}(e))}$ on an object $\mathsf{obj}(e) \in Obj$ at a replica $\mathsf{repl}(e) \in ReplicaID$
- $\mathsf{ro} \subseteq E \times E$ is a replica order, which is a union of irreflexive and total orders on events at each replica;
- $\mathsf{vis} \subseteq E \times E$ is an acyclic visibility relation such that $\forall e, f \in E.e \xrightarrow{\mathsf{vis}} f \implies \mathsf{obj}(e) = \mathsf{obj}(f)$;

We use the notation $e \xrightarrow{r} f$ for $(e, f) \in r$. The relation ro gives the order in which the events happened on the replica where the corresponding operation has been issued. The relation vis reflects which events can influence the result of other events; $e \xrightarrow{\mathsf{vis}} f$ means that f is aware of e and thus e can influence f.

We define the abstract execution of an access control system using a data store by a tuple $A_{AC} = (A_D, E, \mathsf{repl}, \mathsf{obj}, \mathsf{subj}, \mathsf{oper}, \mathsf{tsubj}, \mathsf{ro}, \mathsf{vis})$, where

- A_D is an abstract execution of the underlying data store;
- $A_D.E \subset E \subseteq Event_{AC}$ is a set of events from a countable universe $Event_{AC}$ with $Event_D \subseteq Event_{AC}$;
- each event $e \in E$ executed by subject $\mathsf{subj}(e) \in Subj$ either describes a data store event $e \in A_D.E$ on the underlying data store or an access control event with replica $\mathsf{repl}(e) \in ReplicaID$ performing an operation $\mathsf{oper}(e) \in Op_{\mathsf{policy}(\mathsf{obj}(e), \mathsf{tsubj}(e))}$ with target object $\mathsf{obj}(e) \in Obj$ and target subject $\mathsf{tsubj}(e) \in Subj$;
- $\mathsf{ro} \subseteq E \times E$ is an extension of the data store's replica order $A.\mathsf{ro}$ to the operations on the access control system;
- $\mathsf{vis} \subseteq E \times E$ is an extension of the visibility relation of the data store.

We consider a concrete execution to be correct if it can be justified by an abstract execution with the same operations. A detailed explanation of abstract executions and how to map them to concrete executions of a given system is omitted owing to space constraints but can be found in [6].

Policies and trust

The operator of an information system needs to define rules which restrict the operations that may be performed on the objects by the individual subjects. In a concrete system, the subjects can be users, processes, or applications executing operations on the data store. A security policy assigns to each subject-object pair a specific right $r \in Right$. We require $Right$ to form a lattice, since we need a minimum function for later constructions. The interpretation of the right is given by a function decide : $Right \times Event \rightarrow \{Grant, Deny\}$. We model a policy as a replicated data type with an operation asgn. The asgn operation allows to modify the policy at runtime by assigning a new right for a subject-object-pair.

An abstract execution of an access control system is valid if all events $e \in E$ are valid with respect to the policy visible at repl(e) when e happened. The visible policy can only be defined based on the execution of the system. An *operation context* for an event is a tuple $L_{AC} = (o, E, \text{oper}, \text{vis})$ where $o \in Op_{\text{policy}(o,s)} \cup Op_{\text{type}(o)}$, E is a finite subset of $Event_{AC}$, oper : $E \rightarrow Op_{\text{policy}(o,s)} \cup Op_{\text{type}(o)}$ and vis $\subseteq E \times E$ is acyclic. We can extract the context of an event $e \in A.E$ in an abstract execution of the system by the construction given in [6] based on the visibility relation:

$$\text{ctxt}(A, e) = (A.oper(e), G, (A.oper)|_G, (A.vis)|_G),$$

where $G = (A.vis)^{-1}(e)$ are the events that have been visible when event e happened, and $\cdot|_G$ is the restriction to events in G. The visible policy for an event e can be given as a function $\mathcal{F}_{\text{policy}(s,o)}(L_{AC})$ based on an operation context L_{AC}, which returns the current right of subject $s = \text{subj}(e)$ on object $o = \text{obj}(e)$. An event e is valid if decide($\mathcal{F}_{\text{policy}(s,o)}(\text{ctxt}(A, e)), e) = Grant$

For brevity, we use some short notations: We write decide(A, e) for short to mean the access control decision of event e in the abstract execution A. We write oper(e) = $\text{asgn}_{s,o}(r)$ to mean oper(e) = $\text{asgn}(r) \wedge \text{obj}(e) = o \wedge \text{tsubj}(e) = s$. A superscript on an event denotes the subject that executed the operation oper(e), such that f_1^s is equivalent with f_1 and subj(f_1) = s.

3 Correctness of Access Control in Weakly Consistent Systems

Informally, an access control system is correct if it enforces the security policy on all replicas. To check whether a given abstract execution is valid, it is sufficient to take for each event $e \in Event_{AC}$ the events that happened before e and compute possible current policies when e happened. The policies for e denoted by $\mathcal{F}_{\text{policy}(s,o)}(\text{ctxt}(A, e))$ are based on the right assignments that happened before e on the same object obj(e). Event e is valid according to the security policy if decide($\mathcal{F}_{\text{policy}(s,o)}(\text{ctxt}(A, e)), e) = Grant$.

For strongly consistent systems, it is possible to talk about *the* current security policy. Strong consistency induces a global order of all operations that occur in the system. To find the current policy that applies to an operation op, we take the initial policy and apply all policy modifications that happened before op. According to the global order, this means that in this case ro = vis for all replicas.

For weakly consistent systems, there is not such a total order between all operations. At each replica, there is a total order in which operations are applied, but this order can vary for different replicas. We might have different vis-relations describing different orders in which events of remote replicas get visible on other replicas restricted by additional correctness conditions for abstract executions. Depending on the vis-relation, we might get different possible policies for an event leading to different decisions about the validity of the same event. We need to disambiguate the policy for events thereby preserving the protective properties of a policy modification.

We want to preserve two properties of the access control system: (1) All policy changes need to be applied on all replicas before applying the subsequent data events and (2) conflicts of concurrent policy modifications are handled conservatively.

3.1   Protection Relation

For an access control system for distributed weakly consistent systems to be correct, operations that depend on policy changes globally must be applied after the policy modifications that possibly restrict the access to the object.

The per-object causality order hbo is defined in [6] as

$$\mathsf{sameobj}(e, f) \Longleftrightarrow \mathsf{obj}(e) = \mathsf{obj}(f)$$
$$\mathsf{hbo} = ((\mathsf{ro} \cap \mathsf{sameobj}) \cup \mathsf{vis})^+$$

We extend the hbo order to the protection relation. For an abstract execution A_{AC} the *protection relation* prot is defined as

$$\mathsf{guarding}(e, f) \Longleftrightarrow \mathsf{oper}(e) \in Op_{\mathsf{policy}(\mathsf{obj}(e), \mathsf{tsubj}(e))} \land \mathsf{oper}(f) \in Op_{\mathsf{type}(\mathsf{obj}(f))}$$
$$\mathsf{prot} = \mathsf{hbo} \cap \mathsf{guarding}$$

Two events e and f are in protection relation if e happened before f, both concern the same object and e is a policy modification and f is a data operation.

3.2   Conservative Conflict Resolution

The data type to store the policy for a subject-object-pair is the policy type with the operation asgn. For an event e with $o = \mathsf{oper}(e)$ and $s = \mathsf{subj}(e)$, the specification of the current policy when e happens is specified by $\mathcal{F}_{\mathsf{policy}(s,o)}(\mathsf{ctxt}(A, e))$ as:

$$\mathcal{F}_{\mathsf{policy}(s,o)}(op, E, \mathsf{oper}, \mathsf{vis}, \mathsf{ar}) = \min\{r \mid \exists e \in E.\ \mathsf{oper}(e) = \mathsf{asgn}_{s,o}(r) \land$$
$$\neg \exists f \in E.\ \mathsf{oper}(f) = \mathsf{asgn}_{s,o}(r') \land e \xrightarrow{\mathsf{vis}} f\}$$

Set E is the set of events on o that are visible when e happens. Informally, we take the set of all rights assigned to the subject-object-pair which have not been overwritten by subsequent assignments to the policy. The result is a set of concurrently assigned rights $\mathsf{rs} \subseteq Right$, for which we required to form a lattice. From rs we take the minimum element with respect to this rights-lattice.

3.3 Correctness Criterion

An access control for weakly consistent systems is correct if it retains the protection relation on all replicas and it conservatively resolves conflicts for policy modifications.

Definition 1. *An abstract execution A of a distributed access control system is correct if*

$$A.\mathsf{prot} \subseteq A.\mathsf{vis} \; and \; \forall e \in A.E. \; \mathsf{decide}(\mathcal{F}_{\mathsf{policy}(s,o)}(\mathtt{ctxt}(A,e)),e) = Grant$$

In a correct access control system, all policy modifications are visible for subsequent data operations, thus can restrict access to the effect of subsequent events. For conflicting updates of the same policy, the system needs to integrate the updates in a way, that preserves the protective property of all policy modifications. This property is guaranteed by preserving the information about events that happened concurrently (neither $e \xrightarrow{\mathsf{vis}} f$ nor $f \xrightarrow{\mathsf{vis}} e$) and taking the minimum over these concurrently assigned rights.

4   Protection-Preserving Access Control

In this section we discuss why the two properties of a correct access control system for weakly consistent systems stated in Sect. 3 are needed.

We assume that there is an initial access control policy, which grants only specific events. A sensible default might be to have an administrative user that has the rights to assign new rights to other subjects.

A data operation f may depend on a policy modification e in two different ways:

1. f is valid because e is a change in the policy that permits it:

$$e \xrightarrow{\mathsf{ro}} f^s \wedge \mathsf{oper}(e) = \mathbf{asgn}_{s,o}(r) \wedge \mathsf{decide}(r,f) = Grant$$

2. e protects the modification of the state of an object resulting from f by revoking access for a specific subject:

$$e \xrightarrow{\mathsf{ro}} f_1 \wedge \mathsf{oper}(e) = \mathbf{asgn}_{s,o}(r) \wedge \mathsf{decide}(r,f_2) = Deny \wedge \mathsf{obj}(f_1) = \mathsf{obj}(f_2) = o$$

The first case only concerns the consistency between the local security policy and the data state. Wobber et al. [21] have discovered this relation in the implementation of their access control system for weakly consistent replication. Their implementation blocks a data operation on a replica until the respective policy update arrives. In contrast, our system model requires consistency of the access control decisions, thus we require that $e \xrightarrow{\text{vis}} f$ on all replicas.

The second case is more interesting since it can lead to leakage of information. Event e is a right assignment which protects the effect of f_1 by denying access in form of f_2 by s to o. When transferred to other replicas, this relation between e and f_1 should not get lost, since $\neg(e \xrightarrow{\text{vis}} f_2)$ means that f_2 and thereby access for s is allowed on the remote replica. If f_1 is storing confidential information and f_2 accesses this information, e not being visible leads to information leakage on the remote replica. Please note that $e \xrightarrow{\text{prot}} f_1$, thus by retaining the protection relation in the visibility relation we effectively prevent this leak.

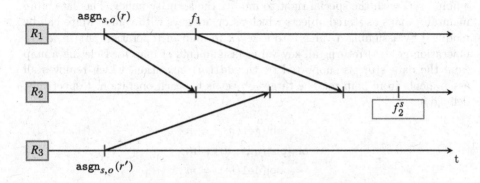

Fig. 3. Concurrent right assignment violating the protection relation.

The protective property of a right assignment could be violated by synchronizing a concurrent policy modification. The situation is sketched in Fig. 3. We assume that $e_1 \xrightarrow{\text{prot}} f_1$ with $\text{oper}(e_1) = \text{asgn}_{s,o}(r)$, $\text{oper}(e_2) = \text{asgn}_{s,o}(r')$, $\text{obj}(f_2) = \text{obj}(f_1)$, $\text{decide}(r, f_2) = Deny$ and $\text{decide}(r', f_2) = Grant$. The rights assignments e_1 and e_2 happen concurrently on replicas R_1 and R_3. In a strongly consistent system, the order in which the operations happen would globally be fixed. This implies that $e_1 \xrightarrow{\text{ro}} e_2$ meaning r' explicitly overrules r thereby explicitly permitting f_2 or $e_2 \xrightarrow{\text{ro}} e_1$ explicitly denying f_2 executed by s. In weakly consistent systems, both right modifications happen without knowledge of one another, so both semantics could be intended. To be conservative, we have to assume the more restrictive semantics, meaning the goal is to deny f_2 if executed by s.

The order in which these two policy modifications are applied on R_2 is arbitrary, which means that $e_1 \xrightarrow{\text{vis}} e_2$ and $e_2 \xrightarrow{\text{vis}} f_2$ is also possible. In this case, integrating the concurrent policy modifications in a last-writer-wins fashion would violate the protective property of e_1 to restrict access to the effect of f_1. The problem in this case is the concurrent modification of the policy.

Our model avoids the problem. Instead of last-writer-wins, we take an approach where all concurrent assignments are retained and the minimum of the assigned rights is taken as the result of the read operation on a policy. This integrates the concurrent policies in a way that makes sure, that the commonly agreed rights cannot be extended by policy modifications invisible to the other replicas.

5   Example

To illustrate the formal model, we will discuss now how to instantiate ProPreAC for a typical system with hierarchical read-write-own policies.

Consider a system with three subjects: Alice, Bob and Eve. In this example, the subjects are actual users which interact with the system. Alice and Bob are admin users with the special right to modify the security policy. The data store maintains maps as stored objects which associate keys with values. Maps can be modified by assigning a value v to a key k in map m (operation $\mathtt{put}(m,k,v)$). Operation $\mathtt{get}(m)$ returns all key-value assignments of map m. Deleting a map from the data store is supported by the $\mathtt{del}(m)$ operation, which removes all assignments from map m. The target object is for each operation, respectively, defined as:

$$\mathsf{obj}(\mathtt{get}(m)) = m$$
$$\mathsf{obj}(\mathtt{put}(m,k,v)) = m$$
$$\mathsf{obj}(\mathtt{del}(m)) = m$$

Further, we assume that the data store ensures eventual consistency of the map objects under concurrent modification (e.g., by implementing Map CRDTs [3]). For the sake of the example, we assume that when issuing two $\mathtt{put}$ operations on distinct keys k_1 and k_2 concurrently, both assignments are retained.

A classical policy model in access control systems is the read-write-own hierarchy. A user which has read access to an object can read the object. The write access also grants the permission to read the object, and in addition the user can also modify the object. The own access grants the same rights as the write access and in addition allows to delete the object. This system is based on a total order of the different access rights, that is $Right = \{none,\ read,\ write,\ own\}$ where $none < read < write < own$.

The decide function is defined as follows regarding operations on a map m:

$\mathsf{decide}(read, \mathtt{get}(m)) = Grant$

$\mathsf{decide}(write, \mathtt{get}(m)) = \mathsf{decide}(write, \mathtt{put}(m,\ k,\ v)) = Grant$

$\mathsf{decide}(own, \mathtt{get}(m)) = \mathsf{decide}(own, \mathtt{put}(m,\ k,\ v)) = \mathsf{decide}(own, \mathtt{del}(m)) = Grant$

All other combinations are denied.

Let us assume that users Alice and Bob have write access to a map m, whereas Eve has only read access to m. In addition, Alice and Bob have the permission to assign new permissions for m, and may thus modify the security policy. Consider now two replicas R_1 and R_2, both having converged to the same state with an identical security policy:

$$P\,|^{old}_{Alice,m} = \{write\}$$
$$P\,|^{old}_{Bob,m} = \{write\}$$
$$P\,|^{old}_{Eve,m} = \{read\}$$

Now, the system state evolves as follows: On R_1, Alice first sets the permission of Eve for m to *none*, because she thinks that Eve is not trustworthy, and afterwards writes a value v_1 to key k_1 in map m which Eve should not read. In parallel, Bob first sets the permission of Eve for m to *write*, because he thinks that Eve is trustworthy, and shares a value v_2 with Eve by writing it to key k_2 in m. Figure 4 illustrates the situation.

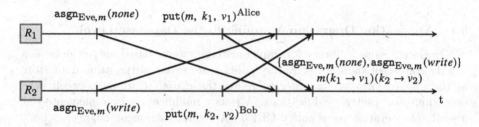

Fig. 4. Concurrent modification of Read-Write-Own policy.

After forwarding the data state and the policy modifications to the respective other replica, the common converged state looks like this: The data state for map m is extended by the two write operations $\mathsf{put}(m, k_1, v_1)$ and $\mathsf{put}(m, k_2, v_2)$. When reading from m, both the assignment to k_1 and to k_2 are visible. The policy state is updated by both rights assignments, from R_1 and from R_2, thereby overwriting previous rights assignments. Since these right assignments happened concurrently, both assignments are taken into account when determining the actual rights. When asked for the current policy for Eve, the system computes the minimum of rights assigned to Eve, which in this case is the right *none*. In this state, the operation $\mathsf{get}(m)$ is not allowed to be performed by Eve since $\mathsf{decide}(none, \mathsf{get}(m)) = Deny$. This is consistent with the fact that the assignment (k_1, v_1) should not be readable by Eve because of the protection relation between the event $\mathsf{asgn}_{Eve,\,m}(none)$ and the event $\mathsf{put}(m, k_1, v_1)^{Alice}$.

6   Implementation

In this section, we sketch how our model ProPreAC can be efficiently implemented in state-of-the-art weakly consistent storage systems. We call our implementation ACGreGate and base it on an eventually consistent data store.

To implement the model discussed in Sect. 4, we require tracking of the causality regarding policy modifications and data operations. Causality tracking using vector clocks as implemented in Amazon Dynamo [7] is known to not scale very well. The problem is that the corresponding meta data grows either linearly with the number of clients, or it grows linearly with the number of servers but is then less accurate. Tracking the information per server does not allow to express concurrent operations on the same server which under-approximates the actual system concurrency. Almeida et al. [4] propose a more efficient and accurate solution using dotted version vectors. This technology allows to track causality of operations accurately by combining server-based version vectors with more detailed tracking of individual operations. Gonçalves et al. [10] presents an implementation of this technology which features additionally low overhead in the distribution of the causality information.

6.1   Application Operation Mapping to the Database Level

ACGreGate acts as a library for implementing systems based on Antidote as a weakly consistent data store. Access policies are saved in the same data store as the application data in order to retain the causal relations between data operations and policy modifications. A policy modification is implemented as a setRight operation on a policy CRDT. A rights assignment $\mathbf{asgn}(r)_{s,o}$ boils down to a data-store operation setRight(r) on the policy object indexed by key (s,o). The key in this case is a tuple of a value representing the subject s, for example, a user name, and a value representing the object o.

In real applications, the security policies are usually not defined on the level of database operations, but on the level of the application's functions. A right in this case is therefore the permission to perform a specific operation of the application. ProPreAC, on the other hand, is based on operations of the data store and their relation to right assignments allowing these operations. This gap between application and database level can be closed by the implementation in two ways:

1. using the information about valid database operations for each application function and checking whether the current subject is authorized to execute the database operation for some application level function, or
2. authorizing access to the application level operation and logging database level operations for auditing purposes.

The first approach requires additional information about the database operations each application function is allowed to trigger. This information initially has to be given by the developer of the application. Depending on the application, programming language, and tool support it might be viable to extract the executed database operations from the source code of the application. The implementation of this approach can be done without further interaction with the application just by intercepting database operations sent by the application to the data store.

The second approach relies only on the information available from the security policies on the application level. ACGreGate has to be notified by the application about the operation to be executed. The access control system then checks the access of users to application level functions based on the application policies. The access control system intercepts all database operations. If the user has the required capabilities, the database operations are logged and relayed to the data store. This creates an auditing log of all operations that have been executed by each user under some permission. If the authorization procedure has not been successful, the user does not have the required capabilities and all corresponding database operations are discarded. After the application level function finished executing, ACGreGate is notified, blocks the database operations again and waits for the next authorization request.

6.2 Alternative Approach for Unknown Operation Mapping

In general, we want to restrict the waiting time to a minimum when applying operations. The knowledge about the database operations executed by an application operation helps to do that. But the correctness of the access control system can be guaranteed by using a causal+ capable data store [14]. This can be useful in case we do not have the relation between the application level operations and the executed database operations. In Sect. 3 we defined the protection relation as an extension of the per-object causality relation:

$$\mathsf{prot} = \mathsf{hbo} \cap \mathsf{guarding}$$

From this, we can deduce that the protection relation is a subset of the causality relation. This means that a system that preserves the causality relation automatically also preserves the protection relation. If the relation between application operations and database operations is not available, we can still implement a correct access control system by implementing causal consistency. causal+ consistency differs from causal consistency in that it requires the convergence of all replicas to the same state. In this sense, we rely on causal+ consistency in order to implement ProPreAC correctly in absence of the application-database-operation relation.

6.3 Convergence of the Policy State

We are currently implementing ACGreGate based on Antidote [20]. Antidote already has support for causal+ consistency, meaning the implementation already takes care of retaining the protection relation. The remaining problem is to conservatively integrate concurrent policy changes, as described in Sect. 3.

To implement this, we take research on convergent replicated data types (CRDTs; [18]) as enabler. The policies are implemented as a CRDT which supports the following operations: get() and setRight(R) with $R \in Right$. The setRight operation allows to modify the policy by setting a new rights assignment. Rights assignments that happened before are overwritten by this operation. Remote updates are incorporated into the local policy similar to the semantics defined in Sect. 3. All rights assignments which are causally related with the remote operation to incorporate are removed while concurrent assignments are retained before adding the new assignment to the policy. This possibly results in multiple concurrent right assignments. The get operations yields the current right assignment by taking the minimum over all concurrent rights assignments.

7 Related Work

In the area of access control for weakly consistent systems, there are two major tracks of related work: weakly consistent data stores and collaborative editors.

Eventually Consistent Data Stores. With the implementation of cloud systems, weakly consistent data stores have moved into the focus of distributed systems research. Though many protocols and implementation schemes have been proposed and implemented, the topic of access control for these systems has received surprisingly little attention. The original version of Amazon Dynamo [7] did not offer authentication and authorization capabilities. Several other related eventually consistent data stores offer meanwhile techniques to implement access control, but the granularity is not fine enough to provide access control on the application level. Riak KV [3], MongoDB [2] and Couchbase [1] all support the management of users, roles and permissions. But the smallest granularity is on the level of buckets or collections, comparable with tables in relational data bases. Typical permissions on this level allow to read, write, modify, or delete any value of the bucket or collection. A more fine-grained permission level relating to the operations on the application level is not supported.

Regarding eventually consistent data stores, Samarati et al. [15] describe a high-level approach to authorization. The general idea is to optimistically accept all operations and compensate the operations which were executed despite the security policy by performing rollbacks. While this approach guarantees convergence of the security policy, it is not clear for each operation how to undo the effect of this operation after it has been executed. One of the problems is the potential binding between operations and effects in the data store and changes of the real world. For example, a banking system allows to withdraw money from an account and the ATM outputs the money. In this case, it is hard to undo the withdrawal because the person with the money has already walked away. In addition, the guarantees given by such an optimistic system remain unclear. Effects of operations can be perceived by a user of the data store before the rollback, thereby possibly leaking sensible information.

Wobber et al. [21] present an access control model for weakly consistent mutually distrustful replicated systems. Their focus work is on partial replication with different access policies per replica. While we consider a different setting of fully replicated systems, similar problems can be identified. The causality between a policy and the subsequent operation that are permitted by the policy is captured by their model by waiting for the required policy change to arrive. However, the causality between a policy change that restricts the visibility of the effect of an operation and the subsequent execution of this operation is not captured. As such, the model still allows leaking sensitive information because of the possible violation of the protection relation between a policy change and a subsequent data operation.

Collaborative Editors. Imine et al. [11] present an access control model for distributed collaborative editors. The similarities to data stores lies in the fact that the modifications of the document in the editor can be seen as data operations and the document needs to be eventually consistent on all distributed editor instances. As such, the editors can be seen as replicas managing the document as the data state. In this setting, the policy modifications consider objects such as a character or section of text. To prevent divergence, all operations on an object are ordered by the authoring editor instance. This implies a one-to-one relation between parts of the text and the responsible editor instance, which again leads to a single point of failure. A addition, the model only considers modifying operations; all users are allowed to read the complete document. The implementation by Imine et al. [11] is very similar to an implementation of causality tracking for a data store. In contrast, our model considers read operations, which allows us to talk about leakage of information because the policy can restrict the read access, thereby protecting data modifications. Further, we introduce neither bottlenecks nor single-points-of-failure by building on the causality relation.

8   Conclusion and Future Work

We introduced ProPreAC, an access control system for weakly consistent replicated information systems. To the best of our knowledge, it is the first system that considers a causal relation between policy modifications and subsequent data operations to prevent information leakage and unauthorized data modification.

We presented a formal model of access control in weakly consistent replicated systems and formulated a definition of the correctness for access control in such a system. The definition is strongly based on the protection relation between a policy modification which restricts access to an object and a subsequent data operation modifying the object. ProPreAC preserves the protective properties of such policy modifications, thereby guaranteeing correct enforcement of the security policy. We showed how to instantiate our system with different policy schemes such as hierarchical read-write-own policy schema, thus illustrating that the model is flexible and applicable for different schemes. Finally, we gave a sketch of how an efficient implementation of the access control model for state-of-the-art replicated data stores like Riak [3] can be achieved. In contrast to currently employed access control systems, ProPreAC supports high availability, does not hinder scalability and allows to implement fine-granular and flexible security policies as required by modern information systems.

In future work, we will show that our model can be implemented such that it scales well in distributed environments with massive interaction. Additionally, the model can be extended to support additional security properties. Malicious operations can, for example, be undone if the data store offers a log of previous values for each object. Stronger properties like the global invariant that there is at least one user with administrative rights need additional synchronization.

References

1. Couchbase, December 2015. http://www.couchbase.com/
2. MongoDB for GIANT Ideas | MongoDB, December 2015. https://www.mongodb.org/
3. Riak KV December 2015. http://basho.com/products/riak-kv/
4. Almeida, P.S., Baquero, C., Gonçalves, R., Preguiça, N., Fonte, V.: Scalable and accurate causality tracking for eventually consistent stores. In: Magoutis, K., Pietzuch, P. (eds.) DAIS 2014. LNCS, vol. 8460, pp. 67–81. Springer, Heidelberg (2014). doi:10.1007/978-3-662-43352-2_6
5. Brewer, E.A.: Towards robust distributed systems (abstract). In: Proceedings of the Nineteenth Annual ACM Symposium on Principles of Distributed Computing, p. 7. PODC 2000, NY, USA. ACM, New York (2000)
6. Burckhardt, S., Gotsman, A., Yang, H., Zawirski, M.: Replicated data types: Specification, verification, optimality. In: Proceedings of the 41st ACM SIGPLAN-SIGACT Symposium on Principles of Programming Languages, pp. 271–284. POPL 2014, NY, USA. ACM, New York (2014)
7. DeCandia, G., Hastorun, D., Jampani, M., Kakulapati, G., Lakshman, A., Pilchin, A., Sivasubramanian, S., Vosshall, P., Vogels, W.: Dynamo: Amazon's highly available key-value store. In: Proceedings of Twenty-first ACM SIGOPS Symposium on Operating Systems Principles, pp. 205–220. SOSP '07, NY, USA. ACM, New York (2007)
8. Ferraiolo, D., Kuhn, R.: Role-based access control. In: 15th NIST-NCSC National Computer Security Conference, pp. 554–563 (1992)
9. Gilbert, S., Lynch, N.: Brewer's conjecture and the feasibility of consistent, available, partition-tolerant web services. SIGACT News $33(2)$, 51–59 (2002)
10. Gonçalves, R., Almeida, P.S., Baquero, C., Fonte, V.: Concise server-wide causality management for eventually consistent data stores. In: Bessani, A., Bouchenak, S. (eds.) DAIS 2015. LNCS, vol. 9038, pp. 66–79. Springer, Heidelberg (2015). doi:10.1007/978-3-319-19129-4_6
11. Imine, A., Cherif, A., Rusinowitch, M.: A flexible access control model for distributed collaborative editors. In: Jonker, W., Petković, M. (eds.) SDM 2009. LNCS, vol. 5776, pp. 89–106. Springer, Heidelberg (2009). doi:10.1007/978-3-642-04219-5_6
12. Jin, X., Krishnan, R., Sandhu, R.: A unified attribute-based access control model covering DAC, MAC and RBAC. In: Cuppens-Boulahia, N., Cuppens, F., Garcia-Alfaro, J. (eds.) DBSec 2012. LNCS, vol. 7371, pp. 41–55. Springer, Heidelberg (2012). doi:10.1007/978-3-642-31540-4_4

13. Jin, X., Sandhu, R., Krishnan, R.: RABAC: role-centric attribute-based access control. In: Kotenko, I., Skormin, V. (eds.) MMM-ACNS 2012. LNCS, vol. 7531, pp. 84–96. Springer, Heidelberg (2012). doi:10.1007/978-3-642-33704-8_8

14. Lloyd, W., Freedman, M.J., Kaminsky, M., Andersen, D.G.: Don't settle for eventual: scalable causal consistency for wide-area storage with COPS. In: Proceedings of the Twenty-Third ACM Symposium on Operating Systems Principles, pp. 401–416. SOSP 2011, NY, USA. ACM, New York (2011)

15. Samarati, P., Ammann, P., Jajodia, S.: Maintaining replicated authorizations in distributed database systems. Data Knowl. Eng. **18**(1), 55–84 (1996)

16. Samarati, P., de Vimercati, S.C.: Access control: policies, models, and mechanisms. In: Focardi, R., Gorrieri, R. (eds.) FOSAD 2000. LNCS, vol. 2171, pp. 137–196. Springer, Heidelberg (2001). doi:10.1007/3-540-45608-2_3

17. Saunders, G., Hitchens, M., Varadharajan, V.: An analysis of access control models. In: Pieprzyk, J., Safavi-Naini, R., Seberry, J. (eds.) ACISP 1999. LNCS, vol. 1587, pp. 281–293. Springer, Heidelberg (1999). doi:10.1007/3-540-48970-3_23

18. Shapiro, M., Preguiça, N., Baquero, C., Zawirski, M.: Conflict-free replicated data types. In: Défago, X., Petit, F., Villain, V. (eds.) SSS 2011. LNCS, vol. 6976, pp. 386–400. Springer, Heidelberg (2011). doi:10.1007/978-3-642-24550-3_29

19. Shapiro, M., Preguiça, N.M., Baquero, C., Zawirski, M.: Convergent and commutative replicated data types. Bull. EATCS **104**, 67–88 (2011b)

20. SyncFree: Antidote reference platform(2016). https://github.com/SyncFree/antidote

21. Wobber, T., Rodeheffer, T.L., Terry, D.B.: Policy-based access control for weakly consistent replication. In: Proceedings of the 5th European Conference on Computer Systems, pp. 293–306. EuroSys 2010, NY, USA. ACM, New York (2010)

Privacy-Aware Trust Negotiation

Ruben Rios[✉], Carmen Fernandez-Gago, and Javier Lopez

Network, Information and Computer Security (NICS) Lab,
University of Malaga, Málaga, Spain
{ruben,mcgago,jlm}@lcc.uma.es

Abstract. Software engineering and information security have traditionally followed divergent paths but lately some efforts have been made
to consider security from the early phases of the Software Development
Life Cycle (SDLC). This paper follows this line and concentrates on the
incorporation of trust negotiations during the requirements engineering
phase. More precisely, we provide an extension to the SI* modelling
language, which is further formalised using Answer Set Programming
specifications to support the automatic verification of the model and the
detection of privacy conflicts caused by trust negotiations.

Keywords: Secure software engineering · Requirements engineering ·
Goal-oriented modelling · Privacy · Trust

1 Introduction

In recent years, the number of vulnerabilities and attacks present in software
systems have led to a growing interest in incorporating security from the early
phases of the SDLC. Also, the notions of trust and privacy are gaining momen-
tum due to the proliferation of new computing paradigms where devices from
different security domains interact with each other and exchange valuable information. Our work deals with the confluence between secure software engineering,
privacy and trust.

This paper presents a framework for identifying privacy threats caused by the
uncontrolled disclosure of information during a trust negotiation. Trust negotiation systems [15] model how the exchange of information between entities,
wishing to establish a relationship, is done. Our framework is capable of modelling such systems and detecting potential threats automatically early in the
specification and design of the system. Thus, it facilitates the incorporation of
privacy-aware trust negotiations in the development of socio-technical systems.
To that end, we build our framework as an extension of SI* [6], which is designed
to capture the objectives and relationships between various entities within an
organisational setting and already supports the definition of some security concepts, such as delegation and trust.

The proposed framework models trust negotiations as a relationship between
two entities that pursue a common goal[1]. To that end, they need to exchange

---

[1] N.B. That we assume that the goal is always common. The consideration of different
goals is out of the scope of the paper.

© Springer International Publishing AG 2016
G. Barthe et al. (Eds.): STM 2016, LNCS 9871, pp. 98–105, 2016.
DOI: 10.1007/978-3-319-46598-2_7

information that may be sensitive and thus impact their privacy. Therefore, informational resources are labelled with a particular sensitivity level that defines how important it is to keep control of this information. The framework detects inconsistencies with the privacy policy by comparing it with the sensitivity level of the resources being exchanged during a trust negotiation.

The rest of this paper is organised as follows. Section 2 introduces the related work in the area whereas Sect. 3 deeps into SI*, which is the basis of our work. Our proposal for a privacy-aware trust negotiation methodology is presented in Sect. 4 and its formalisation in Sect. 5. Section 6 concludes the paper and outlines the future work.

2   Related Work

A common approach to requirements engineering is to follow a goal-oriented methodology based on concepts such as actors and goals rather than on programming concepts. The KAOS framework [14] is based on temporal logics and Tropos [3] is founded on the i* organisational modelling framework [16]. These frameworks have been extended to deal with security requirements. The notions of obstacle [13] and anti-goal [12] have been introduced to KAOS. Secure Tropos [7] extends Tropos by making explicit ownership relationships and actor entitlements. The modelling language used by Secure Tropos is SI* [6], which incorporates a number of security concepts. New goal-oriented methodologies have recently been proposed, such as STS [10], which puts more emphasis on authorisation and the notion of document.

Although research on security engineering is extensive, privacy has traditionally been left out. The only support to privacy in most of these frameworks, including SI* and STS, is considering it as data confidentiality. Notwithstanding, several privacy engineering methods exist. Authors in [8] tackle privacy issues by defining a set of best practices in the different stages of the development process. LINDDUN [4] defines a mapping among privacy threats and the software components in order to elicit privacy requirements. Pris [5] models privacy requirements as organisational goals and later privacy patterns are used for identifying architectures.

The closest approach to ours is the one followed by PP-Trust-$\mathcal{X}$ [11]. The main difference with our proposal is that our framework detects privacy conflicts during the requirements engineering phase rather than at runtime. To the best of our knowledge no other works address this problem early in the SDLC.

3   The SI* Modelling Language

We provide next an overview of the SI* modelling language [6], that is, a description of core elements and some extensions, which are relevant to our work.

3.1 SI* Core Elements

SI* defines a set of concepts, which are necessary to identify the actors[2] involved in the system, their goals, entitlements and the relationships between them. An *agent* is an active entity of the system, which plays a particular *role*. This is represented by means of the *play* relationship. The notion of *service* is used to refer to either a goal, a task or a resource. A *goal* is a desirable situation or interest expressed by an entity, a *task* is a set of actions that can be executed to fulfil a goal, and a *resource* is an artefact produced or used by a goal or task. The connection between services and actors are expressed by means of three relationships: *own* denotes the authority of entities over resources and goals; *provide* represents the ability of an actor to accomplish a goal or to provide a resource; and *request* denotes the interest of an entity over a goal or resource.

There are some additional predicates to denote that a goal can be attained by fulfilling a set of subgoals, and predicates to deal with social relationships such as delegation and trust. The formalisation of the aforementioned elements is done using answer set programming (ASP) syntax [2], as shown on the left side of Table 1. Note that only the most relevant predicates are provided here.

Table 1. Relevant SI* predicates

Goal model
actor(Actor: a)
agent(Agent: a)
role(Role: r)
service(Service: s)
goal(Goal: g)
task(Task: t)
resource(Resource: r)
Actor properties
play(Agent: a, Role: r)
own(Actor: a, Service: s)
request(Actor: a, Service: s)
provide(Actor: a, Service: s)
Goal refinement
subgoal(Service: s_1, Service: s_2)
AND_decomp(Service: s, Service: s_1, Service: s_2)
OR_decomp(Service: s, Service: s_1, Service: s_2)
means_end(Service: s_1, Service: s_2)
Social relations
del_perm(Actor: a_1, Actor: a_2, Service: s)
del_exec(Actor: a_1, Actor: a_2, Service: s)
trust_perm(Actor: a_1, Actor: a_2, Service: s)
trust_exec(Actor: a_1, Actor: a_2, Service: s)

Resource model
stored_in(Resource: r, Resource: r_1)
part_of(Resource: r, Resource: r_1)
require(Resource: r, Resource: r_1)
Permission model
permission(Actor: a, Resource: r, PType: pt)
del_perm(Actor: a, Actor: a_1, Resource: r, PType: pt)
trust_perm(Actor: a, Actor: a_1, Resource: r)
Security and Threat model
secure_req(Resource: r, SProperty: sp)
secure_req(Goal: g, SProperty: sp, Resource: r)
threat(Actor: a, Resource: r, SProperty: sp)
threat(Actor: a, Goal: g, SProperty: sp, Resource: r)
Asset model
asset(Service: s, Actor: a)
sensitivity(Service: s, SLevel: sl, Actor: a)
secure_req(Service: s, SProperty: sp, Actor: a)
Trust model
trust_perm(Actor: a, Actor: a_1, Service: s, PType: pt)

---

[2] The notion of *actor* is inherited from i* and is used only when it is not necessary to distinguish between the concepts of agent and role.

3.2   SI* Extensions

Although SI* is a very powerful language, some extensions have been proposed to support the modelling of new scenarios.

Asnar et al. [1] introduced different levels of permissions on resources and relationships between them. The *stored_in* relationship indicates the physical location of an informational resource, *part_of* denotes that a resource is composed of other resources, and *require* denotes that a resource needs another resource to function. Moreover, resources are marked with a *security requirement* label that indicates the security property (confidentiality, integrity and availability) that must hold for it. Actors can be provided with three different types of *permissions*: access, modify or manage permission. Finally, the *threat* predicate holds if an actor violates the security property on a resource. Paci et al. [9] introduce two additional extensions to detect insider threats in organisations. The first one is based on the notion of *asset*, which is a service for which the owner specifies the *sensitivity level* as well as a *security property* that denotes the level of protection demanded by the actor for protecting the service. The second extension is a *trust* model that enables to specify the trust level that an actor places on another actor with respect to a given permission on a particular asset. A summary of the aforementioned predicates is presented on the right side of Table 1.

4   Trust Negotiation Extension

We present here our privacy-aware extension of SI* for trust negotiations.

4.1   Overview

A trust negotiation [15] is a *dual relationship* in which the participants exchange (accredited) information in order to establish trust as a means to achieve a goal.

Based on the above definition, we propose to model trust negotiations based on existing features of the SI* modelling language, as shown in Fig. 1. In this figure we can distinguish two main components that play a fundamental role in the modelling of trust negotiations. First, the trust relationship in which data is demanded by each of the actors and the goal to be accomplished. Second, the informational resources owned by the actors, which need to be under control. For that reason, these are marked with a privacy requirement label and a sensitivity level to indicate the risk of sharing these data.

4.2   Trust Negotiaton Relationship

Trust negotiations pose a natural tension due to the conflicting objectives of privacy and trust. On the one hand, trust is founded on the availability of information about other actors. On the other hand, privacy refers to the ability to keep control of sensitive information. As a result, trust negotiations are ruled by the amount of information that each participant *demands* and the amount of data that is willing to *offer*.

This type of relationship can be represented with a notation that is consistent with SI*. Actors can be represented as circles, the goal as a squared oval. These elements are connected by a labelled arc. The arc is further parameterised with the information being requested. Since a trust negotiation is a dual relationship it would be necessary to have one arc in each direction. However, for the sake of clarity and simplicity, we propose an alternative notation with a single arc, as depicted in Fig. 1[3].

4.3   Privacy-Aware Data Disclosure

The modelling of trust negotiation must also take into consideration the ownership of data and whether there are any privacy requirements for these data. Similar to previous extensions that incorporate *security requirement* labels, we propose the use of a *privacy requirement* label to indicate that a particular resource must maintain a specific level of privacy.

Privacy violations are usually associated with a loss of control over data. To this end, we adopt the *part_of* relationship to represent the composition of data resources. Data resources may be additionally labelled with a *sensitivity level* to indicate how valuable this information is. Moreover, the sensitivity is related to the level of detail of data offered. For the sake of simplicity, we consider only 3 sensitivity levels: *Low*, *Medium*, and *High*; and, consequently, we also deal with 3 levels of granularity for each data type. This depends on the data type being considered. Note that the requirements engineer can easily extend this feature to incorporate as many sensitivity and granularity levels as desired.

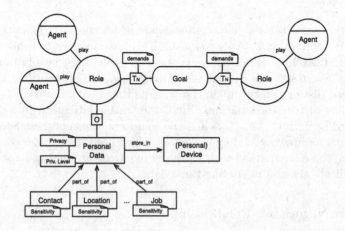

Fig. 1. Trust negotiation representation in SI*

---

[3] Note that pentagons point to the party whose information is being demanded.

5   Reasoning Support

We present in this section how verification of the model can be done.

5.1   Predicates

First, a predicate for representing the trust negotiation relationship itself is needed. The predicate *trust_neg* indicates that actors[4] a_1 and a_2 can initiate a negotiation to achieve a common goal g. Note that it is not reasonable to have a trust negotiation where the two actors are the same. This will be reflected later in the rules presented in Sect. 5.2.

The predicate *offers* denotes that actor a is willing to offer resource r up to a given granularity level $l \in \{Low, Medium, High\}$. The granularity level is inversely proportional to the *sensitivity* of a resource. Similarly, the predicate *demands* indicates that an actor a requests a resource r with at least a given granularity l. This predicate indicates to which actor the resource is demanded since an actor can be involved in several trust negotiations. However, the predicate *offers* does not consider this as it expresses the level of detail that the agent will release regardless of who is involved in the negotiation. Finally, the predicate *privacy_req* denotes the level of privacy that needs to be satisfied for a particular resource. These are predicates P_1 to P_5.

P_1:   trust_neg(Actor: a_1, Actor: a_2, Goal: g)
P_2:   offers(Actor: a, Resource: r, Level: l)
P_3:   demands(Actor: a_1, Actor: a_2, Resource: r, Level: l)
P_4:   sensitivity(Resource: r, Level: l)
P_5:   privacy_req(Resource: r, Level: l)
P_6:   satisfy(Actor: a_1, Actor: a_2)
P_7:   data_exposure(Actor: a, Resource: r, Level: l)
P_8:   establish_trust(Actor: a_1, Actor: a_2, Goal: g)
P_9:   privacy_threat(Actor: a, Resource: r, Level: l)

Besides the aforementioned predicates, other intermediate predicates are needed. The predicate *satisfy* denotes that an actor satisfies the demands of another actor. The predicate *data_exposure* indicates that the resource r belonging to an actor a is exposed to a certain degree l. Two additional predicates indicate whether the trust negotiation process can be fulfilled (*establish_trust*) and whether there is a privacy breach (*privacy_threat*) with respect to the established privacy policy. These are predicates P_6 to P_9.

5.2   Rules

The first set of rules, from R_1 to R_3, express that the sensitivity of a resource is inversely proportional to its granularity level. Rule R_4 denotes that one actor

---

[4] Actors are used for simplicity but the actual predicates and rules should consider roles and agents as arguments.

satisfies the demands of another actor if the resource is offered with at least as much granularity as desired[5]. The actors that demand and offer resources cannot be the same.

R_1: offers(A, R, *High*) $\leftarrow$ owns(A, R) $\wedge$ sensitivity(R, *Low*)
R_2: offers(A, R, *Medium*) $\leftarrow$ owns(A, R) $\wedge$ sensitivity(R, *Medium*)
R_3: offers(A, R, *Low*) $\leftarrow$ owns(A, R) $\wedge$ sensitivity(R, *High*)
R_4: satisfy(A_1, A_2) $\leftarrow$ offers(A_1, R, G_{L_1}) $\wedge$ demands(A_2, A_1, R, G_{L_2})
                                 $\wedge$ ($G_{L_1} \succeq G_{L_2}$) $\wedge$ ($A_1 \neq A_2$)
R_5: establish_trust(A_1, A_2, G) $\leftarrow$ trust_neg(A_1, A_2, G) $\wedge$ satisfy(A_1, A_2)
R_6: data_exposure(A_1, R, E_L) $\leftarrow$ offers(A_1, R, E_L) $\wedge$ satisfy(A_1, A_2)
R_7: data_exposure(A_1, R, E_L) $\leftarrow$ offers(A_1, R_1, E_L) $\wedge$ satisfy(A_1, A_2)
                                 $\wedge$ part_of(R_1, R)
R_8: sensitivity(R, *Low*) $\leftarrow$ not sensitivity(R, _) $\wedge$ resource(R)
R_9: sensitivity(R_1, S_L) $\leftarrow$ not sensitivity(R_1, _) $\wedge$ resource(R_1)
                                 $\wedge$ sensitivity(R, S_L) $\wedge$ part_of(R_1, R)
R_{10}: privacy_threat(A, R, E_L) $\leftarrow$ privacy_req(R, P_L) $\wedge$ data_exposure(A, R, E_L)
                                 $\wedge$ ($E_L \succeq P_L$)

R_5 states that it is possible to establish a trust relationship whenever the trust negotiation has been satisfied. Rules R_6 and R_7 express the amount of information being exposed due to the fulfilment of a trust negotiation.

Rules R_8 and R_9 consider the case of having resources without a predefined sensitivity level. The former assigns a *Low* sensitivity level while the latter impose the same sensitivity level as the one defined for the parent resource. Note that the '_' symbol represents that this argument is irrelevant for the rule to be triggered. Finally, rule R_{10} states that the privacy policy is violated when the level of exposure of a resource exceeds its desired privacy level.

6   Conclusion

This paper presents a framework to include trust negotiation models in the early phases of the SDLC. The framework is based on the SI* modelling language and enables the automatic detection of privacy threats due to disclosure of data beyond a sensitivity level. The detection of privacy threats can aid in the refinement of privacy policies in the system.

We are currently working on extending the features of our framework to capture more complex scenarios. A future research line will be to consider multiple data exchanges when an actor is engaged in multiple trust negotiations.

Acknowledgements. This work has been partially funded by the European Commission through the Marie Curie Training Network NeCS (H2020-MSCA-ITN-2015-675320), the Spanish Ministry of Economy and Competitiveness through PERSIST (TIN2013-41739-R) and PRECISE (TIN2014-54427-JIN), which is co-financed by FEDER.

---

[5] We use the $\succeq$ symbol to compare ordinal values: $High \succ Medium \succ Low$.

References

1. Asnar, Y., Li, T., Massacci, F., Paci, F.: Computer aided threat identification. In: 13th IEEE Conference on Commerce and Enterprise Computing, pp. 145–152 (2011)
2. Brewka, G., Eiter, T., Truszczyński, M.: Answer set programming at a glance. Commun. ACM **54**(12), 92–103 (2011)
3. Castro, J., Giorgini, P., Kolp, M., Mylopoulos, J.: Tropos: a requirements-driven methodology for agent-oriented software. In: Henderson-Sellers, B., Giorgini, P. (eds.) Agent-Oriented Methodologies. Idea Group, Hershey (2005)
4. Deng, M., Wuyts, K., Scandariato, R., Preneel, B., Joosen, W.: A privacy threat analysis framework: supporting the elicitation and fulfillment of privacy requirements. Requir. Eng. **16**(1), 3–32 (2011)
5. Kalloniatis, C., Kavakli, E., Gritzalis, S.: Addressing privacy requirements in system design: the PriS method. Requir. Eng. **13**, 241–255 (2008)
6. Massacci, F., Mylopoulos, J., Zannone, N.: Security requirements engineering: the SI* modeling language and the secure tropos methodology. In: Ras, Z.W., Tsay, L.-S. (eds.) Advances in Intelligent Information Systems. SCI, vol. 265, pp. 147–174. Springer, Heidelberg (2010)
7. Mouratidis, H., GiorginiI, P.: Secure tropos: a security-oriented extension of the tropos methodology. Int. J. Softw. Eng. Know. **17**(02), 285–309 (2007)
8. Notario, N., Crespo, A., Martín, Y., del Álamo, J.M., Métayer, D.L., Antignac, T., Kung, A., Kroener, I., Wright, D.: PRIPARE: integrating privacy best practices into a privacy engineering methodology. In: International Workshop on Privacy, Engineering, pp. 151–158 (2015)
9. Paci, F., Fernandez-Gago, C., Moyano, F.: Detecting insider threats: a trust-aware framework. In: 8th International Conference on Availability, Reliability and Security (ARES), pp. 121–130, September 2013
10. Paja, E., Dalpiaz, F., Giorgini, P.: Modelling and reasoning about security requirements in socio-technical systems. Data Knowl. Eng. **98**, 123–143 (2015)
11. Squicciarini, A., Bertino, E., Ferrari, E., Paci, F., Thuraisingham, B.: PP-Trust-X: a system for privacy preserving trust negotiations. ACM Trans. Inf. Syst. Secur. **10**(3), 1–50 (2007)
12. van Lamsweerde, A.: Elaborating security requirements by construction of intentional anti-models. In: 26th International Conference on Software Engineering, ICSE 2004, pp. 148–157. IEEE Computer Society, Washington, DC (2004)
13. van Lamsweerde, A., Letier, E.: Handling obstacles in goal-oriented requirements engineering. IEEE T Softw. Eng. **26**(10), 978–1005 (2000)
14. van Lamsweerde, A., Darimont, R., Letier, E.: Managing conflicts in goal-driven requirements engineering. IEEE T Softw. Eng. **24**(11), 908–926 (1998)
15. Winslett, M., Yu, T., Seamons, K.E., Hess, A., Jacobson, J., Jarvis, R., Smith, B., Yu, L.: Negotiating trust on the web. IEEE Internet Comput. **6**(6), 30–37 (2002)
16. Yu, E.: Modelling strategic relationships for process reengineering. Ph.D thesis. University of Toronto, Canada (1996)

Securely Derived Identity Credentials on Smart Phones via Self-enrolment

Fabian van den Broek, Brinda Hampiholi$^{(\boxtimes)}$, and Bart Jacobs

Institute for Computing and Information Sciences,
Radboud University, Nijmegen, The Netherlands
{f.vandenbroek,brinda,bart}@cs.ru.nl

Abstract. In the last decade traditional identity documents have been equipped with an embedded NFC-chip to enable wireless access to the relevant data. This applies in particular to passports, following the ICAO standard, but increasingly also to other identification documents, such as driver's licenses. Such electronic identity (eID) documents can now be used as "mother cards" by the users to remotely enrol and obtain derived credentials which can in turn be used for identification and authentication, notably on smart phones. These self-enrolment possibilities are becoming popular, because they are easier and cheaper than traditional, face-to-face enrolments.

This paper first describes a protocol for obtaining credentials on smart phones from an eID document, that has been implemented using the "IRMA" attribute-based credential technology. This basic protocol cannot exclude that someone enrols with another person's eID document. Subsequently several mechanisms are discussed for securing a proper binding between the user and the eID document used for enrolment.

1 Introduction

User authentication is a process that confirms the binding between a user and his presented identity to an authenticating entity, for instance, to a service provider. Typically, a service provider authenticates a user by verifying the presented credentials, e.g., a password or a proof of knowledge which are considered as evidences for the user's claimed identity. To ensure that the service providers are guaranteed of the credentials' authenticity during authentication, the credentials have to be issued to the user (i.e., to the user's authenticating device) in a secure manner after verifying the user's identity during an enrolment phase. Thus, secure and trustworthy enrolment plays a very important role in any authentication ecosystem.

Secure enrolment consists of verifying the real-world identity of a user (also called identity-proofing) and registering the user before issuing an identity credential. Traditionally, face-to-face enrolments are required whenever important (physical) identity documents or credentials are issued to users. For example, a passport is issued after the user has applied for it and a government authority has verified the user's identity during a face-to-face meeting at the authority's office.

G. Barthe et al. (Eds.): STM 2016, LNCS 9871, pp. 106–121, 2016.
DOI: 10.1007/978-3-319-46598-2_8

Such an enrolment gives strong trust assurance to an authenticating entity about the passport holder's claimed identity and about the link between the user and the passport. However face-to-face enrolments are not user-friendly and more importantly, they are very expensive in terms of time, costs and resources. So in recent years there is a push towards remote self-enrolment of users where, of course, security requirements remain strong, but are harder to guarantee.

This paper investigates secure self-enrolment of users in which users can derive their identity credentials from their ICAO[1] standard electronic identification (eID) documents (e.g. e-passports), onto their authenticating devices. In this paper, we follow the definition of 'derived credential' found in NIST Special Publication 800-63-1 [1]:

> *"A credential issued based on proof of possession and control of a token associated with a previously issued credential, so as not to duplicate the identity proofing process".*

The trust for the new credential on an authenticating device is derived from the strong identity binding associated with the authenticated eID document during enrolment. For this paper we consider smart phones as authenticating devices, because they can directly connect with enrolment services and can contain capabilities to communicate with eID documents. This paper abstracts from the specific credentials obtained through self-enrolment and its results can be applicable to different types of credentials. However, the motivation for this topic comes from our earlier work in the field of Attribute Based Credentials (ABCs) [2] within an ongoing research project called IRMA[2] (I Reveal My Attributes). ABCs have many nice properties, but for this paper it is important to know that these credentials are authentic and non-transferable. But, of course the credentials are only as trustworthy as their issuance process, which is why we are interested in secure self-enrolment.

Self-enrolment via eIDs is convenient for a user as it can be done from any location and is very inexpensive, both time- and cost-wise. It is also secure, in principle, as one builds self-enrolment on top of an earlier face-to-face enrolment that was carried out for eID issuance.

A high level picture of our approach to eID-based self-enrolment is given in Fig. 1. The first three steps constitute the enrolment phase, which the user goes through only once for obtaining his credentials. The last 'showing' steps on the right suggest how the issued credentials can be used, selectively, to authenticate to multiple service providers. This paper focuses on these first three enrolment steps, and will especially elaborate the user's interaction with the Enroller and the Issuer. Details will be given in Sect. 3.

---

[1] International Civil Aviation Organization standard document 9303 (http://www.icao.int/publications/Documents/9303_p3_v2_cons_en.pdf).

[2] See https://www.irmacard.org/ for more information.

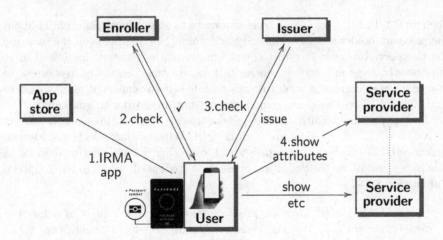

Fig. 1. Self-enrolment using a standard eID document and a smart phone with NFC capability to get derived credentials on the phone.

1.1 Our Contribution

Taking our implementations of several experimental forms of self-enrolment within the IRMA context as a starting point, we explore how to guarantee a higher level of trust by combining several options that are available, in principle, to a wider audience. The conclusion that emerges is:

1. attribute-based authentication technology provides a natural setting (ecosystem) for self-enrolment, providing different attributes for different authentication scenarios;
2. several methods exist or are appearing (such as, eID documents with PIN, biometric checks, existing logins) that make trusted self-enrolment a viable new approach in identity management;
3. trusted self-enrolment requires more than a single protocol, and can be realised by combining several self-enrolment protocols, involving possibly overlapping attributes; they lead to higher levels of trust if they yield consistent outcomes; in this way the separate protocols reinforce each other.

2   Background

Attribute-based credentials (ABCs). ABCs can be considered a privacy-enhancing technology (PET). An *attribute* is a characteristic or a qualification of a person. Attributes can either be identifying (e.g., 'full name', 'address') or non-identifying (e.g., 'student', 'age over 18'). Collectively, these attributes can constitute the identity of a person. An attribute-based credential is a cryptographic container of a few attributes that is signed by an authoritative party. The creation of an attribute-based credential is called *issuing*. This is an interactive cryptographic protocol in which an issuer authority digitally signs the user's credentials with his private key. The credentials are issued in such a way that they are associated to the user's secret key that is securely stored on the user's authentication device. Thus, ABCs are authentic and non-transferable. One special thing about an ABC is that the attributes can be selectively disclosed; thus, the ABCs achieve data minimization and privacy protection via contextual authentication.

ICAO standard. The International Civil Aviation Organization (ICAO) runs a 'machine readable travel documents' programme. Its main purpose is to develop and maintain open specifications for automated access to data in passports. This includes embedded chips that can be accessed wirelessly, via Near Field Communication (NFC).

These chips contain the information that is printed on the main page of the passport, such as name, date of birth, picture, date of issuance etc., but possibly more, like fingerprints. Access to these fingerprints is restricted, but the other data can be accessed without prior authorisation. The data in the passport are digitally signed, so that their integrity can be checked. In the current context two protocols are of special importance. For more information, see [3].

– *Basic Access Control (BAC).* The user data in the embedded chip in a passport are cryptographically protected. The required cryptographic keys can be derived from the combination of: document number, date of birth, expiry number. These can be obtained by scanning the machine readable zone at the bottom of the main passport page. They can also be provided manually, like in the screenshot on the left in Fig. 3. The protocol that derives the relevant keys and uses them for data transfer is called Basic Access Control (BAC). It is implemented in any device that reads e-passport (including the IRMA app).
– *Active Authentication (AA).* The data that are read via BAC includes a document-specific public key. The associated private key is securely stored inside the chip in the passport. The so-called Active Authentication protocol uses this key pair to verify the authenticity of the passport via a standard challenge-response check[3] to ensure that the passport is not a clone.

3 Basic Self-enrolment with eID Documents

Our self-enrolment protocol allows the user to enrol remotely (from any location) through his smart phone using his eID document to get authentic, derived credentials on his smart phone. The entities that are involved in this protocol are:

– *User* - Entity who initiates self-enrolment with his eID document and his smart phone in order to get authentic derived credentials on his phone;
– *Enroller* - Entity who verifies the user's identity (i.e. eID document), carries out enrolment for the user before the credentials can be issued to him;

---

[3] See also https://www.commoncriteriaportal.org/files/ppfiles/c0247_epp.pdf.

- *Issuer* - Entity who issues derived credentials to the user upon getting an enrolment confirmation message from the Enroller.

Note that in specific scenarios the Enroller and Issuer can be the same entity.

In our basic self-enrolment protocol, we assume that the user's eID document has an NFC chip and that the user's smart phone supports NFC, so that the eID document can be read by/via the phone. Below we describe the protocol that summarizes the communication between the user's phone, Enroller and an Issuer during self-enrolment. See also Fig. 2.

1. A user connects to the Enroller securely (e.g. via TLS) through his phone, requests for derived credentials using his eID document, enters the BAC (see Sect. 2) data present in the eID: document number, date of birth and document expiry date on his phone, and holds his eID document against (the NFC reader of) his phone.
2. The Enroller reads the user's eID via the user's phone's NFC interface and performs the following checks on the eID:
   - a check for data integrity: by verifying the digital signature on the (hashes of the) data groups, the Enroller verifies if the eID data are not altered;
   - a check for authenticity: using the ICAO-defined active authentication (see Sect. 2), the Enroller verifies if the eID is not cloned;
   - a check of the user's eID against a database of revoked (e.g. lost/stolen) eID documents. This check is possible only if the Enroller has access to such a database, which is typically maintained by public authorities.
3. If the above eID checks are successful, then the Enroller sends a digitally signed user-identity confirmation message to the Issuer. This message contains the user's eID data that the Issuer can sign and issue to the user as derived credentials.
4. The Issuer verifies the Enroller's signature on the confirmation message, connects to the user's phone and issues signed eID credentials to the user's phone — so that the phone is ready to be used as an authentication device.

The above protocol considers the user's eID document as a *mother card* from which an Issuer derives user's identity credentials and issues them securely to the user's phone. After this issuance, the user can use his phone as his authenticating device and authenticate to any entity with the issued credentials. The self-enrolment protocol, although remotely done, ensures that the user is in possession of a valid eID and that the identity credentials are derived onto his phone from that authentic source.

The above approach may give clearly separated roles between public and private parties. Public authorities are the traditional trusted root for identity information about citizens. They remain so in our basic enrolment protocol, via the eID documents that they issue. Private parties may develop smart phone apps for derived identity credentials and play the roles of Enroller and Issuer, and thus build innovative identity management systems on top of the publicly issued e-documents.

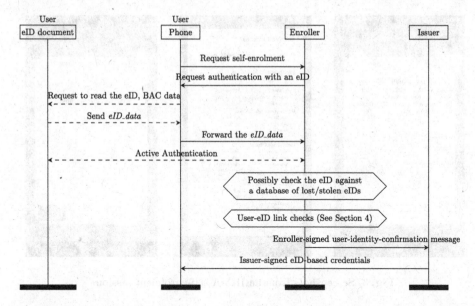

Fig. 2. Basic self-enrolment protocol using a standard eID document. The dashed arrows in the figure indicate the phone as a NFC reader and the solid arrows indicate the phone as the currently enrolling user-device (potential credential carrier).

3.1 Implementation of Basic Self-enrolment Protocol

We have implemented the basic self-enrolment protocol in an attribute-based credential (ABC) [2] framework based on a technology called IRMA that has been developed at Radboud University, Nijmegen, Netherlands. IRMA has created an efficient and simple smart card and smart phone implementation of ABCs, based on Idemix from IBM [4–6]. The fundamental idea of credential design and a broader non-technical description of the IRMA technology is given in Alpar et al. [7]. Our implementation[4] uses:

- eID documents such as passports, identity cards or driver's licenses as the standard identity documents;
- Android-based smart phones enabled with NFC as the user-devices;
- an IRMA (Android) app;
- an Enroller server;
- an Issuer server.

In our implementation, the user chooses to enrol with his eID document via his smartphone's IRMA app[5] and enters the BAC data manually or by scanning a QR code that is printed on the latest version of Dutch driver's license. The

---

[4] IRMA self-enrolment implementation details can be found at https://github.com/ credentials/irma_mno_server/blob/master/README.md.
[5] More details on IRMA smartphone app can be found at https://www.irmacard.org/ irmaphone/.

Fig. 3. Screenshots from an IRMA self-enrolment session

IRMA app essentially functions as a remote card reader for the enroller, reading some data from the eID document and sending it to the Enroller server. This server then verifies the validity of the document, extracts some user's personal data from it, and requests the Issuer server to issue some credentials containing the extracted data to the smart phone[6]. Some of the screenshots of the IRMA app handling self-enrolment are provided in Fig. 3 below.

3.2   Weakness of Basic Self-enrolment

Although the basic self-enrolment protocol is user-friendly, inexpensive for both user and the Enroller, and results in authentic credentials on the user's smart phone, it has an important weakness: a malicious user might use someone else's eID document (stolen, lost or borrowed) and carry out the protocol. This would lead to the malicious user wrongfully getting the eID owner's credentials issued to his phone as his identity credentials. From then onward, the user can impersonate the eID-owner during online authentications with his phone. This attack is possible because there is little binding between the user and the identity document (or the mother card) that is used for the enrolment. We will address this weakness by considering several user-binding solutions described in Sect. 4.

3.3   Deriving Credentials from Common Access Card (CAC)

On a conceptual level, our self-enrolment approach has some overlap with methods developed for deriving credentials from special US-identity cards such as Common Access Card (CAC), but it also differs in several essential aspects.

---

[6] How IRMA enrolment works can be seen in action in the Youtube video https://www.youtube.com/watch?v=q6IihEQFPys, see especially from 1:24 to 1:52.

A CAC is a Personal Identity Verification (PIV) card issued by the U.S. Department of Defense that is meant for closed user groups (e.g. employees of government agencies). An application that uses CAC as the mother card to derive PIV credentials on mobile devices is Entrust Mobile Derived Credential solution[7]. It requires the user to undergo a derived credential enrolment process which involves his PC (desktop or laptop) that is connected to a CAC via the card reader, his mobile device and Entrust's Self Service Module (SSM). The enrolment takes place as follows.

1. The user navigates to the SSM's web page through the web browser on his PC and authenticates to the SSM using his PIV/CAC smartcard. The CAC gets activated by the user-specific PIN.
2. The SSM validates PIV credential on the card and lets the user select the link to request a derived PIV credential.
3. To ensure a secure user-device binding, the SSM uses 'Email with password via encrypted email' activation method in which two emails are sent to the user's pre-registered email address:
   - the first email is unencrypted and contains an encrypted link back to the SSM's web page for issuance of the derived credential, that can be decrypted using the password in the second email;
   - the second email is encrypted and contains a one-time password. This email can be decrypted only with the PIV credentials found on the user's CAC smartcard.
4. On entering the correct password on the mobile device, the user obtains the derived PIV credential from the SSM.

Entrust's enrolment is available only to a closed group of government agency's employees who already have a CAC smartcard and a government-issued secure email account. This type of enrolment achieves user and device binding by sending one-time password to the pre-registered email address of the user.

   In comparison with the enrolment process described above, our self-enrolment implementation:

- is not restricted to a closed group with separate channels — via pre-issued email address;
- uses the phone's NFC capability to read out the ICAO standard eID document (e-passport or a driver's license) that are in principle available for everyone;
- supports eID documents without the PIN code activation — although eIDs with PIN are emerging, see Subsect. 4.1;
- works in the context of attribute-based credentials (ABCs) instead of PKI certificates.
- does not achieve user-binding in its current form.

---

[7] https://www.entrust.com/wp-content/uploads/2014/10/Mobile-Derived-Credential-WEB2-Nov15.pdf.

4   User-Binding Solutions

In this section, we describe several solutions that can achieve the much needed user-eID binding during self-enrolment.

4.1   PIN Code Check During Self-enrolment

Probably the simplest solution for achieving user-binding is to equip an ICAO standard identity document with a PIN that is only known to the owner of the document — like for Common Access Cards (CACs). In the Netherlands, electronic driver's licenses with an experimental PIN are currently being tested for strong online authentication. Such a PIN is typically delivered to the user via a separate channel, like a (secure) PIN mailer. While using the eID document during enrolment, the user will have to enter the PIN to unlock either some of its data fields (other than mandatory data fields required for a passport functionality) or some specific functionality such as signing. For instance, the electronic identification card (nPA) in Germany requires the user to enter a correct PIN to unlock its signature function[8]. This aspect can be added to basic self-enrolment, whereby the user signs a fresh consent statement, in order to ensure the Enroller that the user is the legitimate owner of the eID document. In essence, this adds user-binding by having the user prove knowledge of the PIN. We can include such a PIN verification in the basic self-enrolment protocol in addition to the authenticity and integrity checks on the eID document.

4.2   Biometric Check During Self-enrolment

A second option is to extend our basic self-enrolment protocol with biometric checks in order to achieve user binding. ICAO documents digitally store a photo of the user and optionally fingerprints as well. Since fingerprints can usually only be read from the eID by authorised states, we focus on biometric face verification. We describe a possible scenario in several steps.

1. As in the basic self enrolment protocol, a user initiates enrolment via his phone, upon which the Enroller remotely accesses the user's eID via the phone's NFC interface and performs the eID checks.
2. If the eID checks are successful, the Enroller reads and stores the eID data that includes the user's identity data and his photo.
3. Next, the Enroller requests the user to present a biometric evidence in the form of a live video or some other form of face recognition.
4. Then the Enroller matches the user's photo from the eID to the user's biometric evidence from the video.

---

[8] http://www.die-eid-funktion.de/unterscheidung_der_eid_funktion_und_der_qes.php.

5. If there is a match, then the Enroller proceeds to issue a signed confirmation, which guarantees the Issuer that the eID document is bound to the user and that his identity has been checked by the Enroller.
6. Finally, the Issuer signs the user's identity data (attributes) and issues them as credentials to the user's phone.

We briefly consider two methods, namely WebID video legitimation technology[9] and iProov[10], that could be used for performing the biometric check during self-enrolment.

WebID solution. WebID's video legitimation procedure involves a human verifier (e.g., an employee of the Enroller's organization) who does the task of identifying users over video calls. Regardless of the physical separation, sensory perception of the users is possible, since the user who is to be identified and the employee sit opposite one another "face-to-face" through this video transmission and communicate with one another. The user is asked to hold both the front and rear sides of a valid official identity card or passport in front of the webcam. To allow this to be both automatically and manually verified the ID must be tilted several times and moved so that the hologram and further security features can be checked. The identity number is also recorded and photos are made to secure the evidence. Finally a unique transaction number (TAN) is sent to the user by e-mail or text message, with which the legitimation can be confirmed online. The video-legitimation procedure provided by WebID Solutions has been examined and approved by BMF (German Federal Ministry of Finance) and BaFin (German Federal Financial Supervisory Authority). The basis for this type of legitimation is the new interpretation of Sect. 6[11] of the Anti-Money-Laundering Act by the BMF dating from March 2014. A major bank ING-DiBa in Germany has chosen to adopt WebID's solution[12] with which, on opening a new account, customers of ING-DiBa can verify their identity directly online with video transmission from home via their own computer, tablet or smart phone.

Due to its real-time biometric checking capability involving the user and the employee, WebID's video legitimation could be added to our self-enrolment protocol.

iProov Verifier. iProov[13] is a biometric-based authentication solution that checks if the user's face corresponds to the face that was originally enrolled. The user can use any of his personal devices that has front-facing camera to use iProov where he just has to click and stare at the device to authenticate himself. iProov uses Flashmark technology that enables the user's screen flashing a

---

[9] https://www.webid-solutions.de/en/.

[10] https://www.iproov.com/.

[11] III. Interpretation of Sect. 6 (2) no. 2 of the GwG ("not personally present") (https://www.bafin.de/SharedDocs/Veroeffentlichungen/EN/Rundschreiben/ rs_1401_gw_verwaltungspraxis_vm_en.html).

[12] https://www.webid-solutions.de/en/assets/site/files/presse/140908_pm_ing_e.pdf.

[13] https://www.iproov.com/what-we-do.

sequence of colours on the user's face and during flashing, the video is streamed to the iProov servers. The iProov server:

- matches the user's face against the enrolment image;
- analyses the reflection of the display light on the user's face;
- examines the pattern of reflection to check it comes from a real face;
- checks the one-time sequence of colours to ensure it is the same as the session Flashmark.

If all the above checks are successful, iProov servers mark the user authentication successful.

A technology such as iProov can also be added to our basic self-enrolment protocol at the Enroller, where the user's real time image from the video is then compared against the user's photo read from the eID document. iProov is an experimental technology that is still being evaluated.

4.3 Data Consistency Checks During Self-enrolment

Another solution to bind the eID document, the user and his device i.e. smart phone is to compare a part of the data from the eID document — say, name or date of birth — to some other reliable data source. If the data match, the enrolment succeeds; else it fails. The data source could come from the phone itself, if it has reliable, i.e. authentic and non-transferable, data of the user. We will explore this direction further in Sect. 6. The current section focuses on using an outside data-source to verify the enrolment data against. We will first sketch the general idea and then shortly discuss two possible enrollers in this scenario, namely mobile network operators (MNOs) and banks.

We assume the Enroller has access to an external data-source which contains authentic data of the enrolling user that can be matched against his eID data. In this scenario the Enroller also requires an additional way of authenticating the user. Possible enrollers could be institutions such as universities or the government, or companies such as MNOs or banks. We now generically describe the self enrolment protocol with such an Enroller.

1. A user requests the Enroller to carry out self-enrolment through his phone; the Enroller remotely accesses the user's eID via the user's phone's NFC interface and performs the eID checks as before, in Sect. 3.
2. Additionally, the Enroller requires the user authenticate. A successful authentication results in retrieving the user data from the Enroller's records. This data is then matched against the data read from the user's eID. If matched correctly, it goes to step 3. Otherwise, the Enroller aborts the process with a suitable error message to the user.
3. The Enroller digitally signs a user-identity confirmation message that consists of the user's eID data and sends it to the Issuer.
4. The Issuer verifies the Enroller's signature on the confirmation message, connects to the user's phone and issues the eID credentials.

Naturally, the reliability of such a scheme is dependent on the reliability of the external data-source and the additional authentication step mentioned above. In the following two paragraphs we look at two parties that, under some assumptions, could fulfil the role of an Enroller.

MNO-mediated self-enrolment. Mobile providers, also called Mobile Network Operators (MNOs), could function as the Enroller. Major MNOs in countries like the Netherlands, carry out face-to-face identity proofing for personal subscriptions. This is done at an MNO office or at the user's home, when the SIM (Subscriber Identity Module) card is delivered. Thus we assume that MNOs have authentic identity data and authentic SIM identities of the subscribers in their databases, obtained via a separate channel involving face-to-face authentication. During an enhanced self-enrolment, the enrolling user's eID data could be verified against the MNO's subscriber data in addition to the usual eID checks described in Sect. 3.

This approach has been discussed and evaluated in detail with a major MNO in the Netherlands. In the end the MNO decided not to implement this enhanced enrolment protocol because its database of subscriber data is well-protected and could not be used for experiments.

Bank-mediated self-enrolment. Banks could also fill the role of the Enroller. In many countries, opening a first bank account with a bank requires a face-to-face identity proofing session. Additionally, many banks have strong online authentication methods, such as authenticator tokens (e.g. ABN AMRO bank's e-identifier[14]), for authenticating online banking transactions. So, during self-enrolment, a bank could use the eID data to look up the user data in its customers database and then require the user to perform an additional authentication step towards the bank. Depending on the authentication process of a particular bank, this could provide strong user-binding. Within the Netherlands, the main banks have started an experimental joint authentication service called iDIN[15], where the different banks authenticate their clients with their existing e-banking tokens, but the result is a uniform identity message. This makes the development of a bank-mediated self-enrolment much simpler. It is experimentally supported in the IRMA ecosystem.

5 Evaluation of the User-Binding Solutions

In this section, we briefly evaluate the user-binding solutions described in the previous section, based on their security, trustworthiness, ease of deployment and use.

---

[14] https://www.abnamro.nl/nl/prive/betalen/edentifier/index.html.
[15] http://www.connective.eu/financial/idin/.

PIN Check. Assuming that there are (or will be) eID documents that support PINs, with a restricted number of PIN entry attempts, PIN checks can provide a secure and simple way to achieve user-binding in our self-enrolment scenario. The trust assurance provided by the user PINs depends on how reliably and confidentially they have been generated in the first place and transported to the users. Further, it also depends on how securely the users store and maintain their PINs.

The downside of PINs is that users often forget them. If the PIN was delivered through a PIN mailer, this mail might have been lost at the time of enrolment, hence, making it impossible for the user to carry out self-enrolment. This requires (expensive) help center contacts and re-issuing.

Biometric Check. In the biometric checks that we have considered in this paper, the Enroller compares the photo that is digitally read from the eID document to the person's face that appears in a real time video session during enrolment. The trust assurance level of this biometrically enhanced protocol depends on the quality of the biometric comparison mechanisms. In any case, we would either need a human verifier or a server at the Enroller's end to perform the biometric comparison, communicate with the user and make sure that the owner of the eID document and the communicating user are the same person.

In the case of a human verifier, the result of the biometric check is reliable and convincing but the video addition will be costly, since it requires additional personnel, and will increase the length (in time) of each enrolment, especially when it leads to queues for the video procedure. An automated biometric check using a server is relatively cheap and fast but it has a greater chance of producing unreliable result due to false positives/negatives.

Data Consistency Check. In general an additional data-consistency check seems a cheap way to strengthen self-enrolment. However, it requires at least (1) trustworthy, authentic user data and (2) an additional authentication of the user to the Enroller. MNOs and banks seem natural fits for these roles, which we separately discuss and evaluate below. Entrust's CAC-based self-enrolment that is described in Sect. 3.3, which uses a one-time password transmitted to a pre-issued e-mail address of the user, essentially also falls in this category.

MNO-mediated self-enrolment. Assigning an MNO as the Enroller can be seen as an advantage in terms of security as the MNO can additionally verify whether a user's eID data matches the user data in his SIM subscription. This check ensures that the phone (SIM card) that will eventually store the issued derived credentials belongs to the enrolling user. Thus, an MNO-mediated self-enrolment gives additional guarantees about the link between the user, his identity document and his SIM card i.e. it provides not only user binding but also device binding.

Moreover, we assume that the user has undergone a prior face-to-face enrolment at the MNO when he bought the SIM card and signed the subscription contract. This assumption results in self-enrolment being more secure and trust-worthy as it is now built upon two previous face-to-face enrolments, one for the eID document and one for the SIM subscription. The downsides of MNO-mediated user-binding are: (1) it is limited only to the MNOs which carry out face-to-face enrolments of its subscribers for obtaining SIM subscription; (2) it is not applicable to users who own prepaid/anonymous SIM cards: they can be obtained without the user having to go through an enrolment at the MNO.

Bank-mediated self-enrolment. With a bank in the position of the Enroller, we also assume a prior face-to-face enrolment of the user during the opening of the bank account. The bank-mediated self-enrolment can potentially offer the strongest user-binding, based on an out-of-band authentication using a secure authentication token, a bank card and a PIN. Alternatively, it could offer authentication based on username/password. This difference in security level of the authentication methods makes evaluation hard. Still, even in a user-name/password scenario, it is an additional authentication of a separate fac-tor (something you know), in addition to the possession of the passport. The downside of such a system is the plurality of authentication mechanisms offered by banks. This means development of such a system can be costly, because the authentication mechanisms of all participating banks need to be supported. Additionally, this means all these authentication mechanisms will need to be evaluated separately and the resulting process may not provide a uniform user experience. To be viable, a uniform system of an authenticating service combin-ing several banks, such as the Dutch iDIN, seems necessary.

6   Combining Several Self-enrolment Approaches

Since none of the above presented enhancements for self-enrolment is clearly "the best" it is worthwhile to look into ways to combine these approaches. Since we are working within an ABC framework, we also have the ability to use prior issued credentials during a self-enrolment in order to strengthen the confidence in the user's identity that is presented to a service provider during an authentication.

The enrolment procedure now involves several steps — which is typical for attribute-based systems: the user first obtains credentials from some online iden-tity provider. Next, in an enhanced version of our self-enrolment, these existing credentials are read by the Enroller and compared to the ones from the eID document. In this way several enrolment steps can be built upon each other, to create a reliable and consistent set of attributes.

In IRMA ecosystem, we have an implementation where we use a (federated) identity provider (or the Issuer) such as SURFconext[16], where the user has a login and the Issuer already has some of the user's data that he can issue to the user's IRMA app as authentic credentials. These credentials can then be used within a self-enrolment session to compare with the eID data. Essentially this

---

[16] https://www.surf.nl/en/services-and-products/surfconext/index.html.

comes down to an additional data-consistency check (as described in Sect. 4.3) with the data provided by the phone.

Within such a multi-step enrolment system one can support credentials of varied trust assurance levels, corresponding to the number (and nature) of the self-enrolment steps that the user performed. The credentials obtained from an online identity provider (e.g. SURFconext) has low assurance but they can be used within an eID-based self-enrolment as mentioned above to obtain higher assurance credentials. Optionally, these credentials could then be used within yet another self-enrolment session, for instance involving a biometric verification to obtain even higher assurance credentials. It would then be up to service providers to decide which assurance level they accept for their service. For instance, an online ticket service would likely accept lower assurance level credentials whereas a higher assurance level credential would be required to review your own patient data at a hospital portal.

7   Conclusion

In this paper, we start from a basic self-enrolment scheme which allows a user with an eID document and an NFC-enabled smart phone to enrol himself from any location (e.g. sitting at home) by connecting to an Enroller entity online. Subsequently, he can get derived credentials issued by an Issuer entity to his smart phone. This type of enrolment is user-friendly, cheap and commercially viable when compared to traditional face-to-face enrolments. Based on the experiences with our smartphone implementation of this basic self-enrolment protocol in an attribute-based credential (ABC) framework, we can claim that it is also practical and efficient. Furthermore, the paper discusses several enhancements of the basic self-enrolment involving different user-eID document binding solutions — which should prevent a malicious user from using someone else's eID document for enrolment.

Which solution works best in which situation depends on various factors, such as availability of a PIN on eID documents, costs, effort, and willingness of different parties to cooperate. Since no solution offers a panacea, the solution that best fits the existing IRMA self-enrolment implementation is the one from Sect. 6, where eID data is compared to the credentials from a previous self enrolment, to achieve higher assurance levels for user credentials.

References

1. Burr, W.E., Dodson, D.F., Newton, E.M., Perlner, R.A., Timothy Polk, W., Gupta, S., Nabbus, E.A.: SP 800-63-1. Electronic authentication guideline (2011)
2. ABC4Trust. Attribute-Based Credentials tutorial (2011). http://www.dime-project.eu/en/Home/dime/events/list/tutorial-on-attributebased-credentials
3. Hoepman, J.-H., Hubbers, E., Jacobs, B., Oostdijk, M., Schreur, R.W.: Crossing borders: security and privacy issues of the european e-passport. In: Yoshiura, H., Sakurai, K., Rannenberg, K., Murayama, Y., Kawamura, S. (eds.) IWSEC 2006. LNCS, vol. 4266, pp. 152–167. Springer, Heidelberg (2006). doi:10.1007/11908739_11

4. IBM Research Zürich Security Team. Specification of the Identity Mixer cryptographic library. Technical report, IBM Research, Zürich, February 2012
5. Vullers, P., Alpár, G.: Efficient selective disclosure on smart cards using idemix. In: Fischer-Hübner, S., Leeuw, E., Mitchell, C. (eds.) IDMAN 2013. IFIP AICT, vol. 396, pp. 53–67. Springer, Heidelberg (2013). doi:10.1007/978-3-642-37282-7_5
6. Camenisch, J., Lysyanskaya, A.: An efficient system for non-transferable anonymous credentials with optional anonymity revocation. In: Pfitzmann, B. (ed.) EUROCRYPT 2001. LNCS, vol. 2045, pp. 93–118. Springer, Heidelberg (2001). doi:10.1007/3-540-44987-6_7
7. Alpár, G., Jacobs, B.: Credential design in attribute-based identity management. In: Bridging Distances in Technology and Regulation, 3rd TILTing Perspectives Conference, pp. 189–204 (2013)

Distributed Immutabilization of Secure Logs

Jordi Cucurull[(⊠)] and Jordi Puiggalí

Scytl Secure Electronic Voting, Pl. Gal.la Placídia, 1–3, 1st floor,
08006 Barcelona, Spain
{jordi.cucurull,jordi.puiggali}@scytl.com

Abstract. Several applications require robust and tamper-proof logging systems, e.g. electronic voting or bank information systems. At Scytl we use a technology, called immutable logs, that we deploy in our electronic voting solutions. This technology ensures the integrity, authenticity and non-repudiation of the generated logs, thus in case of any event the auditors can use them to investigate the issue. As a security recommendation it is advisable to store and/or replicate the information logged in a location where the logger has no writing or modification permissions. Otherwise, if the logger gets compromised, the data previously generated could be truncated or altered using the same private keys. This approach is costly and does not protect against collusion between the logger and the entities that hold the replicated data. In order to tackle these issues, in this article we present a proposal and implementation to immutabilize integrity proofs of the secure logs within the Bitcoin's blockchain. Due to the properties of the proposal, the integrity of the immutabilized logs is guaranteed without performing log data replication and even in case the logger gets latterly compromised.

Keywords: Secure logging · Blockchain · Distributed immutabilization · Integrity · Trust

1 Introduction

There are several applications that require a robust and tamper-proof logging system, e.g. electronic voting systems [15] or bank information systems. At Scytl we have applied a logging solution, the immutable logs [4], in our electronic voting systems [7] that ensures the integrity, authenticity and non-repudiation of the generated logs.

In the event the logger or its private key gets compromised, the data logged before this point could be truncated or altered without being detected if no additional measures are applied. The most common solutions to this problem are (1) storage and/or replication of the information in a location where the logger only has write-only permissions [1], (2) implementation of third party notary services [16] or (3) usage of advanced cryptographic mechanisms based on aggregated signatures that are implemented as one-way functions [10]. The first solution guarantees that a manipulation of the log is not possible, due to

© Springer International Publishing AG 2016
G. Barthe et al. (Eds.): STM 2016, LNCS 9871, pp. 122–137, 2016.
DOI: 10.1007/978-3-319-46598-2_9

the medium used to store the logs, or that it will be detected, due to their replication. However, the log replication requires the deployment and management of a specific infrastructure, composed of one or more servers, for this purpose. This solution does not protect against colluding entities with the logger. Thus, if a large enough distributed infrastructure needs to be deployed to prevent that a sufficient number of malicious nodes collude, this infrastructure can be expensive and difficult to maintain. The second solution relies on the usage of a trusted service which stores integrity proofs. This service could also collude with the attacker to manipulate the logs. And the third solution ensures that a log truncation will be detected because it is not possible to restore an existing aggregated signature at the point at which the log is truncated (see the reference for more details). This is presented as a two-options solution, one more efficient and dependent on a trusted party based on the usage of Message Authentication Codes (MACs), and one more computationally expensive based on public key signature and a PKI. However, in this article we explore an alternative solution based on the use of an existing efficient secure logging technology, which combines MACs and Digital Signatures (DAs), and the Bitcoin blockchain, which provides off-the-shelf distributed immutabilization. The solution consists of publishing log integrity proofs within the blockchain. Thus any manipulation of the logs is detected and collusion is not possible due to the distributed nature of the mechanism.

The blockchain is the underlying technology used by the crypto-currency Bitcoin [11] as a public ledger of all the economic transactions performed. The transactions are immutabilized, within a sequence of blocks, in a distributed manner by a set of nodes, called miners. The miners compete to perform this operation and obtain rewards and fees for each block generated. The main advantage of the blockchain is that it guarantees the integrity and non-repudiability of all the transactions registered without the need of a trusted entity.

In this article we take advantage of both technologies, the secure logs and the blockchain, to make a proposal and implementation to immutabilize integrity proofs of the secure logs within the blockchain. This guarantees the integrity of the immutabilized logs, when no replication is enabled, even in case the logger gets latterly compromised. There are other proposals that also take advantage of the off-the-shelf immutabilization capacity provided by the blockchain. For example, Zyskind et al. [18] propose a system to protect personal data, using Distributed Hash Tables (DHTs) to store the data and the blockchain to keep the access rights to it. There is also a specification, the Colored Coins [3], that extends the Bitcoin by the possibility of tagging coins and associate metadata to the transactions which may include a link to a digital asset in the BitTorrent network. There are simple services, such as Proof of existence[1], that provide immutabilization of single documents in the blockchain for a fee. And there are more complex services, such as Factom [17], which provides immutabilization and chaining of any type of data for a certain amount of fees. In this case the service is implemented as a permissioned blockchain [8] with public access, that

---

[1] https://proofofexistence.com.

contains references to external documents. This blockchain is connected to the main Bitcoin blockchain for enhanced verifiability. However, the work we have performed, which also uses the blockchain to immutabilize data, is different from the previous ones since: (1) it is specifically devoted to immutabilize logs, thus it presents several challenges: (a) the information must be kept chained in the same order as it is generated and (b) the system must support the speed at which the logs are generated given the speed constraints of the Bitcoin blockchain. And (2) our proposal does not require additional infrastructure, such as intermediate databases or private and/or permissioned blockchains.

The article is structured in six sections: Sect. 2 explains the immutable logs and the blockchain; Sect. 3 explains the proposal; Sect. 4 presents the implementation and tests performed; Sect. 5 discusses some issues dealt with during the definition of the proposal and its implementation; and, finally, Sect. 6 concludes the article with the conclusions and future work.

2   Background

This section presents the two technologies used throughout the proposal of distributed logs immutabilization.

2.1   Secure Logs

The secure logs are an event logging technology called immutable logs [4]. This technology implements cryptographic measures to preserve the integrity and authenticity of logs, without compromising the performance of the system. The system is based on chaining the log entries using a combination of Message Authentication Codes (MACs) and Digital Signatures (DAs). Each logger has a pair of signing keys, thus the log authenticity and non-repudiation is guaranteed.

The logging process comprises two types of log entries, the regular ones (see Eq. 1) and the checkpoints (see Eq. 2). Each log entry (L_i) is chained with the previous one using a MAC cryptographic function (specifically a HMAC [12] in the implementation used). The input of the MAC is the log entry text ($LogInfo_i$) concatenated with the integrity proof of the previous entry (h_{i-1}). A different random session key (K_j) is used for a number of consecutive entries. This scheme prevents any modification, deletion or addition of intermediate entries.

$$L_i = (LogInfo_i, h_i) \quad where \quad h_i = HMAC(K_j, (h_{i-1}|LogInfo_i)) \quad (1)$$

The checkpoints are a special type of entry that are used to guarantee the authenticity and non-repudiation of the last block (j) of entries. A checkpoint (Chk_j) is issued every a certain number of lines or given time, depending of the logger configuration. In each checkpoint the MAC session key used to chain the last block of entries is disclosed and a new one, kept secret by public key encryption (P_{enc}), is generated. Finally, a digital signature of the entry is also created with the signing key (S_{sig}). Thus, any log entry manipulation or deletion is detected during the verification process.

$$Chk_j = L_i = (LogInfo_i, K_{j-1}, E(P_{enc}, K_j), Sig_j, h_{i-1}, h_i) \qquad where$$

$$h_i = HMAC(K_b, (h_{i-1}|K_{j-1}|LogInfo_i))$$
$$Sig_j = S(S_{sig}, (h_{i-1}|K_{j-1}|E(P_{enc}, K_j)|h_i|Loginfo_i))$$

(2)

The main advantage of the secure logs, compared with only digitally signed logs, is that they allow to detect the exact location of any manipulation attempt and isolate it, from the rest of the log entries that remain intact, while keeping a good performance. These logs can also be replicated by sending them to a central log server which centralizes all the log information, to ensure logs availability and provide log monitoring. The log replication also ensures that a compromised logger cannot modify former entries, e.g. by truncating and regenerating the chain of log entries.

2.2   Bitcoin Blockchain

Bitcoin [11] is a well-known decentralized cryptocurrency system. The scheme is based on a consensus network where all the nodes agree on the state of the system according to a certain set of rules. No central authority operates it neither has control of the money. A set of nodes called miners are in charge of the system operation and, to be more specific, to the generation of the blockchain that is used as a public ledger.

The operation of the system, at a high level, consists of users generating transactions that represent cryptocurrency transfers, and miners that validate and immutabilize them. Each transaction (see Fig. 1) contains a reference to one or more former transactions, the inputs (I_k), which prove the user has the money he/she is spending, and the quantity and receivers of the money to spend, the outputs (O_l). The inputs are a list of tuples that include a transaction identifier (Tx_{id}) and the index of an output (ϕ_p) in that transaction. Several types of transaction outputs exist, but the most common (Pay-to-PubkeyHash) refers to a Bitcoin address $(@_l)$, which is the hash of a public key, and the amount of money (θ_l) to give to that address. This type of output can only be spent by the entity that has the matching private key. Thus, each transaction contains the public key and signatures required to redeem the money of the former transactions referred. The ECDSA signing algorithm [14] with the secp256k1 curve is used. The amount of money transferred by a transaction is the sum of all its inputs. However, a small quantity of it, the difference between inputs and outputs, is taken as a publishing fee by the miners. The transactions are sent and validated by the miners through a distributed network that supports the system. After this, they remain publicly available thus all the money exchanges are publicly auditable. Despite the initial functionality of the blockchain is to be a Bitcoin ledger, it is also possible to publish a small quantity of information within each transaction

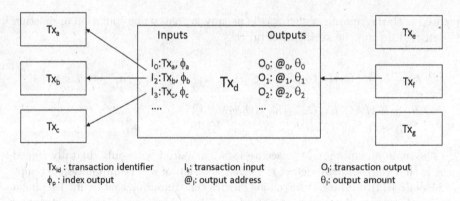

Fig. 1. Transaction detail

output. This is used in the proposal presented in the following section and it is possible by creating a special type of output, called non-spendable output, by using the op-code OP_RETURN. After this op-code they can be included up to 75 bytes of information that are published within the transaction.

The Bitcoin transactions are registered and immutabilized within the blockchain, which provides integrity, public auditability and non-repudiation. The blockchain is a sequence of blocks that are chained by cryptographic means and that contain transactions. The blocks are generated by the miners in a competitive process that requires to solve a Proof of Work (PoW). Each block contains a set of transactions and a header with a reference to the previous block, a nonce used by the PoW and a hash that is the root of a Merkle tree that groups all the transactions to be immutabilized by the block. The transactions are immutabilized in a certain order as leaves of the Merkle tree, however this order depends of the miners and is not chosen by their issuers. The generated PoW consists of finding a cryptographic hash of the block, by trying different nonces, that starts with a certain number of zeroes. The complexity to solve the PoW is adjusted every two weeks in order to produce one block every ten minutes on average. When a miner solves a PoW and publishes a block, it receives a certain amount of Bitcoins both as a reward and from the fees of each transaction included in the block. The PoW, assuming that no entity has more than 51 % of the mining power, is used as a mechanism to (1) prevent that a deliberately chosen entity can publish a certain block in the blockchain, and (2) prevent that formerly published blocks can be modified. Other mechanisms that are not based on the computational performance are also available [2], but they are implemented in alternative coins.

3   Distributed Logs Immutabilization

As explained in Sect. 2.1, the secure logs provide integrity and authenticity to the logs generated. In addition, the logs can be sent to a central server in order to ensure their availability and provide monitoring. But the replication of logs is also a desirable security feature. It ensures that, in the event of a logger compromise, a logger signing key compromise or a log truncation, the manipulation of previously logged entries could be detected by comparing them with the replicated information. However, this solution requires an infrastructure of servers where the information will be replicated, a mechanism to export the logs and a protocol to determine which information is valid when discrepancies are observed among the different copies.

In this section we propose a distributed log immutabilization solution that combines the use of the secure logs [4] with the blockchain. The solution does not require log replication to detect the mentioned manipulations (despite it still supports it if needed for durability and fault tolerance). The proposal takes advantage of the blockchain to distributedly publish and immutabilize log integrity proofs.

3.1   Distributed Immutabilization Proposal

The secure logs periodically issue a special type of log entry called checkpoint. The information included in this entry allows the verification of the block of entries present between the current and the previous checkpoint. Thus our proposal for distributed log immutabilization consists of publishing an integrity proof, i.e. a hash, into the blockchain for every issued checkpoint. These integrity proofs can later be validated with the actual log files in order to see that they were not manipulated. Each log that is immutabilized in the blockchain will have a log identifier to distinguish it from other logs immutabilized by the same entity, thus it is not globally unique.

The integrity proofs registered to the blockchain are SHA256 hashes [13] of the checkpoints (Chk_j) present in the log (see Eq. 2 in Sect. 2.1):

$$H_j = SHA256(Chk_j) \tag{3}$$

One or more checkpoint hashes can be included within a single transaction (Tx_{id}). This accommodates the solution to the blockchain scalability constrains (see Sect. 5) and can reduce the total amount of transaction fees. Each hash is included within a non-spendable output entry (O_l where $l > 0$) of the transaction. The following information is published (see Table 1 for description of the fields):

$$O_l = (prefix, version, logId, H_j) \tag{4}$$

In order to properly validate the logs against the checkpoint hashes published in the blockchain, it is needed to maintain, and enforce, the order of them. Since several checkpoint hashes can be included into a single transaction, the order has to be guaranteed at the level of transaction outputs. The order has also to be kept when multiple transactions are present. Thus, for the first case, the hashes are just included in the transaction as outputs (O_l) in the same order as they appear in the log file, as the order is kept by design of the Bitcoin. And, for the second case, each transaction is linked to the previous one using the transaction input (I_k).

Table 1. Data immutabilized within the transaction output

Name	Bytes	Content	Description
prefix	2	"SL"	OP_RETURN prefix
version	1	1	Version of the data structure
logId	16	-	Unique log identifier
H_j	32	-	Hash of the checkpoint

Hence, the transactions generated by the application are linked forming a chain of transactions (see Fig. 2). As it can be seen, each transaction contains one or more inputs from transactions with spendable outputs used to pay current and future transaction fees, as well as a single output with spendable outputs that will be linked with the next transaction used to register checkpoint hashes. In addition, the transaction contains all the non-spendable outputs required in order to register the checkpoint hashes. It is important to clarify that, the transaction issued, is not directly linked to the next one via its spendable output. This output points to an address, which is different for each transaction issued[2], that belongs to the logger or registrar application. However, the transaction can only be spent by the logger application, thus only the logger can actually link it with the input of the next transaction with checkpoint hashes.

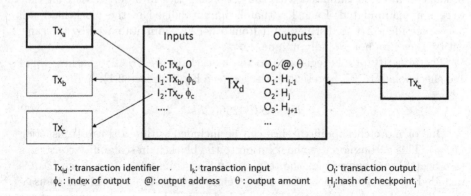

Fig. 2. Transaction link

In order to go through the generated chain of transactions and retrieve the integrity proofs of a given log, it is required to make public the first transaction of the chain and the log identifier, e.g. in a newspaper or by a trusted entity in the blockchain.

---

[2] Although it is not enforced by the implementation of Bitcoin, it is recommended by the community not to reuse Bitcoin addresses. Thus, we decided to regenerate the reception address for each transaction generated.

3.2 Validation Proposal

The validation of the information published consists of retrieving all the published checkpoint hashes, recompute them using the log files and compare they match in content and order. We assume that the content of the logs files and the content of the blockchain is validated following the regular logger and blockchain validation mechanisms. The first transaction issued by the logger and the log identifier must be publicly well-known.

The algorithm used to perform the validation is depicted in Algorithm 1. The algorithm starts by going through all the transactions issued and registered in the blockchain by the logger (the first while in the algorithm). The first transaction (*firstTransaction*) is taken as a trusted beginning of the chain and the log identifier (*logId*) is used to select the appropriate entries (in case checkpoint hashes of different logs were included in the same transaction). The checkpoint hashes are temporally stored (WriteHashes), for later comparison, in a file (*fileHashesBC*). The next transaction is searched and processed (GetNextTransaction). As it can be appreciated in Algorithm 2, finding the next transaction requires to go through the current and following blocks of the blockchain (outer while of the algorithm) until a transaction that has the current one as its input is found (inner while of the algorithm). After the checkpoint hashes are collected from the blockchain (again in Algorithm 1), the checkpoint hashes are recalculated (ComputeHash) from the actual log to validate (second while in the algorithm) and they are temporally stored (WriteHashes) in a file (*fileHashesSL*). Finally the files with the two lists of checkpoint hashes (*fileHashesBC* and *fileHashesSL*) are checked to be identical (CompareFiles). If this is the case the validation is passed.

Data: firstTransaction, logId, logs, blockchain, fileHashesBC, fileHashesSL
Result: boolean result
transaction = firstTransaction;
while *there is transaction* **do**
  hashes = GetHashes(*transaction, logId, blockchain*);
  WriteHashes(*hashes, fileHashesBC*);
  transaction = GetNextTransaction(*transaction, blockchain*);
end
while *There is a log file* **do**
  logFile = GetNextLogFile();
  while *There is a log line to read* **do**
    line = ReadLine(*logFile*);
    if *line is a checkpoint* **then**
      hash = ComputeHash(*line*);
      WriteHashes(*hash, fileHashesSL*);
    end
  end
end
CompareFiles(*fileHashesBC, fileHashesSL*);

Algorithm 1. Validation algorithm

Data: blockchain, currentTransaction
Result: nextTransaction
blockHash = **GetBlockTransaction**(*currentTransaction*);
while *there is a blockHash* **do**
 | block = **GetBlock**(*blockHash*);
 | **while** *there are pending transactions in block and transaction not found* **do**
 | | nextTransaction = **GetTransaction**(*block*);
 | | inputs = **GetTransactionInputs**(*nextTransaction*);
 | | **if** **ListContains**(*inputs, currentTransaction*) **then**
 | | | return nextTransaction;
 | | **end**
 | **end**
 | blockHash = **GetNextBlock**(*block*);
end

Algorithm 2. GetNextTransaction algorithm

If the registration of the checkpoint hashes in the blockchain is performed within a certain timeframe after the secure log checkpoints are generated, then it is also possible to validate the timing is correct. In this case, during validation it is required to gather and compare the timestamp of the log checkpoints, this is part of the log basic information, and the timestamp of the blockchain blocks at which each checkpoint hashes are linked (via a transaction). The timestamps, given a certain margin defined by the validator, must match. The margin depends on the delay between the checkpoint hashes generation and their immutabilization in the blockchain.

4   Implementation and Test

The proposal described in the previous section has been implemented as two real Java applications: an immutabilizer and a validator. These two applications interact with the logs generated by a secure logger and with the Bitcoin Core software.

4.1   Distributed Immutabilizer Application

The immutabilizer application has been built as a standalone Java application that periodically reads the secure log files in order to register integrity proofs of the new checkpoints to the blockchain. The application takes advantage of the btcd-cli4j library[3] as a Java wrapper of the RPC-JSON calls provided by the Bitcoin Core version 0.12.1[4] in order to access and operate the blockchain.

When the application is started, if it is the first time, it generates a new random log identifier and reads all the available log files. Then it calculates the hashes of the checkpoints, creates a transaction that includes them and signs it.

---

[3] https://github.com/priiduneemre/btcd-cli4j.
[4] https://bitcoin.org/en/bitcoin-core/.

From this point, the application periodically reads the log files to detect new lines to register. The period to register checkpoint hashes is configurable, but it should not be higher than the time required for the transaction to get immutabilized and confirmed (usually a transaction is considered confirmed after the sixth block of its inclusion in the blockchain, although it is a configurable parameter too). This means that in production the period should be at least one hour. Each time a transaction is published the state is stored, thus if the application is stopped it can be resumed from the same point and with the same identifier.

The transactions created by the application have as many outputs as hashes plus an additional one that is used as a change address. The fees to pay for the transaction are calculated using the RPC-JSON EstimateFee call that estimates the relative fees to publish a transaction within a certain number of blocks (set to one in our application). If the estimation is not available, a hard-coded value of 0.0002 BTC/kB is selected. The size considered to calculate the fee is 200 bytes for the basic transaction and 60 additional bytes for each output. The idea behind this calculation is to get the transaction included in a block in a timeliness manner without spending too much fees on it. When the fee is calculated the transaction is linked with the previous one, and with additional spendable transactions if not enough Bitcoins where available to pay the fees.

It is also worth commenting that the Bitcoin Core does not provide RPC-JSON calls to use transactions to immutabilize other data than Bitcoin payments. However, there are a set of calls that permit to operate with transactions at binary level. Thus, the approach followed has consisted of creating a transaction dummy output for each data entry to register using the CreateRaw-Transaction RPC-JSON primitive. The transaction, encoded in hexadecimal, is returned and each dummy output is replaced with the manually tailored output that contains the OP_RETURN code and the hash to register.

4.2   Validator Application

The validator application has also been built as an standalone Java application that takes advantage of the btcd-cli4j library as a Java wrapper of the RPC-JSON calls of Bitcoin Core 0.12.1. In this case the application downloads all the checkpoint hashes published to the blockchain, starting from a given initial transaction and for a particular log identifier, creates the checkpoint hashes from the log files and compares them. No timing checks have been implemented.

The application requires the identifier of the first well-known transaction registered by the immutabilizer and the assigned log identifier. Then it follows the algorithm described in Algorithm 1 in order to perform the validation.

4.3   Testing

The testing of the immutabilizer and the validator has been performed with a generator of secure logs and the Bitcoin Core 0.12.1 running as a full node in the Bitcoin testnet.

The generator has been enabled together with the immutabilizer in order to generate logs. The log generator has been set to generate one log every 5 s, one checkpoint every 5 min and to rotate the log files every hour. The log immutabilizer has been setup to generate one transaction every hour linked to confirmed transactions for at least 3 blocks. The log checkpoints integrity were successfully validated against the information published in the blockchain when the validator was executed (currently it is not implemented as a periodic mechanism).

One of the tests we performed comprised the immutabilization of 101 checkpoints generated during around 8 h. The log identifier was:

$$8e4b943f45506c876a93ff4b113da68f$$

and the first transaction generated was:

$$59f5167416ecf96c8101d1cafce92075f4504b37548b92b6157ac966fee102d9$$

which can be seen with a blockchain viewer such as Block Trail[5]. From this transaction the trace of the logs can be followed during 9 transactions, containing the 101 checkpoints generated.

5   Discussion

In this section we discuss the design decisions taken during the design and implementation of the solution, the scalability and costs of the proposal and the security of it.

5.1   Design Decisions

As explained in Sect. 2.2, the blockchain is a continuously-growing distributed database composed of blocks and transactions. The blocks are organized as a sequence, each of them linked with the previous one through a hash. The transactions are linked to a block using their identifier, which is a hash computed from its elements. This organization is appropriate to keep the integrity of the information as well as the order of it. However, it has the disadvantage that finding a specific transaction requires to download and index all the data, that currently accounts around 64 GBs, unless we know in which block is contained.

Thus, one of the first questions we had was about which was the most appropriate manner to organize the integrity proofs, i.e. checkpoint hashes, of our log immutabilizer while keeping their order. The approach chosen was to include the integrity proofs in its natural order within the transactions and to link these transactions as a sequence using the input transaction field. Another option considered was to enforce the order at application level, i.e. including in each entry the current and previous checkpoint hash. However, this was discarded for two reasons: (1) it required to read, process and sort the data included within all the transaction outputs from the first block containing one of our transactions, (2)

---

[5] https://www.blocktrail.com/.

it was oblivious to the Bitcoin mechanisms to keep the order of the data, and (3) it complicated the protection of the data authenticity when different pairs of keys were used for each transaction (see next paragraphs).

Another question was how the authenticity of the integrity proofs could be kept. This can be done by cryptographically signing the transactions issued. In Bitcoin the addresses where a transaction is sent are associated to a pair of cryptographic keys. However, the standard behavior is to automatically generate a new address for each transaction received. Thus a certain entity, e.g. the logger, will have multiple addresses as new transactions are sent to it. The transactions issued are signed with the keys required by the transactions being spent, which belong to the owner of them. This renders the possibility to use a single well-known address for the immutabilizer not advisable. Another possibility, would be to publish all the pairs of keys generated and associated to the logger. However, this does not guarantee the non-repudiability property. Given a certain transaction, the immutabilizer could claim the pair of keys are not their ones, as there is no PKI infrastructure. Hence, the approach taken was the following: (1) the first transaction with log integrity proof entries is made public in a trusted place, and (2) the immutabilizer will only generate transactions with a unique spendable output sent to an address controlled by itself (it is the only one that can spend it). Thus if the first transaction, with the associated address, is trusted, the rest of the transactions ahead can also be trusted. This approach does not allow to return the change of the last transaction when the immutabilization is finished to another entity. Otherwise, the other entity could continue the chain and create additional fake entries. However, we assume the immutabilizer can continue its task with other logs or just manage small quantities of money just to pay a few fees ahead. If this was required it is possible to add a field with opcodes that indicate the beginning and end of the log immutabilization. Another possibility could be to create a transaction to give away the remaining funds without any checkpoint hash published, considering this as a signal that the log immutabilization activity is finished.

Another question was how we could facilitate the visibility of the published data. The chosen solution, as already mentioned, was to make public the very first transaction ID of the integrity proofs published. Hence, the rest of the entries can be found following the mentioned chain. A log identifier was also included in order to discriminate the integrity proofs from the ones of other logs immutabilized. However, the log identifier cannot be solely used since any entity is free to register transactions in the blockchain with any log identifier. Another option was to use a single well-known address as the change address of all the issued transactions. However, due to the regeneration of addresses explained before this option was discarded.

5.2   Scalability and Costs

Another important aspect of the solution is its scalability. The blockchain of Bitcoin is currently setup to support up to 7 transactions per second in total [5]. There is a lot of discussion on how to increase this value, since it is very small for a globally used system. Considering this limitation, we decided to register the log integrity proofs in a periodic manner, at the level of log checkpoint, and including one or more entries per transaction. The logs must also be adjusted to generate a number of checkpoints that do not end up in too large transactions. The larger a transaction is, the more expensive are the fees and the less probability to be included in a block. Thus, this approach allows to adjust the system to have a trade-off between its scalability, security and transaction fees. As example, in our tests we created one transaction every hour of 1 KB on average. Considering the mentioned size and the current 1 MB block size limit, a maximum of 6000 simultaneous logs could be immutabilized at a global scale. This is not a large value, specially considering that the current blocks are already used at almost its maximum capacity.

Another aspect to consider is the operational cost of the solution. Bitcoin has an associated cost related to the publication of transactions. The average fees have a high variance, but if no delays are desired in the confirmation of transactions a rate of 0.0006 BTC/KB has to be paid[6] (checked at 5th of August of 2016). As an example, if we setup our logger to generate 12 checkpoints/hour, 1 Bitcoin transaction/hour, during a period of one month, the cost is around 203 €/month. In the example each transaction has a size of almost 1 KB with a cost of 0.0006 BTC that is approximately 0.31 €. This is an approximated cost, which depends on the system setup, that is obtained from the cost model we detail in Eq. 5. The model considers the number of checkpoints per unit of time (c), number of transactions per unit of time (tx), transaction fees (f) given a maximum publication delay accepted, and time of operation (t). The model considers each transaction with a base size of 0.2 KBs plus 0.06 KBs for each checkpoint included. The selected unit of time is the hour. The final cost obtained may increase due to the foreseeable increase of the transaction fees (f). Currently most of the miners profits come from the reward when a block PoW is solved, but this reward is halved every 210.000 blocks (approximately every 4 years). Thus in the future the reward will be lower and the transaction fees are likely to increase.

$$cost = ((tx * 0.2) + (c * 0.06)) * t * f \qquad (5)$$

5.3 Security

The solution proposed enhances the data integrity, stream integrity (order of the data), forward integrity (ensures pre-compromised data cannot be manipulated), and non-repudiation properties provided by the secure logs for the case of insider attacks. Thus, the threat model addressed is focused on attackers that compromise the logger or with access to the logs and/or private key of it. The threats in this case are: (1) forging the full log, (2) truncation of the log, and (3) forging past log entries.

---

[6] https://bitcoinfees.21.co/.

The forge or replacement of all the logs, as described in threat 1, is not possible since it would require the replacement or modification of the first transaction to refer to an alternative handcrafted chain of immutabilized logs. The first transaction cannot be replaced if its identifier has been conveniently made public and broadcasted at the beginning of the system operation (e.g. the identifier could be published to newspapers, etc.). Even in case this first transaction identifier is replaced, the timestamps of the blocks will not match the expected times, unless the genuine and replaced logs are created and registered to the blockchain at the same time. Furthermore, if the first transaction identifier is not replaced, the modification of this transaction is not an option. The data published in the blockchain is almost impossible to modify after it has been confirmed (usually when six blocks are chained after the one considered confirmed).

Any manipulation of the logs, as mentioned in threats 2 and 3, would be detected as long as it affected the log blocks commited in the blockchain. The reason is that the hashes of the log checkpoints, which cover the integrity of each block of the log, would not match the ones published. It is worth to note that if the manipulation affected the current block or an unpublished block, the attacker still would have the chance to manipulate it. Thus, the more frequently the checkpoint hashes are published in the blockchain, the smaller is the opportunity window to manipulate the data from unpublished blocks of the log.

For more security, it is also possible to publish the identifier of the first transaction in one of the first entries of the logs, thus creating a commitment of the logs with the information published in the blockchain.

Other possible attacks could be tried at the level of Bitcoin. Common attacks, such as the double spending attacks [9] do not apply in this case since the logger issues the transactions against itself, thus there is no threat model that fits with this attack. Another possibility would be the logger to collude with a miner to perform selfish mining [6]. In this case the logger would try to fork and construct a parallel chain of transactions to be immutabilized in a parallel branch of the blockchain. However, this would be too difficult to sustain during the whole live of the logs, since it requires to own at least 1/4th of the total mining power.

6   Conclusions

In this article we have presented a proposal, implemented on top of the Bitcoin's blockchain, that enhances the security of the immutable logs [4]. It provides additional integrity and non-repudiation security properties resilient to log truncation and log re-generation in cases in which the logger or its signing key gets compromised. The proposal is based on publishing log integrity proofs in the blockchain. This protection can also be given by creating a mechanism of log replication at different selected servers operated by independent entities or within a distributed network. However with the blockchain the mentioned security properties can be given off-the-shelf without log replication and scaling up the immutabilization at a global level. In this case the immutabilizers are the Bitcoin miners, entities that are not globally susceptible to respond at the particular interests of a potential compromised logger or attacker. Due to the blockchain design, the information immutabilized cannot be modified by anybody unless it has more than 50 % of the system's mining capacity.

With the proposal and implementation presented it is shown that the blockchain can be used for the purpose described. However, we have also discussed the limitations that currently exist. If the number of transactions and block size supported by the blockchain do not increase, the number of immutabilized logs at a global scale cannot be large and the frequency of immutabilization and number of checkpoints of the log must be kept very low. As a side effect of the limited capacity, the transaction fees are also high in order to guarantee there are no delays in the publication of transactions. Thus, in order to commercially use this solution, the blockchain should offer more capacity than the current one or the user must be willing to pay high operational costs.

Further work can be done in order to improve our specification, for example to support the finalization of logs. Currently, our specification does not comprise the transfer of accumulated funds from one of the transactions used for registering assets to an address non controlled by the logger. Otherwise, the owner of this address could continue the chain with fake integrity proofs for a given log identifier. If a transaction included a signal to indicate the finalization of a log immutabilization, any other integrity proof in the following transactions could be ignored. In addition it would be more efficient by the validator to validate the logs, since it could stop when this sign was found. Regarding the implementation, further work can be done in order to support distributed immutabilization of multiple logs, since currently only a single node is supported. Finally, the validator can be extended to check the timing of the integrity proofs published in the blockchain match the secure log entries within a given time frame.

References

1. Bellare, M., Yee, B.S.: Forward integrity for secure audit logs. Technical report (1997)
2. Bentov, I., Gabizon, A., Mizrahi, A.: Cryptocurrencies without proof of work. In: Proceedings of 3rd Workshop on Bitcoin and Blockchain Research (2016)
3. Colu. Colored Coins Protocol Specification. Accessed June 2016
4. Cornet, A.O., Bosch, J.M.B.: Method and system of generating immutable audit logs, 15 January 2009. US Patent App. 12/096,048
5. Croman, K., Decker, C., Eyal, I., Gencer, A.E., Juels, A., Kosba, A., Miller, A., Saxena, P., Shi, E., Gün, E.: On scaling decentralized blockchains. In: Proceedings of 3rd Workshop on Bitcoin and Blockchain Research (2016)
6. Eyal, I., Sirer, E.G.: Majority is not enough: bitcoin mining is vulnerable. In: Christin, N., Safavi-Naini, R. (eds.) FC 2014. LNCS, vol. 8437, pp. 436–454. Springer, Heidelberg (2014). doi:10.1007/978-3-662-45472-5_28
7. Galindo, D., Guasch, S., Puiggalí, J.: 2015 Neuchâtel's Cast-as-Intended Verification Mechanism. In: Haenni, R., Koenig, R.E., Wikström, D. (eds.) VOTELID 2015. LNCS, vol. 9269, pp. 3–18. Springer, Heidelberg (2015). doi:10.1007/978-3-319-22270-7_1

8. BitFury Group, Garzik, J.: Public versus private blockchains. Part 1: permissioned blockchains. Technical report, BitFury Group, October 2015
9. Karame, G.O., Androulaki, E., Roeschlin, M., Gervais, A., Čapkun, S.: Misbehavior in bitcoin: a study of double-spending and accountability. ACM Trans. Inf. Syst. Secur. **18**(1), 2: 1–2: 32 (2015)
10. Ma, D., Tsudik, G.: A new approach to secure logging. Trans. Storage **5**(1), 2: 1–2: 21 (2009)
11. Nakamoto, S.: Bitcoin: a peer-to-peer electronic cash system (2008)
12. National Institute of Standards and Technology. FIPS 198-1, The Keyed-Hash Message Authentication Code (HMAC), Federal Information Processing Standard (FIPS), Publication 198-1. Technical report, U.S. Department of Commerce, July 2008
13. National Institute of Standards and Technology. FIPS 180-4, Secure Hash Standard, Federal Information Processing Standard (FIPS), Publication 180-4. Technical report, U.S. Department of Commerce, March 2012
14. National Institute of Standards and Technology. FIPS 186-4, Digital Signature Standard (DSS), Federal Information Processing Standard (FIPS), Publication 186-4. Technical report, U.S. Department of Commerce, July 2013
15. Puiggalí, J., Chóliz, J., Guasch, S.: Best practices in internet voting. In: NIST: Workshop on UOCAVA Remote Voting Systems, Washington DC, August 2010
16. Snodgrass, R.T., Yao, S.S., Collberg, C.: Tamper detection in audit logs. In: Proceedings of the Thirtieth International Conference on Very Large Data Bases, VLDB 2004, vol. 30, pp. 504–515. VLDB Endowment (2004)
17. Snow, P., Deery, B., Lu, J., Johnston, D., Kirby, P.: Factom: business processes secured by immutable audit trails on the blockchain. Whitepaper, Factom, November 2014
18. Zyskind, G., Nathan, O., Pentland, A.S.: Decentralizing privacy: using blockchain to protect personal data. In: 2015 IEEE on Security and Privacy Workshops (SPW), pp. 180–184, May 2015

A Stochastic Framework for Quantitative Analysis of Attack-Defense Trees

Ravi Jhawar, Karim Lounis$^{(\boxtimes)}$, and Sjouke Mauw

CSC/SnT, University of Luxembourg, Luxembourg, Luxembourg
{ravi.jhawar,karim.lounis,sjouke.mauw}@uni.lu

Abstract. Cyber attacks are becoming increasingly complex, practically sophisticated and organized. Losses due to such attacks are important, varying from the loss of money to business reputation spoilage. Therefore, there is a great need for potential victims of cyber attacks to deploy security solutions that allow the identification and/or prediction of potential cyber attacks, and deploy defenses to face them. In this paper, we propose a framework that incorporates Attack-Defense trees (ADTrees) and Continuous Time Markov Chains (CTMCs) to systematically represent attacks, defenses, and their interaction. This solution allows to perform quantitative security assessment, with an aim to predict and/or identify attacks and find the best and appropriate defenses to reduce the impact of attacks.

Keywords: Attack-Defense Trees · Markov chains · Security modeling · Quantitative analysis

1 Introduction

Cyber attacks are becoming more and more technically sophisticated, and well organized. Losses due to such attacks are important, varying from the loss of money to business reputation spoilage. On the other side of the coin, in order to fend and stop this destructive cyber attacks wave, research efforts on cyber attacks and security have considerably risen, trying to come with the best solutions that allow security engineers to predict cyber attacks, estimate their likelihood, and find the most feasible defenses to prevent or reduce the negative impact of these cyber attacks. As a consequence of these research efforts, a great number of graphical models have been proposed in the last two decades (e.g., attack trees [14], attack graphs [7], attack-countermeasure trees [17], and attack-defense trees [10]) and have been widely used for cyber security modeling and

The research leading to the results presented in this work received funding from the European Commission's Seventh Framework Programme (FP7/2007–2013) under grant agreement number 318003 (TREsPASS) and Fonds National de la Recherche Luxembourg under the grant C13/IS/5809105 (ADT2P).

© Springer International Publishing AG 2016
G. Barthe et al. (Eds.): STM 2016, LNCS 9871, pp. 138–153, 2016.
DOI: 10.1007/978-3-319-46598-2_10

assessment. In spite of their similarities, these models differ on how to model attacks and defenses, and how to integrate aspects like time, and dependencies between actions within the model. The perfect model should be easy to use, and practically implementable. It should provide a user-friendly and comprehensive representation of real-life security scenarios, and should integrate aspects like time and dependencies as well as security assessment functions. These requirements are well defined by the ADTrees model [10], which extends attack trees [14] with refinable defenses, and allows the representation of sequential dependencies between actions. It also supports security assessments of attributes such as the likelihood, the cost, and/or the efficiency of attacks/defenses.

ADTrees are defined as a graphical methodology used to represent security scenarios by systematically representing the different actions that an attacker may undertake to realize a security goal, and the different actions that a defender may apply to stop the attacker's actions from being realized. It comes with a strong formal framework for reasoning about security scenarios through different types of semantics (propositional, multiset, De Morgan lattice, and equational), and has proven to be simple, easy to use, and yet powerful in its modeling capability. It has been validated in a large industrial case study [4].

To perform quantitative security assessment for evaluating attributes like cost, efficiency, time, and probabilities, ADTrees apply a bottom-up procedure [14]. Unfortunately this procedure can *only* be used for attribute evaluation under the assumption that *all considered actions (attacks/defenses) are independent*. This is a very strong assumption which is unrealistic in practice, since actions are usually dependent, or in the simplest case sequentially dependent. To overcome this limitation, we propose a new approach for security assessment of ADTrees involving dependencies between actions. This approach relies on Continuous Time Markov Chains. Being a powerful model, provided with a useful quantitative analysis approach, CTMCs tend to be the perfect candidate to assess ADTrees involving dependencies. Inspired by authors of [1–3,12,15], we model atomic attacks/defenses using an exponential distribution. In fact, exponential distribution seems to be a suitable distribution to model a great number of attacks/defenses like brute force attacks, adaptive defense mechanisms (e.g., moving target defenses), or countermeasures with delayed impacts like policies execution. In this paper, we propose a framework that combines the graphical and formal methodology of ADTrees with CTMCs, and allows performing a system's security assessment. The framework takes as an input an ADTree representing a security scenario, and transforms it into a CTMC. This CTMC is then used to perform the security assessment through the evaluation of security attributes such as likelihood, the mean time required by an attack scenario, and other attributes that security engineers may define. To achieve this, we define a new semantics for ADTrees in terms of CTMCs. These semantics express how to translate attacks/defenses into individual CTMCs and how to combine these individual CTMCs into one final CTMC representing the entire ADTree.

Related work. Over the last two decades, a number of graphical security models (e.g., attack trees [14], attack graphs [7], and attack-countermeasure trees [17]) have been proposed in the literature and have been widely used for cyber security modeling and assessment. Moreover, due to the development of cyber attacks in terms of techniques, dependencies, and organization, these models have been enriched and elevated in order to correctly model and assess sophisticated cyber attacks. For instance, attack trees have been enriched and augmented with adaptable countermeasures to become ADTrees [10]. Performing quantitative analysis on these models usually goes through applying an analytic approach such as Markov chains [1–3,12,15], Petri-Nets [5,16], or Bayesian networks [11].

The choice of the analytical approach depends mainly on the model itself, the aspects (time, dependencies) that it considers, and the user preference toward the approach. We find that the Markov chains approach has mostly been chosen for assessing these models. For instance, they have been applied in [2,3,15] on attack trees, and in [1,12] on attack graphs to perform quantitative analysis, and have shown their easy and useful applicability. Inspired by the previous works, we have chosen to apply the Markov chains approach on ADTrees for the following reasons: Models used in the previously cited works like attack trees [2, 3,5,15,16], and attack graphs [1,12] do not define the modeling of defenses in their specification.

Although defense specification is not present in those models, some authors [1–3,5,12,15,16] tried to incorporate defenses to model security scenarios. Unfortunately, they have assumed that the defenses can totally, with no delay, mitigate a given attack. In other words, an attack node is simply deleted from the attack model when it is counter-defended. This assumption is too strong since it is not always the case for a defense to immediately stop an attack once the defense is set up. In fact, there exist defenses whose impact comes after a certain delay like a password changing policy. The ADTree model overcomes the limitation of modeling defense by nature, as it allows to model and represent defenses of different types independent of their impact delay. Secondly, compared to attack-countermeasure trees model, an ADTree model allows the refinement of defenses, which is more realistic. Kordy el al. [11] adopted ADTrees model and used Bayesian networks approach to assess the likelihood of security scenarios. This approach requires for each instant of time the construction of a conditional probability table for each action because of the stochastic dependency between actions. This requirement can be time consuming, error prone, and not practical when a large ADTree is evaluated. Thanks to CTMCs, we can represent the same information (conditional probability tables) using a temporal probability function known as CDF (Cumulative Distribution Function). This function is associated to each action, and provides for each given instant of time t the probability of occurrence of the action with respect to its dependencies.

Contributions. To summarize, the contributions of this paper are threefold.

- We define a new semantics of ADTree model in terms of CTMCs. The semantics express the way attacks/defense action must be represented as a CTMC, and how different CTMCs can be composed to represent the entire attack-defense tree.

– We use the composed CTMC that represents the attack-defense scenario to perform quantitative analysis. Given that attack trees are formally a sub-class of attack-defense trees, our analysis technique also applies to attack trees.
– We demonstrate the applicability of our solution using a simple but realistic example study.

Organization. Section 2 presents the basics of the attack-defense tree model and CTMC model. Section 3 defines our semantics for attack-defense trees in terms of CTMCs. Section 4 discusses the analytical approach of CTMCs to perform quantitative security assessment. Section 5 performs quantitative analysis on an example study. Finally, Sect. 6 provides conclusions and perspectives.

2 ADTrees and CTMCs

2.1 ADTrees

ADTrees are a graphical methodology used to represent security scenarios. They can be seen as a two-player game. The first player is qualified by proponent 'p', and the second by opponent 'o' [9]. Depending on the root of the attack-defense tree, if the root is an attack, then the proponent is the attacker, else it is the defender. Graphically, each performed action or accomplished sub-goal is represented by a node depicted by a red circle ($\bigcirc$) if it refers to an attack action/subgoal, or by a green square ($\square$) if it refers to a defense action/subgoal. Any node of either type in an ADTree can be refined (either disjunctively, conjunctively, or sequentially conjunctive), or countered by another node of the opposite type. Nodes that cannot be refined any further are qualified by basic actions. When a node is disjunctively refined, its accomplishment requires at least one of its refinement nodes to be accomplished. A conjunctively refined node requires all its refinement nodes to be realized without any prefixed order. The sequential conjunctive refinement is similar to the latter but requires a pre-defined accomplishment order for its refinement nodes. We depict a conjunctive refinement of a node by an arc over all edges connecting the node and its refinement nodes, and the sequentially conjunctive refinement with a directed arc. When a node is countered with another node of opposite type, they are linked together using a dashed line.

Figure 1 illustrates an ADTree for a simple networked system where the attacker wants to compromise a server host by executing malicious scripts. To achieve his goal, the attacker must first perform reconnaissance in order to gain knowledge about the network's assets (e.g., topology, protocols, addresses, open ports) using some tools like Nmap. On the other side, to prevent the attacker from gaining knowledge on the network, the defender can apply one of the two adaptive defenses. The first defense regularly changes IP addresses of network hosts and the second defense 'Mutable network' dynamically shuffles IP addresses, routing tables and topology of the network. In the second step, the attacker looks for any vulnerabilities using Nesus for instance. Then, using Metasploit for example, he exploits the discovered vulnerability, and executes a

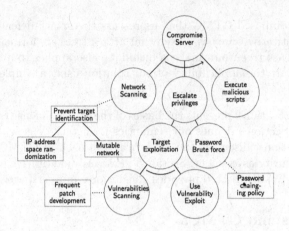

Fig. 1. An example ADTree representing the security scenario

specific designed payload to gain high privileges on the target host. To fend this, the defender frequently performs penetration tests to discover vulnerabilities and develop appropriate patches. As an alternative to target exploitation through vulnerabilities, the attack can brute force the root's password to gain the privilege. The defender implements in this case a policy to periodically change the passwords. This will delay the attacker from succeeding his goal. Finally, if the attacker manage to escalate the privileges, he can execute malicious command and cause harm to the server.

Given that this multi-step attack must be performed in a particular order, we use a sequential conjunction refinement. To realize the 'Escalate Privilege' attack, the attacker must either successfully brute force the root password or (disjunction refinement) exploit a discovered vulnerability and (conjunction refinement) running its dedicated Exploit and payload program.

2.2 Formal Definition of ADTrees

Formally, ADTrees are defined by means of an abstract syntax called ADTerms [10]. The ADTerms in this paper are typed over the signature $\Sigma = (\mathbb{S}, \mathbb{F})$, where:

- $\mathbb{S} = \{p, o\}$ is the set of types (proponent p and opponent o)
- $\mathbb{F} = \{(\vee_k^p)_{k \in \mathbb{N}}, (\wedge_k^p)_{k \in \mathbb{N}}, (\overrightarrow{\wedge}_k^p)_{k \in \mathbb{N}}, (\vee_k^o)_{k \in \mathbb{N}}, (\wedge_k^o)_{k \in \mathbb{N}}, (\overrightarrow{\wedge}_k^o)_{k \in \mathbb{N}}, c^p, c^o\} \cup \mathbb{B}^p \cup \mathbb{B}^o$
  is a set of function symbols.

The unranked functions $(\vee_k^s)_{k \in \mathbb{N}}, (\wedge_k^s)_{k \in \mathbb{N}}$ and $(\overrightarrow{\wedge}_k^s)_{k \in \mathbb{N}}$, where $s \in \mathbb{S}$, represent the disjunctive ($\vee$), conjunctive ($\wedge$), and sequential conjunction ($\overrightarrow{\wedge}$) refinement operators for the proponent and the opponent, respectively. The binary functions c^s connect an action of a given type $s \in \mathbb{S}$ with an action of the opposite type $\overline{s} \in \mathbb{S}$. If we model the proponent as the attacker, then the set $\mathbb{B}^p$ (and respectively $\mathbb{B}^o$)

consists of atomic attacks (and atomic countermeasures). Conventionally $\bar{p} = o$ and $\bar{o} = p$.

Definition 1. *ADTrees are closed terms over the signature $\Sigma = (\mathbb{S}, \mathbb{F})$, generated by the following BNF-grammar, where $b^s \in \mathbb{B}^p \cup \mathbb{B}^o$, and $s \in \mathbb{S}$ is the type of players.*

$$t := b^s \mid \vee^s(t, \ldots, t) \mid \wedge^s(t, \ldots, t) \mid \overrightarrow{\wedge}(t, \ldots, t) \mid c^s(t, t) \tag{1}$$

Example 1. If we label the basic events of the ADTree in Fig. 1 by $b_0^p, b_1^p, b_2^p, b_3^p, b_4^p, b_0^o, b_1^o, b_2^o$, and b_3^o, respectively for Network scanning, Vulnerability scanning, Use vulnerability Exploit, Password brute forcing, Execute dangerous commands, IP randomization, Mutable network, patches development, and finally password policy, then the resulting ADTerm of the ADTree is:

$$t = \overrightarrow{\wedge}^p \left(c^o \left(b_0^p, \vee^o \left(b_0^o, b_1^o \right) \right), \vee^p \left(\wedge^p \left(c^o(b_1^p, b_2^o), b_2^p \right), c^o(b_3^p, b_0^3) \right), b_4^p \right) \tag{2}$$

2.3 Continuous Time Markov Chains

Markov chains [13] are stochastic processes used to model system behavior where probabilistic events are considered. They are called Markovian since the predictions are made based only on the current state of the system, and not on any previous state. A Markov process that transits from one state to another via an exponential rate is called Continuous Time Markov Chain or CTMC.

Definition 2. *A continuous time Markov chain is a tuple (S, G, π), where:*

- *S is a finite disjoint set of states,*
- *$G \colon S \times S \to \mathbb{R}$ is the infinitesimal generator matrix which gives the rate of transition between two states $s \in S$ and $s' \in S$,*
- *$\pi \colon S \to [0, 1]$ is the initial probability distribution on S.*

The proposed semantics for ADTree requires to differentiate between the initial state, intermediate states, and the final states. Therefore, we slightly modify Definition 2 and adapt it to our needs. The new explicit notation (Definition 3) will help us to easily formalize and define our semantics. Moreover, the initial distribution π is usually devoted to the initial state of the system. Therefore, we omit the variable π from the definition, since we arbitrary devote the entire initial distribution to the initial state.

Definition 3. *An enumerated continuous time Markov chain M is a tuple (S, S_0, S_*, G), where:*

- *S is a finite disjoint set of states,*
- *$S_0 \subset S$ is a finite set of initial states,*
- *$S_* \subset S$ is a finite set of final states,*

– $G\colon S \times S \to \mathbb{R}$ is the infinitesimal generator matrix which gives the rate of transition between two states $s \in S$ and $s' \in S$.

We note that there exists a set of intermediate states that we denote by $S_{mid} \subset S$, where $S = S_0 \cup S_{mid} \cup S_*$, and $S_0 \cap S_{mid} \cap S_* = \emptyset$.

The infinitesimal generator matrix G defines the exponential rates $g_{s,s'}$ of the transitions that go from one state $s \in S$ to an other state $s' \in S$. The element $g_{s,s}$ of the infinitesimal generator matrix G are chosen such that each row of the matrix sums to zero. Therefore, the generator matrix G is built as follows:

$$G = \begin{cases} -\sum_{s \neq s'} g_{s,s'} & if \quad s = s', \\ g_{s,s'} & otherwise. \end{cases} \tag{3}$$

Here, each $g_{s,s'} \geq 0$ represents the exponential rate of transition from state $s \in S$ to state $s' \in S$. The inverse $1/g_{s,s'}$ represents the average time needed to transit from $s \in S$ to $s' \in S$ and $|1/g_{s,s}|$ is the average amount of time (sojourn time) spent in state $s \in S$. Furthermore, for a given state $s \in S$, if $\forall s' \in S$, $s' \neq s$, $G(s,s') = 0$, then state $s \in S$ is called an absorbing state and M a continuous time absorbing Markov chain.

3   Markov Chain Semantics for Attack-Defense Trees

We now define the semantics for ADTrees in terms of CTMC. In particular, we first define the semantics for basic events $b^s \in \mathbb{B}^p \cup \mathbb{B}^o$, followed by the semantics for the three refinement operators $(\vee_k^s)_{k \in \mathbb{N}}, (\wedge_k^s)_{k \in \mathbb{N}}$ and $(\overrightarrow{\wedge}_k^s)_{k \in \mathbb{N}}$, where $s \in \mathbb{S}$, and finally the semantics for counteractions c^s (see Sect. 2.2). We then use the semantics of these ADTree components to compose a single CTMC that represents the semantics of the complete ADTree.

Semantics for basic events. Consider a set $\mathbb{M}$ of all possible CTMCs. We can then define a function $\Psi\colon \mathbb{B} \to \mathbb{M}$ that associates, for each basic event $b^s \in \mathbb{B}^p \cup \mathbb{B}^o$, a CTMC defined as $(\{s_0, s_*\}, \{s_0\}, \{s_*\}, G^{b^s})$, where s_0 and s_* are the initial and final states, respectively. The element G^{b^s} represents the infinitesimal generator to the CTMC. It is computed using Eq. 3, and hence given by Eq. 4:

$$G^{b^s} = \begin{bmatrix} -\lambda_{b^s} & \lambda_{b^s} \\ 0 & 0 \end{bmatrix} \tag{4}$$

Figures 2-a and b, illustrate the CTMC corresponding to basic events $b^p \in \mathbb{B}^p$ and $b^o \in \mathbb{B}^o$, respectively. The rates λ_{b^p} and μ_{b^o} represent the exponential rates of an atomic attack and an atomic countermeasure, respectively.

Semantics for conjunctive refinements. We define an unranked function $\wedge_{k \in \mathbb{N}}\colon \mathbb{M}^k \to \mathbb{M}$ which takes k Markov chains and composes them in a way that all k Markov chains should be executed in an irrelevant execution order. Therefore, the composed Markov chain is $(\prod_{i=1}^k S^{b_i}, \prod_{i=1}^k S_0^{b_i}, \prod_{i=1}^k S_*^{b_i}, G^{\wedge_{k \in \mathbb{N}}^s})$. The set $S^{\wedge_{k \in \mathbb{N}}^s}$ contains all possible combinations of the states of the k involved

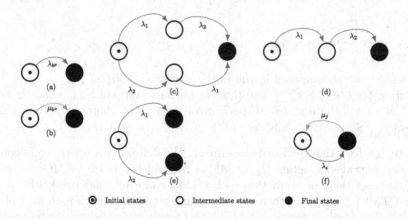

Fig. 2. CTMC-Semantics of basic events, refinements, and countermeasures.

Markov chains. The initial state is equal to $(s_0^{b_1}, s_0^{b_2}, ..., s_0^{b_k})$, and similarly, the final state is $(s_*^{b_1}, s_*^{b_2}, ..., s_*^{b_k})$. The remaining states refer to intermediate (transitive) states.

Figure 2-c illustrates the CTMC obtained by applying the function $\wedge_2^s$ on CTMC M_1^s and M_2^s, where M_1^s and M_2^s are two CTMCs corresponding to two basic events $b_1^s, b_2^s \in \mathbb{B}$. The generator $G^{\wedge_{k\in\mathbb{N}}^s}$ is obtained by the following equation:

$$G^{\overrightarrow{\wedge}_{k\in\mathbb{N}}^s}(s_i, s_j) = \begin{cases} -\sum_{i\neq j} G^{\overrightarrow{\wedge}_{k\in\mathbb{N}}^s}(s_i, s_j) & if \quad i = j, \\ 0 & if \quad i \neq j \quad \wedge \quad |s_i \Delta s_j| > 2, \\ 0 & if \quad s_i \in \Omega, \\ G^{idf}(S^{idf} \cap s_i, S^{idf} \cap s_j) & otherwise. \end{cases} \quad (5)$$

Where Δ is the symmetric difference between two sets, $|S|$ is the cardinality of a given set S, Ω is the set of absorbing states, and $idf = \vartheta(s_i \cap s_j)$ is a function which returns the identifier of the Markov chains from where the input sets belong to. For example, $\vartheta(s_0^1, s_5^2, s_8^2)$ returns $\{1, 2\}$. In summary, this formulation consists in identifying which transition (t_i^{idf}) is linking state s_i to state s_j. Note that this formulation is valid for sequential conjunction and disjunction refinement as well.

Semantics for sequential conjunctive refinements. We define the sequential conjunction refinements using the function $\overrightarrow{\wedge}_{k\in\mathbb{N}}: \mathbb{M}^k \to \mathbb{M}$ which takes k CTMCs as input and composes them sequentially. The final state of the nth CTMC is merged with the initial state of the $n+1^{th}$ CTMC. Figure 2-d illustrates how two CTMCs are composed by $\overrightarrow{\wedge}_2^s$. The result of $\overrightarrow{\wedge}_{k\in\mathbb{N}}$ composition is a CTMC $(S^{\overrightarrow{\wedge}_{k\in\mathbb{N}}^s}, S_0^{\overrightarrow{\wedge}_{k\in\mathbb{N}}^s}, S_*^{\overrightarrow{\wedge}_{k\in\mathbb{N}}^s}, G^{\overrightarrow{\wedge}_{k\in\mathbb{N}}^s})$ where:

- $S^{\overrightarrow{\wedge}_{k\in\mathbb{N}}^s} = S_0^{\overrightarrow{\wedge}_{k\in\mathbb{N}}^s} \bigcup S_*^{\overrightarrow{\wedge}_{k\in\mathbb{N}}^s} \bigcup S_{mid}^{\overrightarrow{\wedge}_{k\in\mathbb{N}}^s}$
- $S_0^{\overrightarrow{\wedge}_{k\in\mathbb{N}}^s} = \prod_{i=1}^k S_0^{b_i}$

$$- \ S_*^{\overrightarrow{\wedge^s}_{k\in\mathbb{N}}} = \prod_{i=1}^{k} S_*^{b_i}$$

$$- \ S_{mid}^{\overrightarrow{\wedge^s}_{k\in\mathbb{N}}} = \bigcup_{i=1}^{k-1} \ S_*^{b_i} \times S_0^{b_{i+1}} \ \bigcup \ S_{mid}^{b_i} \times S_0^{b_{i+1}} \ \bigcup \ S_*^{b_i} \times S_{mid}^{b_{i+1}}$$

The set $S^{\overrightarrow{\wedge^s}_{k\in\mathbb{N}}}$ is composed of the initial state $S_0^{\overrightarrow{\wedge^s}_{k\in\mathbb{N}}} = \{(s_0^{b_1}, s_0^{b_2}, ..., s_0^{b_k})\}$, the final state $\{(s_*^{b_1}, s_*^{b_2}, ..., s_*^{b_k})\}$, and the intermediate states of S_{mid}, which is composed of intermediate states of the k involved Markov chains plus the linking states $\bigcup_{i=1}^{k-1} S_*^{b_i} \times S_0^{b_{i+1}}$ (chains each CTMC with the next CTMC).

Semantics for disjunction refinement. We define a disjunctive refinement using an unranked function $\vee_{k\in\mathbb{N}}: \mathbb{M}^k \to \mathbb{M}$, which takes k CTMCs as input and composes them in a way that each CTMC can evolve independently to the other CTMCs. Therefore, there will be k final states (one from each k involved CTMC). The result of composing k CTMCs by means of a disjunction refinement is $(S^{\vee_{k\in\mathbb{N}}^s}, S_0^{\vee_{k\in\mathbb{N}}^s}, S_*^{\vee_{k\in\mathbb{N}}^s}, G^{\vee_{k\in\mathbb{N}}^s})$, where:

$$- \ S^{\vee_{k\in\mathbb{N}}^s} = S_0^{\vee_{k\in\mathbb{N}}^s} \cup S_*^{\vee_{k\in\mathbb{N}}^s} \cup S_{mid}^{\vee_{k\in\mathbb{N}}^s},$$

$$- \ S_0^{\vee_{k\in\mathbb{N}}^s} = \prod_{i=1}^{k} S_0^{b_i},$$

$$- \ S_*^{\vee_{k\in\mathbb{N}}^s} = \bigcup_{i=1}^{n} S_*^{b_i} \times \prod_{j\neq i} S_0^{b_j},$$

$$- \ S_{mid}^{\vee_{k\in\mathbb{N}}^s} = \bigcup_{i=1}^{n} S_{mid}^{b_i} \times \prod_{j\neq i} S_0^{b_j}.$$

The set $S^{\vee_{k\in\mathbb{N}}^s}$ is composed of the initial state $(s_0^{b_1}, s_0^{b_2}, ..., s_0^{b_k})$, the intermediate states of S_{mid}, and the final states $\{(s_*^{b_1}, s_0^{b_2}, ..., s_0^{b_k}), (s_0^{b_1}, s_*^{b_2}, ..., s_0^{b_k}), ..., (s_0^{b_1}, s_0^{b_2}, ..., s_*^{b_k})\}$. The set S_{mid} is composed of intermediate states of the k involved CTMCs. Figure 2-e illustrates how two CTMCs are disjunctively composed.

Semantics for countermeasures. We represent counter-measuring with an unranked function $c^s(b^p, b^o)$, where $s \in \mathbb{S}$, $b^p \in \mathbb{B}^p$ and $b^o \in \mathbb{B}^o$. If we consider the proponent to be the attacker and the opponent to be the defender, this function will link the atomic attack $b^p \in \mathbb{B}^p$ with an atomic defense $b^o \in \mathbb{B}^o$. Note that besides taking as inputs atomic attacks/defenses, the function c^s can also take as inputs conjunctively, disjunctively or sequential conjunctive refined inputs.

The CTMC-semantics for a countermeasure is characterized using a new unranked function $c^s: \mathbb{M} \times \mathbb{M} \to \mathbb{M}$. This new function takes two CTMCs M^s and $M^{\overline{s}}$ as inputs, one representing the proponent action, and the second representing the opponent action. It links them such that they counter each other. In other words, the final state of the proponent action will be the initial state of the opponent action and vice-versa. Therefore, if the proponent starts his next step before the opponent action is executed, the proponent would skip successfully the countermeasure set by the opponent. However, if the countermeasures is successfully executed (before the proponent manages to move to next step), the proponent is brought to the initial state where he has to re-perform his action. For example, in Fig. 1, if the password changing policy is executed the attacker has to re-perform the brute force attack again.

The constructed CTMC for counter-measuring is defined as follows:

- $S^{c(M^s,M^{\bar{s}})} = S_0^{c(M^s,M^{\bar{s}})} \cup S_{mid}^{c(M^s,M^{\bar{s}})} \cup S_*^{c(M^s,M^{\bar{s}})}$,
- $S_0^{c(M^s,M^{\bar{s}})} = S_0^{M^s} \times (s_1^{M^{\bar{s}}}, s_2^{M^{\bar{s}}}, ..., s_{|S_*^{M^{\bar{s}}}|}^{M^{\bar{s}}})$ where $s_i^{M^{\bar{s}}} \in S_*^{M^{\bar{s}}}$ and $i \in \{1, ..., |S_*^{M^{\bar{s}}}|\}$,
- $S_*^{c(M^s,M^{\bar{s}})} = S_*^s \times S_0^{M^{\bar{s}}}$,
- $S_{mid}^{c(M^s,M^{\bar{s}})} = S_{mid}^{M^s} \times S_0^{M^{\bar{s}}} \cup S_{mid}^{M^{\bar{s}}}$.

Similarly to the other semantics, the set $S^{c(M^s,\bar{s})}$ is composed of the initial state, which contains the initial state of player (proponent/opponent) s and a tuple of all final states of player (opponent/proponent) $\bar{s}$. The final state consists of the final states of the player (proponent/opponent) and the initial state of player (opponent/proponent) $\bar{s}$. It also contains intermediate states from each player's chain. Figure 2-f shows how counter-measuring of an atomic attack with an exponential rate λ is performed against an atomic countermeasure with an exponential rate μ.

We have formulated the generator matrix $G^{c(M^s,M^{\bar{s}})}$ as follows:

$$G^{c(M^s,M^{\bar{s}})}(s_i, s_j) = \begin{cases} -\sum_{i \neq j} Q^{c(M^s,M^{\bar{s}})}(s_i, s_j) & if \quad i = j, \\ \sum G^{M^s}(s_{i'}, s_{j'}) + \sum G^{M^{\bar{s}}}(s_{i''}, s_{j''}) & otherwise. \end{cases} \quad (6)$$

Where $(s_{i'}, s_{j'}), (s_{i''}, s_{j''}) \in s_i \times s_j$ and $\vartheta(s_{i'}) = \vartheta(s_{j'})$ and $\vartheta(s_{i''}) = \vartheta(s_{j''})$.

Overall, this formulation consists in summing the rates of all possible transitions that go from state s_i to state s_j. Since every transition t_i^{idf} belongs to only one CTMC M_{idf}, the execution of t_i^{idf} will only affect states of M_{idf}. Therefore, there will generally be only one transition (one rate), unless it regards a disjunction of countermeasures, where the rates of the involved countermeasures are summed.

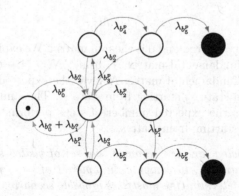

Fig. 3. CTMC obtained by composing individual CTMCs for the ADTree in Fig. 1

Example 2. We use the ADTerm given by Eq. 2 (Sect. 2.2) and apply the new semantics described above to obtain the entire CTMC (see Fig. 3) representing the whole ADTree of Fig. 1. This is merely achieved by first building CTMCs of basic events, then composing them according to the involved refinements operators that links the basic events.

4 Quantitative Security Assessment

In this section, we show how to perform quantitative analysis using Markov chains [18]. We show how to compute and extract matrices that are necessary for the analysis. To achieve this, we consider an enumerated continuous time Markov chain $M = (S, S_0, S_*, G)$, from which we can extract and compute the following structures:

The first structure is called the instantaneous probability matrix $P(t)$. It gives the instantaneous probability to transit from a state s_i to state s_j. In an other words, for each state $s_i \in S$ in a CTMC M, is associated a cumulative distribution function $0 \leq F_X(t) \leq 1$ (where X is a random variable and t is the time) that describes the probability of being in state $s_i \in S$, in time interval $[0-t)$, starting from state $s_j \in S$. The instantaneous probability matrix is computed using the infinitesimal generator matrix G as $P(t) = e^{G \cdot t}$.

Application. *We exploit this matrix to draw the cumulative distribution function (CDF) of each final state (representing the final goal) starting from the initial state. Therefore, we can compute at any time the probability of success for each possible attack scenario leading to a final state (final goal).*

The second structure is the mean probability transition matrix P, where each element $P_{i,j}^{i \neq j}$ is equal to $|g_{ij}/g_{ii}|$ for $i \neq j$, and gives the mean probability to transit from state s_i to state s_j. The elements $P_{i,i}$ however, are null. In an absorbing CTMC, this matrix particularly takes a canonical form defined as:

$$P = \begin{bmatrix} Q & R \\ 0 & Id \end{bmatrix} \tag{7}$$

Here Id is the identity matrix, and 0 is the null matrix. We exploit the submatrix Q to compute the fundamental matrix N, using: $N = (1 - Q)^{-1}$, where each element $n_{i,j}$ in the fundamental matrix N gives the expected number of steps the process visited a state s_j starting from state s_i. The sum of the ith row in matrix N represents the expected number of steps performed to reach any of the absorbing state starting from state s_i.

Application. *Knowing for each scenario, the set of visited states, we can use the fundamental matrix N, to compute the amount of steps performed in each scenario and hence determine the most/less probable scenario, or exert a ranking for the different possible scenarios.*

The third component is the absorbency frequency matrix $B = N \times R$, where each element b_{ij} of B gives the probability of getting absorbed by each absorbing states.

Application. *This matrix will serve to identify the most probable goal if we have many, or to confirm again the most probable scenario and with which steady state probability.*

Finally, using the fundamental Matrix N and the sojourn times $|1/g_{ii}|$ of each state, we can compute the mean time required to reach the final goal starting from the initial state.

Application. *In the context of security modeling, we compute the MTTSF (Mean Time To Security Failure) also known as MTTB (Mean Time To Breach) or MTTA (Mean Time To Attack). We can also compute the mean time for each scenario. The MTTSF is given by:*

$$MTTSF = \sum_{i \in X_t} n_{0,i} \times \frac{1}{|g_{ii}|} \tag{8}$$

Where $n_{0,i}$ is the expected number of steps performed to go from the initial state s_0 to state s_i.

5 Security Assessment of the Networked System

We report on the analysis conducted to evaluate the security of the scenario discussed in Sect. 2.1. In particular, we consider the ADTree in Fig. 1 and its CTMC representation in Fig. 3 to perform security assessment. To achieve this, we go through three cases: one (case 1), where we don't consider existence of countermeasures (attack trees), the second (case 2) we add countermeasure 'prevent target identification', and the last case (case 3), in addition to the previously added countermeasure we add two more countermeasures respectively 'Frequent patches' and 'Passwords policy'. The results of our analysis can be used by security engineers to choose appropriate defenses in order to harden the security of

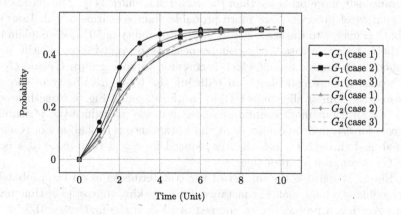

Fig. 4. Cumulative Distribution Function of scenarios group

the system. For the purpose of performing quantitative analysis, we have arbitrarily affected rational values for the different exponential rate of each basic event. Therefore, by denoting atomic attack as $b_0^p \ldots b_5^p$ and countermeasures as b_0^o and b_3^o. We assign exponential rates λ as follows: $\lambda_{b_0^p} = 1$ for $b_0^p = $ Network scanning, $\lambda_{b_1^p} = 2$ for $b_1^p = $ Vulnerability scanning, $\lambda_{b_2^p} = 1$ for $b_2^p = $ Use vulnerability exploit, $\lambda_{b_5^p} = 5$ for $b_5^p = $ Execute malicious scripts. The atomic attack $b_3^p = $ Password brute force attack use an Erlang distribution $Erl(2,3)$, which corresponds to a sequence of two exponentials of rate $\lambda_{b_3^p} = 3$. Therefore, we model this attack with two atomic attacks b_3^p and b_4^p of the same rate equal to 3. The countermeasures $b_0^o = $ IP address randomization, $b_1^o = $ Mutable network, $b_2^o = $ Updates, and $b_3^o = $ Password policy are modeled using exponential distributions $\mu_{b_0^o} = 1$, $\mu_{b_1^o} = 2$, $\mu_{b_2^o} = 1$, and $\mu_{b_3^o} = 1$, respectively. A point that we should highlight, is that the fact of having sub-goals disjunctively refined, and at least one of the refinements is conjunctively refined, induces the replication of the final goal in the constructed Markov chain (see the two black states in Fig. 3). Therefore, there will be more than one state referencing to the same final goal but reached through different scenarios. As shown in Fig. 3, the first final state is reached through $[b_0^p; b_3^p; b_4^p; b_5^p]$. However, the second final state is reached through two different scenarios $[b_0^p; b_2^p; b_1^p; b_5^p]$ or $[b_0^p; b_1^p; b_2^p; b_5^p]$. Therefore, we can define for each final goal (final state) f_i a group of scenarios G_i composed of the same atomic attacks, but conducted in different order.

Probabilistic security attributes. We compute the probability of reaching the final goal over time expressed in terms of CDF. We also try to determine the probability of each group of scenarios, and draw the evolution of their probability of success over time. We compute the most probable scenario and perform a ranking for the possible scenarios. To achieve this, we first use the instantaneous probability matrix to draw the CDF of each final goal f_i. In our example of study, we have determined two groups of scenarios G_1 and G_2.

From Fig. 4, in the two first cases, we see that the group of scenarios G_1 is instantaneously more probable than the group of scenarios G_2. This means that the scenarios of group G_1 are more probable than scenarios of $G2$. However, they both converge to the same steady state probability of 50 %. We explain this from the fact that in case 2, the countermeasure 'prevent target identification' is applied to an atomic attack which is common to both groups G_1 and G_2. In other words, defense contributes in reducing the total probability of the goal over time (the sum of all groups CDFs) as we can see in Fig. 5. Nonetheless, in case 3, we have put more countermeasures in a way to reduce the probability of success for G_1, and we can see that the instantaneous probability of reaching the final goal through G_1 has slightly reduced for $t \geq 3$ time units to a point where G_2 becomes more probable.

In Fig. 5, we can see the impact of the countermeasures on the probability of succeeding the final goal. For instance, for a working time of [0-5] time units, the attacker has a probability to succeed of 97 % in the first case, 91 % in the second case, and finally 86 % in the last case, which is more secure. Note that

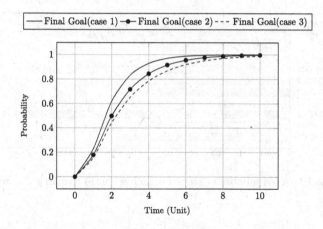

Fig. 5. Cumulative Distribution Function of the final goal

the impact is slightly small since the rates that we have affected are too close to the attacks rates.

Then we use the fundamental matrix N to compute the expected number of steps realized in each scenario of each group, and therefore determine the most probable scenario MPS (we can rank scenarios). The results are depicted in Fig. 6, where we can see that the most probable scenario has the largest amount of steps. In this case, scenario $[b_0^p; b_3^p; b_4^p; b_5^p]$ is the most probable one. Furthermore, the number of steps is increasing each time countermeasures are added. We explain that from the fact that the attacker performs more steps since the execution of a countermeasure forces the attacker to restart from his initial state. Therefore, in each scenario, the number of expected steps is increased as long as countermeasures are added. Moreover, we can rank the three scenarios as follows: $[b_0^p; b_3^p; b_4^p; b_5^p]$, then $[b_0^p; b_1^p; b_2^p; b_5^p]$, and finally scenario $[b_0^p; b_2^p; b_1^p; b_5^p]$. Finally, we use the absorbency frequency matrix B to compute the percentage in which the attacker succeed in reaching his final goal through a particular scenario in the steady state, that is to say, when he is given enough time. This will allow us to testify which group of scenarios is the most probable. The results are shown in Fig. 7 (left side).

The steady state probability is 50 % for the first two cases, where no countermeasures are applied, then when a common countermeasures is applied. The third case shows that it is more probable to perform attacks through G_2 than trough G_1, since this last one contains more countermeasures.

Time based attributes. Finally, we evaluate the mean time to breach the system in terms of MTTSF. Therefore, we make use of Eq. (5) and compute the MTTSF for the three cases. The results are illustrated in Fig. 7 (right side). We can see that the attacker is each time delayed as long as we add countermeasures. Indeed, the countermeasure 'prevent target identification' has delayed the attacker to spend 25.64 % more time units than usual (initial case). In the third

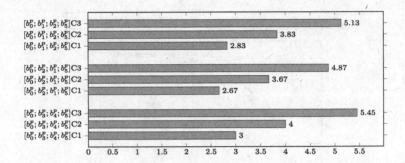

Fig. 6. Expected number of steps for each scenario and for each case

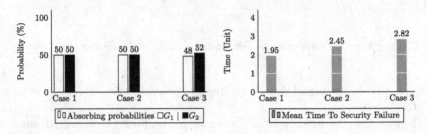

Fig. 7. Absorbing probabilities (left), Mean Time To Security Failure (right)

case, the attacker has to spend 44.62 % more time units compared to the initial non-secure case.

6   Conclusions

We presented a stochastic framework to perform quantitative analysis of ADTrees. We started by defining a new semantics for ADTrees in terms of CTMCs, then showed how to construct a final CTMC representing the entire ADTree. We then applied the analytical approach of CTMC to perform quantitative analysis. We finally demonstrated the usefulness of our solution by means of a simple but realistic example study.

As part of our future work, we will extend our framework to model and quantitatively assess complex security scenarios like social attacks. We will also extend our framework in order to embed it within the ADTool [6,8], which is a free software tool for security modeling and quantitative analysis using ADTrees.

References

1. Abraham, S., Nair, S.: Predictive cyber-security analytics framework: a non-homogenous markov model for security quantification. arXiv preprint arXiv:1501.01901 (2015)

2. Arnold, F., Guck, D., Kumar, R., Stoelinga, M.: Sequential and parallel attack tree modelling. In: Koornneef, F., Gulijk, C. (eds.) SAFECOMP 2015. LNCS, vol. 9338, pp. 291–299. Springer, Heidelberg (2015). doi:10.1007/978-3-319-24249-1_25

3. Arnold, F., Hermanns, H., Pulungan, R., Stoelinga, M.: Time-dependent analysis of attacks. In: Abadi, M., Kremer, S. (eds.) POST 2014 (ETAPS 2014). LNCS, vol. 8414, pp. 285–305. Springer, Heidelberg (2014)

4. Bagnato, A., Kordy, B., Meland, P.H., Schweitzer, P.: Attribute decoration of attack-defense trees. Int. J. Secur. Softw. Eng. 3(2), 1–35 (2012)

5. Dalton II, G.C., Mills, R.F., Colombi, J.M., Raines, R.A.: Analyzing attack trees using generalized stochastic Petri nets. In: IEEE Information Assurance Workshop, pp. 116–123. IEEE (2006)

6. Gadyatskaya, O., Jhawar, R., Kordy, P., Lounis, K., Mauw, S., Trujillo-Rasua, R.: Attack trees for practical security assessment: ranking of attack scenarios with ADTool 2.0. In: Agha, G., Houdt, B. (eds.) QEST 2016. LNCS, vol. 9826, pp. 159–162. Springer, Heidelberg (2016). doi:10.1007/978-3-319-43425-4_10

7. Hughes, T., Sheyner, O.: Attack scenario graphs for computer network threat analysis and prediction. Complexity 9(2), 15–18 (2003)

8. Kordy, B., Kordy, P., Mauw, S., Schweitzer, P.: ADTool: security analysis with attack-defense trees (extended version). arXiv preprint arXiv:1305.6829 (2013)

9. Kordy, B., Mauw, S., Melissen, M., Schweitzer, P.: Attack–defense trees and two-player binary zero-sum extensive form games are equivalent. In: Alpcan, T., Buttyán, L., Baras, J.S. (eds.) GameSec 2010. LNCS, vol. 6442, pp. 245–256. Springer, Heidelberg (2010)

10. Kordy, B., Mauw, S., Radomirović, S., Schweitzer, P.: Foundations of attack–defense trees. In: Degano, P., Etalle, S., Guttman, J. (eds.) FAST 2010. LNCS, vol. 6561, pp. 80–95. Springer, Heidelberg (2011). doi:10.1007/978-3-642-19751-2_6

11. Kordy, B., Pouly, M., Schweitzer, P.: A probabilistic framework for security scenarios with dependent actions. In: Albert, E., Sekerinski, E. (eds.) IFM 2014. LNCS, vol. 8739, pp. 256–271. Springer, Heidelberg (2014)

12. Madan, B.B., Gogeva-Popstojanova, K, Vaidyanathan, K., Trivedi, K.S.: Modeling and quantification of security attributes of software systems. In: International Conference on Dependable Systems and Networks, pp. 505–514. IEEE (2002)

13. Markov, A.: Extension of the limit theorems of probability theory to a sum of variables connected in a chain. In: Howard, R. (ed.) Dynamic Probabilistic Systems (Volume I: Markov Models), pp. 552–577. Wiley, New York (1971)

14. Mauw, S., Oostdijk, M.: Foundations of attack trees. In: Won, D.H., Kim, S. (eds.) ICISC 2005. LNCS, vol. 3935, pp. 186–198. Springer, Heidelberg (2006). doi:10.1007/11734727_17

15. Piètre-Cambacédès, L., Bouissou, M.: Beyond attack trees: dynamic security modeling with Boolean logic Driven Markov Processes (BDMP). In: European Dependable Computing Conference, pp. 199–208. IEEE (2010)

16. Pudar, S., Manimaran, G., Liu, C.-C.: PENET: a practical method and tool for integrated modeling of security attacks and countermeasures. Comput. Secur. 28(8), 754–771 (2009)

17. Roy, A., Kim, D.S., Trivedi, K.S.: Attack countermeasure trees (ACT): towards unifying the constructs of attack and defense trees. Secur. Commun. Netw. 5(8), 929–943 (2012)

18. Stewart, W.J.: Introduction to the Numerical Solutions of Markov Chains. Princeton University Press, Princeton (1994)

Information Security as Strategic (In)effectivity

Wojciech Jamroga[1] and Masoud Tabatabaei[2(✉)]

[1] Institute of Computer Science, Polish Academy of Sciences, Warszawa, Poland
w.jamroga@ipipan.waw.pl
[2] Interdisciplinary Centre for Security and Trust,
University of Luxembourg, Luxembourg, Luxembourg
masoud.tabatabaei@uni.lu

Abstract. Security of information flow is commonly understood as preventing *any* information leakage, regardless of how grave or harmless consequences the leakage can have. In this work, we suggest that information security is not a goal in itself, but rather a means of preventing potential attackers from compromising the correct behavior of the system. To formalize this, we first show how two information flows can be compared by looking at the adversary's ability to harm the system. Then, we propose that the information flow in a system is *effectively information-secure* if it does not allow for more harm than its idealized variant based on the classical notion of noninterference.

1 Introduction

In most approaches to information flow security, information defines the ultimate goal of the interaction between agents. Classical information security properties specify *what* information must not leak, and *how* it could possibly leak (i.e., what channels of information leakage are considered), but they do not give account of *why* the information should not leak to the intruder. For example, the property of *noninterference* [7] assumes that the "low clearance" users cannot learn anything about the activities of the "high clearance" users. In order to violate this, the "low" users can try to analyse their observations and/or execute a sequence of explorative actions of their own. *Nondeducibility on strategies* [30] makes the same assumption about *what* should not leak, but takes also into account covert channels that some "high" users can use to send signals to the "low" agents according to a previously agreed code. *Anonymity* in voting [2,5] captures that an observer cannot learn what candidate a particular has voted for by looking at the voter's behavior, scanning the web bulletin board, coercing the voter to hand in the vote receipt, etc.

As a consequence, the classical properties of information security can only distinguish between relevant and irrelevant information leaks if the distinction is given explicitly as a parameter, e.g., by classifying available actions into sensitive and insensitive [7]. However, it is usually hard (if not impossible) to obtain such a distinction based on the internal characteristics of the actions. We illustrate the point below by means of a real-life example.

© Springer International Publishing AG 2016
G. Barthe et al. (Eds.): STM 2016, LNCS 9871, pp. 154–169, 2016.
DOI: 10.1007/978-3-319-46598-2_11

Example 1. In some phone banking services, the maiden name of the user's mother is used as a part of authentication.[1] Consider now a user posting an essay about some ancestor of hers on her blog, mentioning also the name of the ancestor. If the essay is about the user's mother, it reveals potentially danger-ous information. On the other hand, if the post is about some other member of the user's family (father, grandmother, paternal grandfather, etc.) revealing the name of the person is probably harmless. Note that it is impossible to distinguish between the two pieces of information (say, the mother's maiden name vs. the grandmother's maiden name) based on their internal features. The only differ-ence lies in the context: the first kind of information is used in some important social procedures, while the second one is not.   □

In this paper, we claim that a broader perspective is needed to appropriately model and analyse such scenarios. Agents compete for information not for its own sake, but for reasons that go beyond purely epistemic advantages. More precisely, information is a commodity that the players compete for in an "information security game" but the game is played in the context of a "real" game where information is only a resource, enabling (some) players to achieve their non-epistemic goals. As players obtain new information, their uncertainty is reduced, and they increase their ability to choose a good strategy in the real game.

What would a *significant information leak* be in this view? To answer the question, we draw inspiration from the concept of the *value of information*: a piece of information is worth as much as it increases the expected payoff of the player. Similarly, an information leak is significant if it increases the ability of the attacker to construct a damaging attack strategy in the real game.

Contribution of the Paper. First, we use the concept of *surely winning strate-gies* from game theory to analyze the adversary's strategic ability to disrupt the correct behavior of the system. We will see the *effective security* of the system as the attacker's *in*ability to come up with such a strategy.

Secondly, we use the notion of *effective security* for comparing two systems by looking at the strategic ability of an adversary to harm the goal of the system.

Thirdly, a successful attack strategy can exist due to flawed design of either the control flow or the information flow in the system. Here, we are interested in the latter. That is, we want to distinguish between vulnerabilities coming from the control vs. the information flow, and single out systems where redesigning the flow of information alone can make the system more secure. To this end, we define the noninterferent idealized variant of the system, which has the same control flow as the original system, but with the information reduced so that the system satisfies noninterference. Then, we define the system to be *effectively information-secure* if it is as good as its noninterfering idealized variant. As the main technical result, we show that the concept is well defined, i.e., the maximal noninterferent variant exists for every state-transition model.

---

[1] This is a real-life example from the authors' personal experience. For similar security questions, used by various phone or web services, cf. e.g. [14].

Due to lack of space, we include only proof sketches for most results. The complete proofs, together with additional examples, can be found in the extended version of the paper, available at http://arxiv.org/abs/1608.02247.

2   Related Work

Various formalizations of information flow security have been proposed and studied. The classical concept here is *noninterference* [7] and its variations: *nondeducibility* [28], *noninference* [22], *restrictiveness* [18], *nondeducibility on strategies* [30], and *strategic noninterference* [13]. Probabilistic noninterference and quantitative noninterference have been investigated, e.g., in [9,16,19,23,27,30]. All the above concepts assume that the information flow in the system is secure only when no information ever flows from High to Low players. In this paper, we want to discard irrelevant information leaks, and only look at the significant ones (in the sense that the leaking information can be used to construct an attack on a higher-order correctness property).

The problem of how to weaken noninterference to successfully capture security guarantees for real systems has been also extensively studied. Most notably, postulates and policies for *declassification* (called also *information release*) were studied, cf. [26] for an introduction. This submission can be viewed as an attempt to determine *what information is acceptable to declassify*. In this sense, our results can useful in proposing new declassification policies and evaluating existing ones. We note, however, that the existing work on declassification are mainly concerned by the question *what* information can be released, *when*, *where*, and by *whom*. In contrast, we propose an argument for *why* it can be released. Moreover, declassification is typically about intentional release of information, whereas we do not distinguish between intentional and accidental information flow. Finally, the research on declassification assumes that security is defined by some given "secrets" to be protected. In our approach, no information is intrinsically secret, but the information flow is harmful if it enables the attacker to gain more strategic ability against the goals of the system.

Parameterized noninterference [6] can be seen as a theoretical counterpart of declassification, where security of information flow is parameterized by the analytic capabilities of the attacker. Again, that research does not answer why some information must be kept secret while some other needs not, and in particular it does not take strategic power of the attacker into account.

Economic and strategic analysis of security properties is a growing field in general, cf. [21] for an introduction. A number of papers have applied game-theoretic concepts to define the security of information flow [3,4,11–13,17]. However, most of those papers [3,11,12,17] use games only in a narrow mathematical sense to provide a proof system (called the *game semantics*) for deciding security properties. We are aware of only a handful of papers that investigate the impact of participants' incentives and available strategies on the security of information flow. In [1,10], economic interpretations of privacy-preserving behavior are proposed. [4] uses game-theoretic solution concepts (in particular, Nash equilibrium) to prescribe the optimal defense strategy against attacks on information security. In contrast, our approach is analytic rather than prescriptive, as we do not propose how to manage information security. Moreover, in our view, privacy is not the goal but rather the means to achieve some higher-level objectives. Finally, [13] proposes a weaker variant of noninterference by allowing the High players to select an appropriate strategy, while here we look at the potential damage inflicted by adverse strategies of the Low users.

Our idea of looking at the unique most precise non-interfering variant of the system is related on the technical level to [6]. There, attackers displaying different analytical capabilities are defined by abstract interpretation, which leads to a lattice of noninterference variants with various strength. Attackers with weakened observational powers were also studied in [31].

3 Preliminaries

3.1 Simple Models of Interaction

Since we build our proposal around the standard notion of noninterference by Goguen and Meseguer [7], we will use similar models to represent interaction between actions of different agents. The *system* is modeled by a multi-agent asynchronous transition network $M = \langle St, s_0, \mathfrak{U}, \mathfrak{A}, Obs, obs, do \rangle$ where: St is the set of *states*, s_0 is the initial state, $\mathfrak{U}$ is the set of *agents* (or *users*), $\mathfrak{A}$ is the set of *actions*, Obs is the set of possible *observations* (or *outputs*); $obs : St \times \mathfrak{U} \to Obs$ is the observation function. $do : St \times \mathfrak{U} \times \mathfrak{A} \to St$ is the transition function that specifies the (deterministic) outcome $do(s, u, a)$ of action a executed by user u in state s. We will sometimes write $[s]_u$ instead of $obs(s, u)$. Also, we will call a pair *(user, action)* a *personalized action*. We construct the multi-step transition function $exec : St \times (\mathfrak{U} \times \mathfrak{A})^* \to St$ so that, for a finite string $\alpha \in (\mathfrak{U} \times \mathfrak{A})^*$ of personalized actions, $exec(s, \alpha)$ denotes the state resulting from execution of α from s on. We may sometimes write $s \xrightarrow{\alpha} t$ instead of $exec(s, \alpha) = t$, and $exec(\alpha)$ instead of $exec(s_0, \alpha)$.

Three remarks are in order. First, Goguen and Meseguer's models define agents' observations based on states only, whereas it is often convenient to also model the information flow due to observing each others' actions. Secondly, the models are fully asynchronous in the sense that if each user "submits" a sequence of actions to be executed then every interleaving of the submitted sequences can occur as the resulting behavior of the system. No synchronization is possible. Thirdly, the models are "total on input" (each action label is available to every user at every state), and hence no synchronization mechanism can be encoded via availability of actions. Especially the last two features imply that models of Goguen and Meseguer allow for representation of a very limited class of systems.

We start by using the purely asynchronous models of Goguen and Meseguer. Then, in Sect. 6, we extend our results to a broader class of models by allowing partial transition functions.

3.2   Noninterference

We now recall the standard notion of noninterference from [7]. Let $U \subseteq \mathfrak{U}$ and $\alpha \in (\mathfrak{U} \times \mathfrak{A})^*$. By $Purge_U(\alpha)$ we mean the subsequence of α obtained by eliminating all the pairs (u, a) with $u \in U$.

Definition 1 (Noninterference [7]). *Let M be a transition network with sets of "high clearance" agents H and "low clearance" agents L, such that $H \cap L = \emptyset, H \cup L = \mathfrak{U}$. We say that H is non-interfering with L iff for all $\alpha \in (\mathfrak{U} \times \mathfrak{A})^*$ and all $u_l \in L$, $[exec(\alpha)]_{u_l} = [exec(Purge_H(\alpha))]_{u_l}$. We denote the property by $NI_M(H, L)$.*

Thus, $NI_M(H, L)$ expresses that L can neither observe nor deduce what actions of H have been executed.

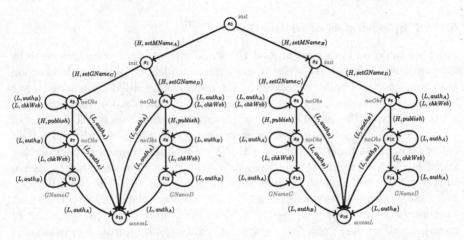

Fig. 1. Transition network M_a in which the High player publishes her grandmother's maiden name on her blog. Only the observations of L are shown

Example 2. Consider a simplified version of the phone banking scenario from Example 1. There are two users: H who has an account in the bank, and L who may try to impersonate H. H can access her account by correctly giving the maiden name of her mother. Moreover, H runs a blog, and can publish some of her personal information on it. We consider two alternative variants: one where H publishes her grandmother's maiden name on the blog (Fig. 1), and one where she publishes her mother's maiden name (Fig. 2). We assume that the possible names are A and B in the former case, and C and D in the latter. Each model begins by initialization of the relevant names. The observations of L are shown beside each state. The observations for H are omitted, as they will be irrelevant for our analysis.

Note that, for mathematical completeness, we must define the outcome of every user-action pair in every state. We assume that there are two "error states"

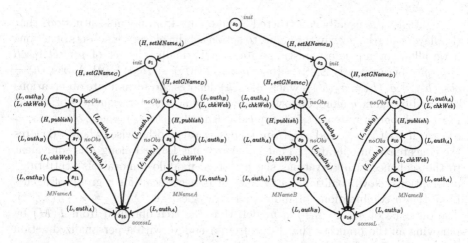

Fig. 2. Transition network M_b in which H publishes her mother's maiden name

s_{HErr}, s_{LErr} in models M_a and M_b (not shown in the graphs). Any action of H not depicted in the figure leads to s_{HErr}, and any action of L not depicted in the figure leads to s_{LErr}. We will later use the error states in the definition of the players' goals, in such a way that L will always want to avoid s_{LErr} and H will want to avoid s_{HErr}. This way we can (however imperfectly) simulate some synchronization in the restricted framework of Goguen and Meseguer.

Neither M_a nor M_b satisfies noninterference from H to L. For instance, in the model of Fig. 1, if $\alpha = \langle (H, setMName_A), (H, setGName_D), (H, publish), (L, chkWeb) \rangle$, the observation of L after sequence α is $GNameD$, but the observation of L after $Purge_H(\alpha) = \langle (L, chkWeb) \rangle$ is $noObs$, which is clearly different.   □

3.3 Strategies and Their Outcomes

Strategy is a game-theoretic concept which captures behavioral policies that an agent can consciously follow in order to realize some objective [15]. Let $T(M)$ be the *tree unfolding* of M. Also if $U \subseteq \mathfrak{U}$ is a subset of agents, let T' be a *U-trimming* of tree T iff T' is a subtree of T starting from the same root and obtained by removing an arbitrary subset of transitions labeled by actions of agents from U. For the moment, we assume that each subset of agents $U \subseteq \mathfrak{U}$ is assigned a set of available coalitional strategies Σ_U. The most important feature of a strategy $\sigma_U \in \Sigma_U$ is that *it constrains the possible behaviors of the system*. We represent it formally by the *outcome function* $out_M(\sigma_U)$ that removes the executions of the system that strategy σ_U would never choose. Therefore, for every $\sigma_U \in \Sigma_U$, its outcome $out_M(\sigma_U)$ is a U-trimming of $T(M)$.

Let h be a node in tree T corresponding to a particular finite history of interaction. We denote the sequence of personalized actions leading to h by $act^*(h)$. Furthermore, $act^*(T) = \{act^*(h) \mid h \in nodes(T)\}$ is the set of finite sequences of personalized actions that can occur in T.

Strategies are usually constructed as mappings from possible situations that the player can recognize in the game, to actions of the player (or subsets of actions if we allow for nondeterministic strategies). Formally, the set of *perfect recall strategies* of agent u is $\Sigma_u^{\mathfrak{Rec}} = \{\sigma_u : nodes(T(M)) \to \mathcal{P}(\mathfrak{A}) \setminus \{\emptyset\} \mid obs_u(h) = obs_u(h') \Rightarrow \sigma_u(h) = \sigma_u(h')\}$, where $obs_u(h)$ denotes the accumulate observations collected by agent u along history h. How to define obs_u for sequences of states? For asynchronous systems, this is typically defined as $obs_u(q) = [q]_u$, $obs_u(h \circ q) = obs_u(h)$ if $last(h) = q$, and $obs_u(h \circ q) = obs_u(h) \circ [q]_u$ otherwise (where $\circ$ denotes the concatenation operator). That is, what u has learned along h is equivalent to the sequence of observations she has seen, modulo removal of "stuttering" observations. Now, coalitional strategies of perfect recall for a group of agents $U \subseteq \mathfrak{A}$ are combinations of individual strategies, i.e., $\Sigma_U^{\mathfrak{Rec}} = \times_{u \in U}(\Sigma_u^{\mathfrak{Rec}})$. The outcome of $\sigma_U \in \Sigma_U^{\mathfrak{Rec}}$ in model M is the tree obtained from $T(M)$ by removing all the branches that begin from a node h with a personalized action $(u, a) \in U \times \mathfrak{A}$ such that $a \notin \sigma_U(h)$.

3.4 Temporal Goals and Winning Strategies

A goal is a property that some agents may attempt to enforce by selecting their behavior accordingly. We base our approach on the concepts of *paths* and *path properties*, used in temporal specification and verification of systems [20]. Let $paths(M)$ denote the set of infinite sequences of states that can be obtained by subsequent transitions in M. Additionally, we will use $paths_M(\sigma)$ as a shorthand for $paths(out_M(\sigma))$.

Definition 2 (Temporal goal [20]). *A goal in M is any $\Gamma \subseteq paths(M)$. Note that $paths(M) = paths(T(M))$, so a goal can be equivalently seen as a subset of paths in the tree unfolding of M.*

Most common examples of such goals are safety and reachability goals.

Definition 3 (Safety and reachability goals [20]). *Given a set of safe states $\mathbb{S} \subseteq St$, the safety goal $\Gamma_\mathbb{S}$ is defined as $\Gamma_\mathbb{S} = \{\lambda \in paths(M) \mid \forall i.\lambda[i] \in \mathbb{S}\}$. Moreover, given a set of target states $\mathbb{T} \subseteq St$, the reachability goal $\Gamma_\mathbb{T}$ can be defined as $\Gamma_\mathbb{T} = \{\lambda \in paths(M) \mid \exists i.\lambda[i] \in \mathbb{T}\}$.*

Definition 4 (Winning strategies). *Given a transition network M, a set of agents $U \subseteq \mathfrak{A}$ with goal Γ_U, and a set of strategies $\Sigma_U^{\mathfrak{Rec}}$, we say that U have a (surely winning) strategy to achieve Γ_U iff there exists a strategy $\sigma_U \in \Sigma_U^{\mathfrak{Rec}}$ such that $paths_M(\sigma_U) \subseteq \Gamma_U$.*

Example 3. Consider the models in Figs. 1 and 2, and suppose that L wants to access H's bank account. This can be expressed by the reachability goal $\Gamma_\mathbb{T}$ with $\mathbb{T} = \{s_{15}, s_{16}\}$ as the target states. In fact, L also wins if H executes an out-of-place action (cf. Example 2 for detailed explanation). In consequence, the winning states for L are $\mathbb{T} = \{s_{15}, s_{16}, s_{HErr}\}$. Note that L has no strategy that guarantees $\Gamma_\mathbb{T}$ in model M_a (although information is theoretically leaking to

L as the model does not satisfy noninterference). Even performing the action *chkWeb* does not help, because L cannot distinguish between states s_{11} and s_{13}, and there is no single action that succeeds for both s_{11}, s_{13}. Thus, L does not know whether to use $auth_A$ or $auth_B$ to get access to H's bank account.

On the other hand, L has a winning strategy for $\Gamma_{\mathbb{T}}$ in model M_b. The strategy is to execute *chkWeb* after H publishes her mother's maiden name, and afterwards do $auth_A$ in states s_{11}, s_{12} (after observing *MNameA*) or $auth_B$ if the system gets to s_{13}, s_{14} (i.e., after observing *MNameB*).   □

4   Security as Strategic Property

The property of noninterference looks for *any* leakage of *any* information. If one can possibly happen in the system, then the system is deemed insecure. In many cases, this view is too strong. There are lots of information pieces that can leak out without bothering any interested party. Revealing the password to your web banking account can clearly have much more disastrous effects than revealing the price that you paid for metro tickets on your latest trip to Paris. Moreover, the relevance of an information leak cannot in general be determined by the type of the information. Think, again, of revealing the maiden name of your mother vs. the maiden name of your grandmother. The former case is potentially dangerous since the maiden name of one's mother is often used to grant access to manage banking services by telephone. Revealing the latter is quite harmless to most ends and purposes.

In this paper, we suggest that the relevance of information leakage should be judged by the extent of damage that the leak allows the attackers to inflict on the goal of the system. Thus, as the first step, we define the security of the system in terms of damaging abilities of the Low players.

In order to assess the relevance of information flow from High to Low, we will look at the resulting strategic abilities of Low. Moreover, we assume that the goal of L is to violate a given goal of the system. The goal can be a functionality or a security requirement, or a combination of both. Moreover, it can originate from a private goal of the High players, an objective ascribed to the system by its designer (e.g., the designer of a contract signing protocol), or a combination of requirements specified by the owner/main stakeholder in the system (for instance, a bank in case of a web banking infrastructure).

Definition 5 (Effective security). *Let M be a transition network with some Low players $L \subseteq \mathfrak{A}$, and let Γ be the goal of the system. We say that M is effectively secure for (L, Γ) iff L does not have a strategy to enforce $\overline{\Gamma}$, where $\overline{X}$ denotes the complement of set X. That is, the system is effectively secure iff the attackers do not have a strategy that ensures an execution violating the goal of the system. We will use $ES(M, L, \Gamma)$ to refer to this property.*

Besides judging the effective security of a system, we can also use the concept to compare the security level of two models.

Definition 6 (Comparative effective security). *Let M, M' be two models, and Γ be a goal in M, M' (i.e., $\Gamma \subseteq paths(M) \cup paths(M')$). We say that:*

- *M has strictly less effective security than M' for (L, Γ), denoted $M \prec_{L,\Gamma} M'$, iff $ES(M', L, \Gamma)$ but not $ES(M, L, \Gamma)$.*
- *M' is at least as effectively secure as M for (L, Γ), denoted $M \preceq_{L,\Gamma} M'$, iff $ES(M, L, \Gamma)$ implies $ES(M', L, \Gamma)$;*
- *M is effectively equivalent to M' for (L, Γ), denoted $M \simeq_{L,\Gamma} M'$, iff either both $ES(M, L, \Gamma)$ and $ES(M', L, \Gamma)$ hold, or both do not hold.*

Thus, if in one of the models L can construct a more harmful strategy then the model displays lower effective security than the other model. Conversely, if both models allow only for the same extent of damage then they have the same level of effective security. This way, we can order different alternative designs of the system according to the strategic power they give away to the attacker.

Example 4. Consider models M_a, M_b from Figs. 1 and 2, and let the goal Γ be to prevent L from accessing H's bank account. Thus, Γ is the safety goal $\Gamma_{\mathbb{S}}$ with $\mathbb{S} = St \setminus \{s_{15}, s_{16}, s_{HErr}\}$, and therefore $\overline{\Gamma} = \Gamma_{\mathbb{T}}$ with $\mathbb{T} = \{s_{15}, s_{16}, s_{HErr}\}$. As we saw in Example 3, L has no strategy to guarantee $\overline{\Gamma}$ in M_a, but she has a surely winning strategy for $\overline{\Gamma}$ in M_b. Thus, M_b is strictly less effectively secure than M_a, i.e., $M_b \prec_{L,\Gamma} M_a$.

5   Effective Information Security

We will now propose a scheme that allows to determine whether a given model of interaction leaks relevant information or not. We use the idea of refinement checking from process algebras, where a process is assumed correct if and only if it refines the ideal process [25]. A similar reasoning scheme is also used in analysis of multi-party computation protocols (a protocol is correct iff it is equivalent to the ideal model of the computation [8]).

5.1   Ability-Based Security of Information Flows

Definition 6 allows for comparing the effective security of two alternative information flows. However, we usually do not want to compare several alternative information flows. Rather, we want to determine if a single given model M reveals relevant information or not. A natural idea is to compare the effective security of M to an *ideal model*, i.e. a variant of M that leaks no relevant information by construction. Then, a model is effectively information-secure if it has the same level of effective security as its idealized variant:

Definition 7 (Effective information security). *Let M be a transition network with some Low players $L \subseteq \mathfrak{U}$, and let Γ be the goal of the system. Moreover, let $Ideal(M)$ be the idealized variant of M. We say that M is effectively information-secure for (L, Γ) iff $M \simeq_{L,\Gamma} Ideal(M)$.*

How do we construct the idealized variant of M? The idea is to "blur" observations of Low so that we obtain a variant of the system where the observational capabilities of the attackers are minimal.

5.2   Idealized Models Based on Noninterference

We begin by recalling the notion of *term unification* which is a fundamental concept in automated theorem proving and logic programming [24]. Given two terms t_1, t_2, their unification $(t_1 \equiv t_2)$ can be understood as a declaration that, from now on, both terms refer to exactly the same underlying object. In our case the terms are observation labels from the set *Obs*. A unification can be seen as an equivalence relation on observation labels, or equivalently as a partitioning of the labels into equivalence classes. The application of the unification to a model yields a similar model where the equivalent observations are "blurred".

Definition 8 (Unification of observations). *Given a set of observation labels Obs, a unification on Obs is any equivalence relation $\mathcal{U} \subseteq Obs \times Obs$.*

Given a model $M = \langle St, s_0, \mathfrak{U}, \mathfrak{A}, do, Obs, obs \rangle$ and a unification $\mathcal{U} \subseteq Obs \times Obs$, the application of $\mathcal{U}$ to M is the model $\mathcal{U}(M) = \langle St, s_0, \mathfrak{U}, \mathfrak{A}, do, Obs', obs' \rangle$, where: $Obs' = \{[o]_{\mathcal{U}} \mid o \in Obs\}$ replaces Obs by the set of equivalence classes defined by $\mathcal{U}$, and $obs'(q, u) = [obs(q, u)]_{\mathcal{U}}$ replaces the original observation in q with its equivalence class for any $u \in \mathfrak{U}$.

Our reference model for M will be the variant of M where noninterference is obtained by the minimal necessary "blurring" of L's observations.

Definition 9 (Noninterferent idealized model). *Having a transition network M and a set of "low" players L, we define the noninterfering idealized variant of M as $\mathcal{U}(M)$ such that:*

(i) $NI_{\mathcal{U}(M)}(H, L)$, and
(ii) for every $\mathcal{U}' \subsetneq \mathcal{U}$ it is not the case that $NI_{\mathcal{U}'(M)}(H, L)$.

We need to show that the concept of noninterferent idealized model is well defined. The proof is constructive, i.e., given a model M, we first show how one can build its idealized variant, and then show that it is unique.[2]

Theorem 1. *For every transition network M, there is always a unique unification $\mathcal{U}$ satisfying properties (i) and (ii) from Definition 9.*

The proof of Theorem 1 needs some preliminary steps. First, we recall the concept of unwinding relations [29]. Unwinding relations are important because they characterize noninterference in purely structural terms. Moreover, existence of an unwinding relation is usually easier to verify than proving noninterference directly. We then use the concept of unwinding relation to define relation R_M^* on the states of a transition network M. We use this relation to construct and prove the uniqueness of the idealized variant of M.

---

[2] We will only sketch the proofs due to lack of space. The complete proofs can be found in the extended version of the paper, available at http://arxiv.org/abs/1608.02247.

Definition 10 (Unwinding for Noninterference [29]). $\sim_{NI_L} \subseteq St \times St$ *is an* unwinding relation *iff it is an equivalence relation satisfying the conditions of* output consistency (OC), step consistency (SC), *and* local respect (LR). *That is, for all states* $s, t \in St$:

(OC) *If* $s \sim_{NI_L} t$ *then* $[s]_L = [t]_L$;
(SC) *If* $s \sim_{NI_L} t$, $u \in L$, *and* $a \in \mathfrak{A}$ *then* $do(s, u, a) \sim_{NI_L} do(t, u, a)$;
(LR) *If* $u \in H$ *and* $a \in \mathfrak{A}$ *then* $s \sim_{NI_L} do(s, u, a)$.

Proposition 1 ([29]). $NI_M(H, L)$ *iff there exist an unwinding relation* $\sim_{NI_L}$ *on the states of* M *that satisfies (OC), (SC) and (LR).*

Next we define R_M^* on the states of a transition network M. The definition goes as follows: first we relate any two states of M' if one of them can be reached from the other one by a sequence of High personalized actions. Then in each step we relate the pair of states that are reached by a similar Low personalized action from any two states that are already related. Also, we enforce transitivity on the set. We continue adding related states until the relation becomes stable. The mathematical definition of R_M^* is as follows:

Definition 11 (Relation R_M^* for a transition network M). *Given a model* $M = \langle St, s_0, \mathfrak{U}, \mathfrak{A}, do, Obs, obs \rangle$ *and sets of High players* H *and Low players* L, *we define the relation* $R_M^* \subseteq St \times St$ *as the least fixpoint of the following function* F, *transforming relations on* St:

$$F(R) = R_0 \cup$$
$$\{(t_1, t_2) \mid \exists (s_1, s_2) \in R, l \in L, a \in \mathfrak{A}.do(s_1, l, a) = t_1, do(s_2, l, a) = t_2\} \cup$$
$$\{(t_1, t_2) \mid \exists s \in St.(t_1, s) \in R \& (s, t_2) \in R\},$$

where $(s_1, s_2) \in R_0$ *iff for some sequence of personalized actions of High players* α, *either* $s_1 \xrightarrow{\alpha} s_2$, *or* $s_2 \xrightarrow{\alpha} s_1$.

It can be shown that it is sufficient to unify Low's observations in states connected by R_M^* in order to obtain a non-interferent model. In consequence, R_M^* generates the minimal unification that achieves the task. Now, by using relation R_M^*, we define the unification of observations $\mathcal{U}_M^*$ that will provide the noninterferent idealized variant of M.

Definition 12 (Unification for noninterference $\mathcal{U}_M^*$). *We define the unification of observations* $\mathcal{U}_M^* \subseteq Obs \times Obs$ *as follows. For any* $o_1, o_2 \in Obs$, *we have* $(o_1, o_2) \in \mathcal{U}_M^*$ *iff there exist* $s_1, s_2, t_1, t_2 \in St$ *and* $l \in L$ *such that:* (a) $obs(s_1, l) = o_1$, (b) $obs(s_2, l) = o_2$, (c) $(s_1, t_1) \in R_M^*$, (d) $(s_2, t_2) \in R_M^*$, *and* (e) $obs(t_1, l) = obs(t_2, l)$.

It then holds that $\mathcal{U}_M^*(M)$ satisfies the noninterference property (Proposition 2) and no refinement of $\mathcal{U}_M^*$ achieves that (Proposition 3).

Proposition 2. *Given a model M, and $\mathcal{U}_M^*(M) = \langle St, s_0, \mathfrak{U}, \mathfrak{A}, do, Obs^*, obs^* \rangle$ defined as in Definition 12 on M, it holds that $NI_{\mathcal{U}_M^*(M)}(H, L)$.*

Proposition 3. *Given a model M, and sets of players H and L, for any unification of observations U where $U(M) = \langle St, s_0, \mathfrak{U}, \mathfrak{A}, do, Obs', obs' \rangle$, if $NI_{U(M)}(H, L)$ then $\mathcal{U}_M^* \subseteq U$.*

We can now complete the proof of Theorem 1.

Proof (of Theorem 1). We want to prove that, given a model M, set of players H and L, and any unification of observations $\mathcal{U}$, if $\mathcal{U}(M)$ is a noninterfering idealized variant of M, then $\mathcal{U} = \mathcal{U}_M^*$. Assume that $\mathcal{U}(M)$ is a noninterfering idealized variant of M. By property (i) of Definition 9 and Proposition 3 we infer that $\mathcal{U}_M^* \subseteq \mathcal{U}$. Also, by Proposition 2, we have that $NI_{\mathcal{U}_M^*(M)}(H, L)$. Therefore by property (ii) of Definition 9 it holds that $\mathcal{U} = \mathcal{U}_M^*$.

Example 5. Consider models M_a; M_b in Fig. 1. We recall that both models are not noninterferent. In the noninterferent idealized variant of M_a, observations $noObs$, $MnameC$, and $MNameD$ of L are unified and replaced by the equivalence class $\{noObs, MNameD, MNameD\}$. The idealized variant of M_b is constructed analogously by unification of $noObs$, $MnameA$, and $MNameB$. Clearly, L has no surely winning strategy to guarantee $\overline{\Gamma} = \Gamma_{\mathbb{T}}$ for $\mathbb{T} = \{s_{15}, s_{16}, s_{HErr}\}$ in both $Ideal(M_a)$ and $Ideal(M_b)$.

Recall from Example 4 that L has no winning strategy for $\overline{\Gamma}$ in M_a, but she has one in M_b. So, $M_a \simeq_{L,\Gamma} Ideal(M_a)$, but $M_b \not\simeq_{L,\Gamma} Ideal(M_b)$. Thus, M_a is effectively information-secure for (L, Γ), but M_b is not. □

It is important to notice that noninterferent variants are indeed idealizations:

Proposition 4. *For every M, L, and Γ, we have that $M \preceq_{L,\Gamma} Ideal(M)$.*

Proof. Note that because M and $Ideal(M)$ differ only in their observation functions. Also we have that for any pair of states $s_1, s_2 \in St$, if $[s_1]_L^M = [s_2]_L^M$ then $[s_1]_L^{Ideal(M)} = [s_2]_L^{Ideal(M)}$. Therefore all the strategies of L in $Ideal(M)$ are also L's strategies in M. Thus for any for any goal $\Gamma \subseteq paths(M)$, if L have a surely winning strategy to enforce $\overline{\Gamma}$ in $Ideal(M)$ then they also have a surely winning strategy for $\overline{\Gamma}$ in M. □

6   Extending the Results to a Broader Class of Models

As mentioned before, the models of Goguen and Meseguer are "total on input," i.e., each action label is available to every user at every state. This makes modeling actual systems very cumbersome. In this section, we consider a broader class of models, and show how our results carry over to the more expressive setting. That is, we consider *partial transition networks (PTS)* $M = \langle St, s_0, \mathfrak{U}, \mathfrak{A}, Obs, obs, do \rangle$ which are defined as in Sect. 3.1, except that the transition function $do : St \times \mathfrak{U} \times \mathfrak{A} \rightharpoonup St$ can be a partial function. By

$do(s, u, a) = undef$ we denote that action a is unavailable to user u in state s; additionally, we define $\mathsf{act}(s, u) = \{a \in \mathfrak{A} \mid do(s, u, a) \neq undef\}$ as the set of actions available to u in s. Moreover, we assume that players are aware of their available actions, and hence can distinguish states with different repertoires of choices – formally, for any $u \in \mathfrak{U}, s_1, s_2 \in St$, if $obs(s_1, u) = obs(s_2, u)$ then $\mathsf{act}(s_1, u) = \mathsf{act}(s_2, u)$.

We begin by a suitable update of the definition of noninterference:

Definition 13 (Noninterference for partial transition networks). *Given a PTS M and sets of agents H, L, such that $H \cup L = \mathfrak{U}, H \cap L = \emptyset$, we say that H is non-interfering with L iff for all $\alpha \in (\mathfrak{U} \times \mathfrak{A})^*$ and all $u_l \in L$, if $exec(\alpha) \neq undef$ then $[exec(\alpha)]_{u_l} = [exec(Purge_H(\alpha))]_{u_l}$. We denote the property also by $NI_M(H, L)$, thus slightly overloading the notation.*

Note that Definition 1 is a special case of Definition 13. We now define the noninterferent idealized variant based on the *total extension* of a PTS.

Definition 14 (U-total extension). *Given a PTS $M = \langle St, s_0, \mathfrak{U}, \mathfrak{A}, Obs, obs, do \rangle$ and a subset of users $U \subseteq \mathfrak{U}$, we define the U-total variant of M as $total_U(M) = \langle St, s_0, \mathfrak{U}, \mathfrak{A}, Obs, obs, do' \rangle$ where the transition function $do'(.)$ is defined as follows: for every $s \in St$, $v \in \mathfrak{U}$ and $a \in \mathfrak{A}$, $do'(s, v, a) = s$ if for some $u \in U$ we have $v = u$ and $do(s, u, a) = undef$, otherwise $do'(s, v, a) = do(s, v, a)$.*

Definition 15 (Noninterferent idealized model for PTN). *Given a partial transition network M and a set of "low" players L, we define the noninterferent idealized variant of M as $\mathcal{U}(total_L(M))$ such that:*

(i) $NI_{\mathcal{U}(total_L(M))}(H, L)$, and
(ii) for every $\mathcal{U}' \subsetneq \mathcal{U}$ it is not the case that $NI_{\mathcal{U}'(total_L(M))}(H, L)$.

Theorem 2. *For every partial transition network M, there is always a unique unification $\mathcal{U}$ satisfying properties (i) and (ii) from Definition 15.*

The proof is similar to the proof of Theorem 1, with the difference that we use $R^*_{total_L(M)}$ instead of R^*_M for constructing the idealized variant. However, as we use the concept of unwiding relation as the basis for using the R^* relation for constructing the idealized variant, we first need to modify the definition of the unwinding relation in Definition 10 and its corresponding proposition, Proposition 1 to adapt them to the new model:

Definition 16 (Unwinding for Noninterference in PTN). $\sim_{NI_L} \subseteq St \times St$ *is an unwinding relation iff it is an equivalence relation satisfying the conditions of output consistency (OC), step consistency (SC), and local respect (LR). That is, for all states $s, t \in St$:*

(OC) *If $s \sim_{NI_L} t$ then $[s]_L = [t]_L$;*
(SC) *If $s \sim_{NI_L} t$, $u \in L$, and $a \in \mathfrak{A}$ then $a \in \mathsf{act}(s, u)$ implies $do(s, u, a) \sim_{NI_L} do(t, u, a)$;*

(LR) *If $u \in H$ and $a \in \mathfrak{A}$ then $a \in act(s, u)$ implies $s \sim_{NI_L} do(s, u, a)$.*

Proposition 5. *$NI_M(H, L)$ iff there exist an unwinding relation $\sim_{NI_L}$ on the states of M that satisfies (OC), (SC) and (LR).*

The rest of the proof of Theorem 2 follows analogously.

Example 6. With PTS, the scenario from Example 2 can be modeled directly, without spurious states that ruled out illegal transitions. Thus, our models M_a, M_b for the two variants of the scenario are now exactly depicted in Figs. 1 and 2.

The noninterferent idealized variants of M_a (resp. M_b) is again obtained by the unification of observations $noObs$, $MnameC$, and $MNameD$ (resp. $noObs$, $MnameA$, and $MNameB$). Clearly, L has no surely winning strategy to guarantee $\overline{\Gamma} = \Gamma_{\mathbb{T}}$ for $\mathbb{T} = \{s_{15}, s_{16}\}$ in M_a, $Ideal(M_a)$, and $Ideal(M_b)$. Moreover, he has a surely winning strategy in M_b. In consequence, M_a is effectively information-secure for (L, Γ), but M_b is not.   □

The noninterferent variant was indeed an idealization in simple transition networks of Goguen and Mesguer. Is it still the case in partial transition networks? That is, is it always the case that L has no more abilities in $Ideal(M)$ than in M? In general, no. On one hand, L's observational capabilities are more limited in $Ideal(M)$, and in consequence some strategies in M are no longer uniform in $Ideal(M)$. On the other hand, unification U^* possibly adds new transitions to M, that can be used by L in $Ideal(M)$ to construct new strategies. However, under some reasonable assumptions, $Ideal(M)$ does provide idealization, as shown in the two propositions below. The proofs are relatively simple, and we omit them due to lack of space.

Proposition 6. *Let M be a PTN such that for every state s in M there is at least one player $u \notin L$ with $act(s, u) \neq \emptyset$. Then, for any Γ, we have that $M \preceq_{L, \Gamma} Ideal(M)$.*

Proposition 7. *For any PTN M and safety goal Γ, we have $M \preceq_{L, \Gamma} Ideal(M)$.*

7 Conclusions

In this paper, we introduce the novel concept of *effective information security*. The idea is aimed at assessing the relevance of information leakage in a system, based on how much the leakage enables an adversary to harm the correct behavior of the system. This contrasts with the common approach to information flow security where revealing any information is seen as being intrinsically harmful. We say that two information flows are *effectively equivalent* if the strategic ability of the adversary is similar in both of them. Moreover, one of them is *less effectively secure* than the other one if the amount of information leaked to the adversary in it increases the damaging ability of the adversary.

In order to determine how critical the information leakage is in a given system, we compare the damaging ability of the adversary to his ability in the idealized variant of the model. We define idealized models based on noninterference, and show that the construction is well defined. We prove this first for the deterministic, fully asynchronous transition networks of Goguen and Meseguer, and then extend the results to structures that allow for a more flexible modeling of interaction. The construction includes an algorithm that computes the idealized variant of each model in polynomial time wrt the size of the model.

Note that the concept of effective security is orthogonal to noninterference. The latter can be in principle replaced in our construction by an arbitrary property of information flow. The same reasoning scheme could be applied to noninference, nondeducibility, strategic noninterference, and so on. The pattern does not change: given a property $\mathcal{P}$, we define the idealized variant of M through the minimal unification U such that $U(M)$ satisfies $\mathcal{P}$. Then, M is effectively information-secure in the context of property $\mathcal{P}$ iff it is strategically equivalent to $U(M)$. We leave the investigation of which information security properties have unique minimal unifications for future work. Moreover, we are currently working on a more refined version of effective information security based on coalitional effectivity functions, in which the strategic ability of the adversary is not only compared at the initial state of the system, but across the whole state space.

References

1. Acquisti, A., Grossklags, J.: Privacy attitudes and privacy behavior - losses, gains, and hyperbolic discounting. In: Economics of Information Security. Advances in Information Security, vol. 12, pp. 165–178. Springer, New York (2004)
2. Chaum, D.: Untraceable electronic mail, return addresses, and digital pseudonyms. Commun. ACM **24**, 84–90 (1981)
3. Dimovski, A.S.: Ensuring secure non-interference of programs by game semantics. In: Mauw, S., Jensen, C.D. (eds.) STM 2014. LNCS, vol. 8743, pp. 81–96. Springer, Heidelberg (2014)
4. Fielder, A., Panaousis, E., Malacaria, P., Hankin, C., Smeraldi, F.: Game theory meets information security management. In: Cuppens-Boulahia, N., Cuppens, F., Jajodia, S., Abou El Kalam, A., Sans, T. (eds.) SEC 2014. IFIP AICT, vol. 428, pp. 15–29. Springer, Heidelberg (2014). doi:10.1007/978-3-642-55415-5_2
5. Fujioka, A., Okamoto, T., Ohta, K.: A practical secret voting scheme for large scale elections. In: Seberry, J., Zheng, Y. (eds.) AUSCRYPT 1992. LNCS, vol. 718, pp. 244–251. Springer, Heidelberg (1993). doi:10.1007/3-540-57220-1_66
6. Giacobazzi, R., Mastroeni, I.: Abstract non-interference: parameterizing non-interference by abstract interpretation. In: Proceedings of POPL, pp. 186–197. ACM (2004)
7. Goguen, J.A., Meseguer, J.: Security policies and security models. In: Proceedings of S&P, pp. 11–20. IEEE Computer Society (1982)
8. Goldreich, O., Micali, S., Wigderson, A.: How to play ANY mental game. In: Proceedings of the 19th Annual ACM Symposium on Theory of Computing, STOC 1987, pp. 218–229. ACM (1987)
9. Gray III, J.W.: Probabilistic interference. In: Proceedings of S&P, pp. 170–179. IEEE (1990)

10. Grossklags, J., Christin, N., Chuang, J.: Secure or insure? A game-theoretic analysis of information security games. In: Proceedings of WWW, pp. 209–218. ACM (2008)
11. Hankin, C., Nagarajan, R., Sampath, P.: Flow analysis: games and nets. In: Mogensen, T.Æ., Schmidt, D.A., Sudborough, I.H. (eds.) The Essence of Computation. LNCS, vol. 2566, pp. 135–156. Springer, Heidelberg (2002)
12. Harris, W.R., Jha, S., Reps, T.W., Anderson, J., Watson, R.N.M.: Declarative, temporal, and practical programming with capabilities. In: Proceedings of SP, pp. 18–32. IEEE Computer Society (2013)
13. Jamroga, W., Tabatabaei, M.: Strategic noninterference. In: Federrath, H., Gollmann, D. (eds.) SEC 2015. IFIP AICT, vol. 455, pp. 67–81. Springer, Heidelberg (2015). doi:10.1007/978-3-319-18467-8_5
14. Levin, J.: In what city did you honeymoon? and other monstrously stupid bank security questions. Slate (2008)
15. Leyton-Brown, K., Shoham, Y.: Essentials of Game Theory: A Concise, Multidisciplinary Introduction. Morgan & Claypool (2008)
16. Li, P., Zdancewic, S.: Downgrading policies and relaxed noninterference. In: ACM SIGPLAN Notices, vol. 40, pp. 158–170. ACM (2005)
17. Malacaria, P., Hankin, C.: Non-deterministic games, program analysis: an application to security. In: Proceedings of LICS, pp. 443–452. IEEE Computer Society (1999)
18. McCullough, D.: Noninterference and the composability of security properties. In: Proceedings of S&P, pp. 177–186. IEEE (1988)
19. McIver, A., Morgan, C.: A probabilistic approach to information hiding. In: Programming Methodology, pp. 441–460 (2003)
20. McNaughton, R.: Testing and generating infinite sequences by a finite automaton. Inf. Control 9, 521–530 (1966)
21. Moore, T., Anderson, R.: Economics, internet security: a survey of recent analytical, empirical and behavioral research. Technical report TR-03-11, Computer Science Group, Harvard University (2011)
22. O'Halloran, C.: A calculus of information flow. In: Proceedings of ESORICS, pp. 147–159 (1990)
23. Di Pierro, A., Hankin, C., Wiklicky, H.: Approximate non-interference. J. Comput. Secur. 12(1), 37–81 (2004)
24. Robinson, J.A.: A machine-oriented logic based on the resolution principle. J. ACM 12(1), 23–41 (1965)
25. Roscoe, A.W., Hoare, C.A.R., Bird, R.: The Theory and Practice of Concurrency. Prentice Hall PTR, Upper Saddle River (1997)
26. Sabelfeld, A., Sands, D.: Dimensions and principles of declassification. In: Proceedings of CSFW-18, pp. 255–269. IEEE Computer Society (2005)
27. Smith, G.: On the foundations of quantitative information flow. In: de Alfaro, L. (ed.) FOSSACS 2009. LNCS, vol. 5504, pp. 288–302. Springer, Heidelberg (2009)
28. Sutherland, D.: A model of information. In: Proceedings of the 9th National Computer Security Conference, pp. 175–183 (1986)
29. Meyden, R., Zhang, C.: A comparison of semantic models for noninterference. Theoret. Comput. Sci. 411(47), 4123–4147 (2010)
30. Wittbold, J.T., Johnson, D.M.: Information flow in nondeterministic systems. In: IEEE Symposium on Security and Privacy, p. 144 (1990)
31. Zdancewic, S., Myers, A.C.: Observational determinism for concurrent program security. In: Proceedings of CSFW-16, pp. 29–43. IEEE Computer Society (2003)

Analysing the Efficacy of Security Policies in Cyber-Physical Socio-Technical Systems

Gabriele Lenzini[1](✉), Sjouke Mauw[2], and Samir Ouchani[1]

[1] Interdisciplinary Centre for Security, Reliability and Trust,
University of Luxembourg, Luxembourg, Luxembourg
{gabriele.lenzini,samir.ouchani}@uni.lu
[2] CSC/Interdisciplinary Centre for Security, Reliability and Trust,
University of Luxembourg, Luxembourg, Luxembourg
sjouke.mauw@uni.lu

Abstract. A crucial question for an ICT organization wishing to improve its security is whether a security policy together with physical access controls protects from socio-technical threats. We study this question formally. We model the information flow defined by what the organization's employees do (copy, move, and destroy information) and propose an algorithm that enforces a policy on the model, before checking against an adversary if a security requirement holds.

Keywords: Socio-Technical-Physical Systems · Modelling security and policies

1 Introduction

The data-flow of an ICT organization is defined by what its employees do. They access, copy, share, and move pieces of information and objects that carry information, such as hard disks. In this flow, an organization must avoid to have critical data stolen. To reduce this risk, organizations protect the access to files, or use encryption. Paper documents or electronics are closed in drawers and offices are locked.

They also adopt policies, such as a "clean desk" policy, campaign for best practices, such as "always encrypt emails". However, a critical question remains whether a specific combination of policies and physical/digital controls is effective against certain threats. This question does not have an easy answer, but we advocate that it can be explored by the use of formal methods.

Formal methods have been successfully applied in the analysis of security protocols over the last decades (*e.g.*, see [1]). Recently they have also been proposed to model *Socio-Technical Physical Systems (STPS)* [2] —systems whose operation is defined by the interactions between people, technology, and physical elements— of which ICT organizations are examples. This new research (*e.g.*, see [3–7]) suggests that formal methods can be used in the analysis of the security of STPS and of the processes that define an STPS's daily work flow.

The idea of reasoning about a system's security in combination with policies has also been explored (see [8–12] and Sect. 3). Policies on accesses, on work

© Springer International Publishing AG 2016
G. Barthe et al. (Eds.): STM 2016, LNCS 9871, pp. 170–178, 2016.
DOI: 10.1007/978-3-319-46598-2_12

flows, and on security properties have been formalized and verified over models of STPS. One work in particular, that of Hartel *et al.* [12] considers policies and requirements at the same time. Hartel *et al.* study four specific systems and model check, in SPIN, whether the systems composed with the policies comply with a given requirement.

Here, we aim to provide a formal framework to reason about the efficacy of a policy and of security control mechanisms against an adversary model. Let $\mathscr{S}$ be a model of an STPS, π be a model of a policy, p be a desirable security property, and I be an adversary model. The high-level formalization of the proposition whether $\mathscr{S}$ constrained by policy π is effective in realizing p can be expressed symbolically as follows:

$$\mathscr{S}_{|\pi} \models_I p. \tag{1}$$

Appropriately instantiated, $\mathscr{S}_{|\pi}$ represents the (executions of) $\mathscr{S}$ where π is enforced, while $\models_I p$ is the relation "satisfies requirement p in the presence of adversary I". In absence of π, proposition (1) collapses into $\mathscr{S} \models_I p$, the classical proposition about whether $\mathscr{S}$ satisfies p in the presence of I. We develop a precise formal framework to express the abstract question in (1) and we develop an algorithm to compute $\mathscr{S}_{|\pi}$.

Background. There are a few formal languages upon which we can build. Here, we leverage on the one presented in [6]. There, the authors model an STPS's *state* as a labelled multi-graph. Nodes model offices, objects, or employees of the STPS. Edges represent either doors between offices or a (direct) location relation between nodes saying that "node x is contained/located in node y".

Figure 1 exemplifies an STPS's state and the graph representing it. Here (please, ignore the labels between '[ ]' for now) b is the building and $l_1 - l_4$ are its four rooms. Node l_0 models the outside. Node a_1, in room l_1, and node a_2, in room l_2, are employees. a_2 holds o_2, supposedly a letter. Node o_1, a printer, is in room l_3. I, the intruder, waits outside. Edges d_{04}, d_{12}, d_{13} and d_{24} are the doors between the four rooms.

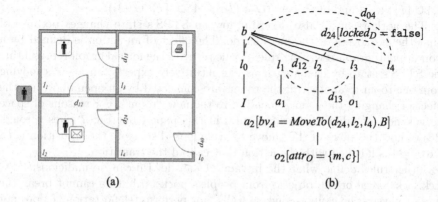

(a)   (b)

Fig. 1. (a) A simplified *STPS's* state; (b) its formal representation.

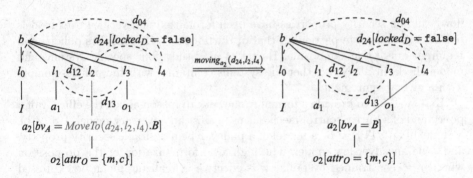

Fig. 2. How the *STPS* in Fig. 1 changes because of agent a_2's moving to l_4.

Nodes and edges of the graph can be labelled to supply additional information. A label on an edge "door" expresses whether the door is locked and what key can lock/unlock it. A label on a node "object" tells us whether the object is movable (m), destroyable (d), or a container (c); in this case, another label tells us whether it is locked and what key can lock/unlock it. A label on a node "agent" tells us what is the "protocol" that defines the agent's behaviour. Agents can, for instance, move, pick up an object, put an object down, or destroy an object and its contents, or exchange an object with another agent. Figure 2 (left side) shows some of the labels (not all of them, though). The door d_{24} is unlocked; o_2 is a container and is movable; agent a_2 is about to move to room l_4.

Formally, an STPS's state is a tuple $\langle Phy, Obj, Act, E \rangle$. *Phy* is composed of nodes representing the physical spaces ($L \cup \{b\}$), door identifiers (D), and two door labelling functions ($locked_D$, and key_D); *Obj* is the nodes that model objects (O) and three object labelling functions ($attr_O$, $lock_O$, and key_O); *Act* is the nodes that model the employees and the intruder ($A \cup \{I\}$), and a set of labelling functions that return the protocols/behaviour of each employee (bv_A). Item E are the edges of the graph: the edges that model the doors ($L \times L$), labelled with door identifiers, and the edges that model the location of employees ($(A \cup \{I\}) \times L$) and of objects ($O \times (L \cup A \cup \{I\} \cup O)$).

The authors of [6] also describe how an STPS's state changes because of what the employees or the intruder do. The effect of an action is defined by a (conditional) graph-rewriting rule. A rule rewrites the formal graph representing the STPS's state by changing it as one intuitively expects: an agent's moving from one room to another, if the rooms are connected by an open door, has the effect of changing the agent's location to the new "room". For reasons of space we will not include the rewriting rules in this paper, but Fig. 2 gives a rough idea of how the effect of the "move to" rule looks like. Note the transition (*i.e.*, arrow $\Rightarrow$) is labelled with the action that caused the transition.

Other rules define what the intruder I can do. He can be malicious, (*e.g.*, pick locks, steal or slip objects from people's pockets) but he cannot break the laws of physics: he cannot traverse walls, nor perform teleportation. I does not follow a protocol. All his actions are enabled, if they are possible.

Starting from a specific initial configuration, by applying the rules that are enabled one can generate *executions of the* STPS. The semantical model of these executions for a specific STPS is a *labelled transition system* $\mathscr{S} = \langle \mathbf{S}, \Gamma, S_0, \Rightarrow \rangle$ where $\mathbf{S}$ is the set of all possible STPS's states, Γ is the set of action labels, $S_0 \in \mathbf{S}$ is the initial state, and $\Rightarrow \ \subseteq \ (\mathbf{S} \times \Gamma \times \mathbf{S})$ is the labelled transition relation between states. It is the smallest relation that satisfies the graph rewriting rules. It must be stressed that $\mathscr{S}$ includes also the transitions due to the intruder.

In [6], $\mathscr{S}$ is a *probabilistic and weighted* labelled transition system. The agent's behaviour is probabilistic *i.e.*, specified by a stochastic process algebra. Actions have a weight, *i.e.*, cost. Costs are important in defining the intruder's strategy. For instance he can pick a lock, which may cost more (*e.g.*, in time) than opening the door with the key. He can also decide to use the key, but then the key must be retrieved (*e.g.*, stolen) first. All the details are in [6] but the intuitive description we have just given here is sufficient for understanding what we are proposing next.

2   Modelling Data and Data Flow

We extend [6] to be able to model data and the flow of data. For this purpose, we introduce *digital objects* and *digital object carriers*. A digital object models a piece of data, such as a file. Data cannot exist by their own: they need to be stored/carried. Digital object carriers are carrying data objects. Hard disks, USB pens, a book, (the mind of) an agent are data carriers. Formally, *Obj* is extended with a new labelling function $type_O$: returns p if the object is physical, d if the object is digital.

Digital objects can be cloned/copied, but they need a carrier that holds them afterwards. Formally, this means to extend *Act*, the language of an employee's or the Intruder's actions with two additional actions: $Clone(o, o')$ and $Clone(o)$. The former creates an identical copy of o into carrier o'; the latter "clones" o in the mind of who executes the action. All the other actions onto objects (*e.g.*, exchange them, destroy them, et cetera) remain applicable with the only constraint that digital objects need a carrier. Due to space limitations, we will not describe the new rules in this paper. The resulting formal semantics is a probabilistic and weighted labelled transition systems extending the one given in [6].

In the setting of this paper, we do not need probabilities or costs. We see little utility in policies that apply with certain probability/cost. Instead, in relation to (1), questioning whether a policy is effective to reduce the risk of a specific attack within a certain probability/cost is a legitimate question. In this paper we do not develop this probabilistic framework. We leave it for future work. Instead, we interpret (1) as the question whether a certain policy, when enforced, is effective in removing attacks (resp., ensuring security) altogether. A non-probabilistic non-weighted labelled transition system (which we still write $\mathscr{S}$ in the remainder of the paper) can be obtained from the model in [6] by substituting any probabilistic choice in all bv_A with a non-deterministic choice and by ignoring costs.

3   Security Policies and Security Requirements

According to the Cambridge Dictionary, a *security policy* is "a plan, or a document, specifying what to do in particular situations, and often how and when to do it". Policies, when enforced or followed, should have the effect of nudging specific practices to become compliant with its provisions.

Policies can be modelled in several ways (*e.g.*, as behavioural patterns [12], as first-order logic assertions [10], as markov decision processes [11]); here we model a policy focusing on the constraints it has on the executions of an STPS. We consider a *security policy* as a statement on what may never happen in the STPS execution. We abstract from the reasons why an STPS's executions appear to be constrained, disregarding how a policy is actually enforced (*e.g.*, access control systems, people having accepted the policy for ethical reasons or for fear of punishment): we assume it is enforced somehow. A *security requirement* instead is a desirable security property that we would like to be valid despite specific threats coming from an adversary. We model a security requirement as a classic security property [1].

We express policies and requirements using the language of *security statements*. It corresponds to Linear Temporal Logic (LTL) with 'Next' and 'Until' operators.

Definition 1. *A security statement is any expression in the language* $L(\varphi)$, *so defined:*

$$\varphi ::= \mathtt{true} \mid \varphi_{SP} \mid \varphi \wedge \varphi' \mid \neg\varphi \mid \bigcirc \varphi \mid \varphi \ \mathrm{U} \ \varphi'$$

$$\varphi_{SP} ::= \neg\varphi_{SP} \wedge \varphi'_{SP} \mid \neg\varphi_{SP} \mid d \in conn(l,l') \mid o \in key_D(d) \mid (x,a) \in Hist_D(d) \mid (x,a) \in Hist_O(o) \mid$$

$$z \in |type_O(o) \mid y \in attr_O(o) \mid loc_O(o) = l \mid o \in key_O(o') \mid o \in cont_O(o') \mid loc_A(a) = l \mid o \in cont_A(a)$$

Operators $\wedge$ and $\neg$ give the full power of propositional logic; operators $\bigcirc$ and U are sufficient to derive the other LTL operators, $\Diamond$ and $\square$. Note that, $L(\varphi_{SP})$ is the sub-language of propositional logic expressions over the STPS's state. In the remainder, we indicate with φ any formula in $L(\varphi)$, and with φ_{SP} any formula in $L(\varphi_{SP})$.

The informal meaning of a state predicate in φ_{SP} can be guessed from the name of the statement. So, for instance, $o \in key_D(d)$ evaluates to true if and only if o is the key that closes/opens door d. The formal semantics is defined in term of $[\![\cdot]\!]_S$, the function returning the truth value of a security statement in a given state $S \in \mathbf{S}$:

$$[\![d \in conn(l,l')]\!]_S \ \text{iff} \ (l,d,l') \in C$$
$$[\![(x,a) \in Hist_D(o)]\!]_S \ \text{iff} \ (x,a) \in Hist_D(o)$$
$$[\![(x,a) \in Hist_O(o)]\!]_S \ \text{iff} \ (x,a) \in Hist_O(o)$$
$$[\![y \in attr_O(o)]\!]_S \ \text{iff} \ y \in attr_O(o)$$
$$[\![z \in type_O(o)]\!]_S \ \text{iff} \ z \in type_O(o)$$

$$[\![loc_O(o) = l]\!]_S \ \text{iff} \ (l,o) \in (E)^+$$
$$[\![loc_A(a) = l]\!]_S \ \text{iff} \ (l,a) \in E$$
$$[\![o \in key_D(d)]\!]_S \ \text{iff} \ o = key_D(d)$$
$$[\![o \in key_O(o')]\!]_S \ \text{iff} \ o = key_O(o')$$
$$[\![o \in cont_O(o')]\!]_S \ \text{iff} \ (o',o) \in (E)^+$$
$$[\![o \in cont_A(a)]\!]_S \ \text{iff} \ (a,o) \in (E)^+$$

$Hist_D$ and $Hist_O$ keep the history of who has locked/encrypted a door or an object.

The semantics of φ is the standard semantics of an LTL formula (*e.g.*, see [13]). Assuming that $\text{Words}(\varphi) = \{\rho \in (2^{\varphi_{SP}})^\omega : \rho \models_I \varphi\}$ is the set of all ω-words (*i.e.*, possible infinite words) over the alphabet $2^{\varphi_{SP}}$ that satisfy φ, the satisfaction relation $\models_I \subseteq (2^{\varphi_{SP}})^\omega \times L(\varphi)$ is the smallest relation satisfying the following properties:

- $\rho \models_I \text{true}$
- $\rho \models_I \varphi_{SP}$ iff $[\![\varphi_{SP}]\!]_{\rho[0]}$
- $\rho \models_I \neg\varphi$ iff $\rho \not\models_I \varphi$
- $\rho \models_I \varphi_1 \wedge \varphi_2$ iff $\rho \models_I \varphi_1$ and $\rho \models_I \varphi_2$

- $\rho \models \bigcirc\varphi$ iff $\rho[1\ldots] \models_I \varphi$
- $\rho \models_I \varphi_1 U \varphi_2$ iff $\exists j \geq 0 : \rho[j\cdots] \models_I \varphi_2$ and $\rho[i\cdots] \models_I \varphi_1, \forall 0 \leq i < j$

Here, for $\rho = S_0 S_1 \ldots \in (2^{\varphi_{SP}})^\omega$, $\rho[j\cdots] = S_j S_{j+1} \ldots$ is the suffix of ρ starting in the $(j+1)^{st}$ symbol S_j. Given $\mathscr{S} = \langle \mathbf{S}, \Gamma, S_0, \Rightarrow \rangle$, we say that a security statement φ is valid in $\mathscr{S}$, written $\mathscr{S} \models_I \varphi$, when $\text{Traces}(\mathscr{S}) \subseteq \text{Words}(\varphi)$, where $\text{Traces}(\mathscr{S})$ is the set of all *prefix closed traces* of $\mathscr{S}$ [13].

From the language of security statements we derive the language of security policies and of security requirements. Since we decided to model the effect of policies as constraints on the execution of an STPS, a security policy is a safety property or a negation of a liveness property. We may consider to extend this language in the future. Instead, we do not impose any restrictions on the language of security requirements.

Definition 2. *A* policy *is a security statement of the form* $\Box\neg\varphi_{SP}$ *or* $\neg\Box(\varphi_{SP} \to \Diamond\varphi_{SP})$.

Definition 3. *A* requirement *is a security statement.*

Example 1. The policy "*o* should be kept in *l*" is written as $(\Box\neg(\exists_{a\in A}.\{o\} \subseteq cont_A(a) \wedge loc_A(a) \neq l)$; the requirement "no one brings *o* outside" as: $\neg(\Diamond loc_O(o) = l_0)$.

4   Policy Constrained Semantics

According to Definition 2, when a policy is enforced, no execution of the system is expected to violate the policy. This should hold only when we consider executions that do not include actions of the intruder, because an intruder is, by definition, someone who is freed from playing by the rules. Such reflections lead to the following definitions:

Definition 4 (Honest Trace). *An* honest trace *is a trace whose underlying sequence of states,* $S_0 \cdot \ldots \cdot S_i \cdot S_{i+1} \cdot \ldots$ *is such that* $(S_i, S_{i+1}) \in \Rightarrow$, *for all* $i \geq 0$ *and where the label of* $\Rightarrow$ *is not the intruder's ID.*

We indicate the set of all honest traces of $\mathscr{S}$ as $\text{Traces}_H(\mathscr{S})$. Here, H is the set of honest agents. Another relevant set of traces for the framework is the set of traces that satisfies a given security statement.

Algorithm 1. Reduce $(\mathscr{S}, \pi) \rightarrow \mathscr{S}_{|\pi}$

Case 1: $\pi = \Box\neg\varphi_{SP}$:
 Forall $S_i \in \mathbf{S} : \exists \rho \in \mathtt{Traces}_H(\mathscr{S}),$
 $\rho = S_0 \cdots S_i \cdots$ **and** $\rho[i \cdots] \models \varphi_{SP}$ **Do**
 $\mathbf{S}' := \mathbf{S}\backslash\{S\};$
 Forall $(S', S_i) \in \Rightarrow$ **Do** $\Rightarrow' := (\Rightarrow \backslash\{(S', S)\}) \cup \{(S', S')\};$
 Forall $(S_i, S') \in \Rightarrow$ **Do** $\Rightarrow' := (\Rightarrow \backslash\{(S', S_i)\})$

Case 2: $\pi = \neg\Box\varphi_{SP} \rightarrow \Diamond\varphi_{SP}$:
 Forall $S_i, S_j \in \mathbf{S} : \exists \rho \in \mathtt{Traces}_H(\mathscr{S})$
 $\rho = S_0 \cdots S_i \cdots S_j \cdots$ **and** $\rho[i\cdots] \models \pi\}$ **Do**
 $\Rightarrow' := (\Rightarrow \backslash\{(S_{j-1}, S_j)\}) \cup \{(S_{j-1}, S_{j-1})\}.$

Definition 5 (Trace satisfying φ). *A trace satisfying φ is a trace in* $\mathtt{Traces}(\mathscr{S}) \cap \mathtt{Words}(\varphi)$. *An honest trace satisfying φ is a trace in* $\mathtt{Traces}_H(\mathscr{S}) \cap \mathtt{Words}(\varphi)$.

We denote the set of all traces satisfying φ by $\mathtt{traces}(\mathscr{S}, \varphi)$, and the set of all honest traces satisfying a φ by $\mathtt{traces}_H(\mathscr{S}, \varphi)$.

We are now interested to distinguishing, in an execution without the intruder, the requirements whose validity can be changed if the policy is enforced from those whose validity is unchanged by it.

Definition 6 (Requirements/Policies Affectedness). *Let φ be a requirement, π a policy, and $\mathscr{S}$ be a model of execution of an STPS. We say that φ is affected by π in $\mathscr{S}$, and we write it $\varphi \hookleftarrow \pi$, when* $\mathtt{traces}_H(\mathscr{S}, \varphi) \subseteq \mathtt{traces}_H(\mathscr{S}, \neg\pi) \neq \emptyset$.

Property 1. Relation $\hookleftarrow$ is reflexive and commutative.

In a system where a policy is parsimoniously enforced, no requirement must change their validity, except those that are affected by the enforcement of π.

Definition 7. *Let $\mathscr{S} = \langle \mathbf{S}, S_0, \Rightarrow \rangle$ be an STPS, π a policy. The system $\mathscr{S}$ constrained by π, written $\mathscr{S}_{|\pi}$, is a new $\mathscr{S}' = \langle \mathbf{S}', S_0, \Rightarrow' \rangle$ that satisfies the following conditions:*

1. *If $\mathscr{S} \not\models_H \pi$ then $\mathscr{S}' \models_H \pi$;*
2. *For all p such that $p \not\hookleftarrow \pi$, if $\mathscr{S} \models_H p$ then $\mathscr{S}' \models_H p$.*

Definition 7 makes it clear that in a system where the policy is enforced the policy holds, and that the validity of properties that are not affected by the policy does not change. The use of the $\models_H$ notation in Definition 7 stresses that the policy is enforced on the system's execution without the interference of the intruder. The intruder can still find its way into breaching security even in the constrained system. Actually, the constrained system will be secure only when $\mathtt{Traces}(\mathscr{S}_{|\pi}) \subseteq \mathtt{Words}(p)$. This is eventually the meaning we intended to give to the proposition in (1).

From an operational point of view we are interested to obtain $\mathscr{S}_{|\pi}$ from $\mathscr{S}$. Algorithm 1, inputs a $\mathscr{S} = \langle \mathbf{S}, S_0, \Rightarrow \rangle$, a π and returns a labelled transition system for $\mathscr{S}_{|\pi}$. The new transitions are labelled with ϵ, the null action.

Proposition 1 (Soundness). $\mathscr{S}' = Reduce(\mathscr{S}, \pi)$ *is a system constrained by* π.

Proof. (sketch) $\mathscr{S}$ satisfies the two conditions in Definition 7. A valid, in $\mathscr{S}$, requirement p that is not affected by π, will not change its validity due to the operations (removing states, and adding loops) that Algorithm 1 implements onto $\mathscr{S}$.

Proposition 2. $Reduce(\mathscr{S}, \pi)$ *can be implemented with worst-case time complexity* $O(|\mathbf{S}|^2 \cdot check(\pi))$. *Here,* $check(\pi)$ *is the complexity of checking* π.

Proof. (sketch) Algorithm 1 is inefficient: the **Forall**s browse far more states than necessary. A more efficient way is to search for the Ss with minimal index in a trace satisfying **Forall**s' conditions. Each **Forall**'s has at most $O(|\mathbf{S}|^2)$ iterations.

5   Conclusion

To reduce the risk that sensitive data are leaked, an ICT organization should protect its files and any item that may contain those files, such as hard disk, books, and USB pens. This can be done by restricting the digital and the physical access to data but also by implementing security policies meant to be enforced on the employees daily job. The research we presented in this paper sets the foundations for reasoning about an organization's security when it enforces its policies. We propose a formal approach: we represent the data flow as it is defined by the daily operation of the employees of an organization in a formal language. Policies are simple formulas that we use to restrict the possible evolution of the system and based on which we check the validity of a security property in the presence of an adversary.

Our theoretical approach focussed on clearly defining the relevant concepts while postponing the design of efficient algorithms. We believe that it is possible to reduce the complexity of our algorithm and to optimize the generation of our *STPS* models. It is worth to mention that, even using our non-optimized algorithm, we managed to run proof-of-concept scenarios by using the PRISM model checker. For reasons of space we could not report on this experience in the current paper. In the future, we will report on our practical experiences in full detail. Another future research question concerns our policy language. We kept our policy language simple to be able to focus on the main concepts in our framework. We will study the expressiveness of our language and study extensions needed to manage real policies. We will also consider the introduction of probabilities and costs in our framework.

Acknowledgments. The research leading to the results presented in this work received funding from the Fonds National de la Recherche Luxembourg, project "Socio-Technical Analysis of Security and Trust", C11/IS/1183245, STAST, and the "European Commissions Seventh Framework Programme", FP7/2007-2013, TREsPASS.

References

1. Cremers, C., Mauw, S.: Operational Semantics and Verification of Security Protocols. Information Security and Cryptography. Springer, Heidelberg (2012)
2. Baxter, G., Sommerville, I.: Socio-technical systems: from design methods to systems engineering. Interact. Comput. **23**(1), 4–17 (2011)
3. De Nicola, R., Ferrari, G.L., Pugliese, R.: KLAIM: a kernel language for agents interaction and mobility. IEEE Trans. Softw. Eng. **24**(5), 315–330 (1998)
4. Meadows, C., Pavlovic, D.: Formalizing physical security procedures. In: Jøsang, A., Samarati, P., Petrocchi, M. (eds.) STM 2012. LNCS, vol. 7783, pp. 193–208. Springer, Heidelberg (2013). doi:10.1007/978-3-642-38004-4_13
5. Sommestad, T., Ekstedt, M., Holm, H.: The cyber security modeling language: a tool for assessing the vulnerability of enterprise system architectures. IEEE Syst. J. **7**(3), 363–373 (2013)
6. Lenzini, G., Mauw, S., Ouchani, S.: Security analysis of socio-technical physical systems. Comput. Electr. Eng. **47**(C), 258–274 (2015)
7. Dimkov, T., Pieters, W., Hartel, P.: Portunes: representing attack scenarios spanning through the physical, digital and social domain. In: Armando, A., Lowe, G. (eds.) ARSPA-WITS 2010. LNCS, vol. 6186, pp. 112–129. Springer, Heidelberg (2010). doi:10.1007/978-3-642-16074-5_9
8. Fong, P.W.L.: Relationship-based access control: protection model and policy language. In: The First ACM Conference on Data and Application Security and Privacy, CODASPY 2011, pp. 191–202 (2011)
9. Jaume, M.: Semantic comparison of security policies: from access control policies to flow properties. In: IEEE Symposium on Security and Privacy, pp. 60–67 (2012)
10. Ranise, S., Traverso, R.: ALPS: an action language for policy specification and automated safety analysis. In: Mauw, S., Jensen, C.D. (eds.) STM 2014. LNCS, vol. 8743, pp. 146–161. Springer, Heidelberg (2014)
11. Tschantz, M.C., Datta, A., Wing, J.M.: Formalizing and enforcing purpose restrictions in privacy policies. In: IEEE Symposium on Security and Privacy, pp. 176–190 (2012)
12. Hartel, P., Eck, P., Etalle, S., Wieringa, R.: Modelling mobility aspects of security policies. In: Barthe, G., Burdy, L., Huisman, M., Lanet, J.-L., Muntean, T. (eds.) CASSIS 2004. LNCS, vol. 3362, pp. 172–191. Springer, Heidelberg (2005). doi:10.1007/978-3-540-30569-9_9
13. Ch, B., Katoen, J.-P.: Principles of Model Checking. MIT Press, Cambridge (2008)

Formal Analysis of Vulnerabilities of Web Applications Based on SQL Injection

Federico De Meo[1]([⊠]), Marco Rocchetto[2], and Luca Viganò[3]

[1] Dipartimento di Informatica, Università degli Studi di Verona, Verona, Italy
federico.demeo@univr.it
[2] iTrust, Singapore University of Technology and Design, Singapore, Singapore
[3] Department of Informatics, King's College London, London, UK

Abstract. We present a formal approach for the analysis of attacks that exploit SQLi to violate security properties of web applications. We give a formal representation of web applications and databases, and show that our formalization effectively exploits SQLi attacks. We implemented our approach in a prototype tool called SQLfast and we show its efficiency on four real-world case studies, including the discovery of an attack on Joomla! that no other tool can find.

1 Introduction

Motivations. According to OWASP (the Open Web Applications Security Project [27]), *SQL injection (SQLi)* is the most critical threat for the security of web applications (*web apps*, for short), and MITRE lists improper SQLi neutralization as the most dangerous programming error [6]. SQLi was first defined in [14] but, also due to the increasing complexity of web apps, SQLis can still be very difficult to detect, especially by manual *penetration testing (pentesting)*.

A number of SQLi scanners have thus been developed to search for injection points and payloads, most notably *sqlmap* [33], which allows human pentesters to find SQLi vulnerabilities by testing the web app with different payloads, and *sqlninja* [34], which focuses on SQL server databases. The combination of the two provides the pentester with a powerful tool suite for SQLi detection. However, neither sqlmap nor sqlninjia (nor other state-of-the-art vulnerability scanners) are able to detect vulnerabilities linked to logical flaws of web apps [12]. This means that even if a scanner can concretely discover a SQLi, it can't link SQLi to logical flaws that lead to the violation of a generic security property, e.g., the secrecy of data accessible only bypassing an authentication phase via a SQLi.

Moreover, determining that a web app is vulnerable to SQLi (and which payload to exploit) might not be enough for the app's overall security. Consider, for instance, a web app that relies on legacy code (when an update is not feasible, e.g., because the legacy code is a core part of the system). If a SQLi is found, an

---

This work was carried out while Marco Rocchetto was at the Università di Verona.

G. Barthe et al. (Eds.): STM 2016, LNCS 9871, pp. 179–195, 2016.
DOI: 10.1007/978-3-319-46598-2_13

investigation should be performed to understand when the SQLi can be exploited and whether this compromises security. This investigation is carried out manually by the pentester in charge of identifying attack scenarios, thus potentially leading to additional omissions, errors and oversights in the security analysis.

A number of formal approaches for the security analysis of web apps, based on the *Dolev-Yao (DY) intruder model* [11], have been implemented recently, e.g., [1,3,4,31,36]. However, the DY model is typically used to reason about security protocols and the cryptographic operators they employ (e.g., for asymmetric or symmetric cryptography, modular exponentiation or exclusive-or) but abstracting away the contents of the payloads of the messages. As a consequence, these approaches cannot properly identify or exploit new SQLi payloads since reasoning about the contents of the messages is crucial to that end.

Contributions. In this paper, we present a formal approach for the analysis of attacks that exploit SQLi to violate security properties of web apps. We define how to formally represent web apps that interact with a database and how the DY intruder model can be extended to deal with SQLi.

In order to show that our formalization can effectively be used to detect security vulnerabilities linked to SQLi attacks, we have developed a prototype tool called *SQLfast (SQL Formal AnalysiS Tool)* and we show its efficiency by discussing four real-world case studies. Most notably, we use SQLfast to detect an attack on Joomla! which, to the best of our knowledge, no state-of-the-art SQLi scanner (e.g., sqlmap or sqlninja) can detect since they do not automatically link different attacks in one attack trace (i.e., they do not find logical flaws linked to SQLi attacks). Another key novel aspect of SQLfast is that it can detect complex attacks in which a first SQLi attack provides data for a second subsequent attack. We show that SQLfast allows us to exploit SQLi combining it with logical flaws of web apps to report sophisticated attack traces in a few seconds and can also deal with Second-Order SQLis, which are notoriously difficult to spot.

Note that we do not search for new SQLi payloads but rather we exploit attacks related to SQLi. This allows us to analyze how an intruder can violate a security property by exploiting one or more attacks related to a SQLi, e.g., credential bypass. Nevertheless, we also (automatically) test our attacks against the web app under analysis and then we use state-of-the-art tools (i.e., sqlmap and curl) to detect the actual payload of all the SQLis exploited.

Organization. In Sect. 2, we discuss a concrete example that shows why we can't stop at the identification of a SQLi. In Sect. 3, we give a categorization of SQLi vulnerabilities, based on which, in Sect. 4, we provide our formalization. In Sect. 5, we discuss SQLfast and its application real-world case studies. In Sect. 6, we sum up and discuss related and future work. The extended version [10] contains full details on our specifications and case studies, and a proof that the formalization of the database correctly handles all the SQLis categorized in Sect. 3.

2 Why Can't We Stop at the Identification of a SQLi? The Case of Joomla!

The identification of a SQLi entry point is generally considered as a satisfactory finish line when dealing with SQLi in web apps. So, one could ask: why not simply stop there (and why bother reading the rest of this paper)? The answer is that a SQLi can be a serious threat *only* if it can be exploited and *only* if it can be used for carrying out an attack. A full understanding of how a potential SQLi vulnerability can afflict the security of a web app is essential in order to implement proper countermeasures. For instance, consider Joomla! [22], a PHP-based Content Management System that allows users to create web apps through a web interface. Joomla! supports different databases, e.g., MySQL [26] and PostgreSQL [30], and a recent assessment [19] has shown that versions ranging from 3.2 to 3.4.4 suffer from a SQLi vulnerability [7].

The execution of a state-of-the-art scanner such as sqlmap on Joomla! can correctly find the vulnerability. However, sqlmap (or any other scanner for SQLi) cannot tell how that SQLi can be usefully exploited in order to carry out a concrete attack. A general description of the consequences of a SQLi attack is given in [8,28] but, whenever a SQLi entry point is found, the penetration tester has to manually investigate the kind of damages that SQLi might cause to the web app. The researchers who discovered the vulnerability of Joomla! [19] also described how it could be exploited in a real attack: it would allow an intruder to perform a session hijack and thus steal someone's session but would not allow him to create his own account or modify arbitrary data on the database. The exploration of different attack scenarios has been entirely performed manually since no automatic tool shows the outcome of the exploitation of a SQLi vulnerability on a specific web app. But who guarantees that a post-SQLi attack can actually be performed and that all possible attacks based on the SQLi have been taken into account by the penetration tester?

This is why we can't stop at the identification of a SQLi and why we can't address the post-SQLi attacks with a manual analysis. Our approach addresses this by automating the identification of attacks that exploit a SQLi.

3 SQL Injections

Some general classifications based on the payloads of the SQLi (and the exploitation scenarios) have been put forth, e.g., [15,27]. Based on these, we can divide SQLi techniques into 6 different categories: (i) Boolean-Based, (ii) Time-Based, (iii) Error-Based, (iv) UNION Query, (v) Second-Order and (vi) Stacked Queries.

Given that our formalization strictly depends on the attack that the intruder wants to perform by using a particular type of SQLi, we now define the two attacks that we have considered:[1]

---

[1] Other possible attacks (e.g., by exploiting a *Cross-Site Scripting (XSS)* inside the payload of some SQLi) are outside the scope of our approach for now, cf. Sect. 6.

– *Authentication bypass attack:* the intruder bypasses an authentication check that a web app performs by querying a database.
– *Data extraction attack:* the intruder obtains data from the database that he should not be able to obtain.

Based on these attack definitions, we will now describe the main details of each category, emphasizing those aspects that are relevant for our formalization. The following table summarizes which attacks can be exploited by a SQLi technique on a specific type of SQL query. Three remarks: (1) since all state-of-the-art DBMS are vulnerable to SQLi, we won't distinguish between different dialects of SQL and simply write "SQL query"; (2) AB abbreviates *authentication bypass* and DE *data extraction*; (3) a scenario in which the intruder extracts information in order to bypass an authentication is considered to be a data extraction attack.

	BB		TB		EB		UQ		SO		SQ	
	AB	DE	AB	DE	AB	DE	AB	DE	AB	DE	AB	DE
SELECT	✓	✓	✓	✓	✓	✓	✓	✓				✓
UPDATE	✓	✓	✓	✓	✓	✓			✓	✓		✓
DELETE						✓						✓
INSERT						✓			✓	✓		✓

In a **Boolean-Based SQLi (BB)**, an intruder inserts into an HTTP parameter, which is used by a web app to write a SQL query, one or more valid SQL statements that make the WHERE clause of the SQL query evaluate to true or false. By interacting with the web app and comparing the responses, the intruder can understand whether or not the injection was successful. In this way, an intruder can perform both authentication bypass and data extraction attacks.

In an authentication bypass attack, the intruder injects a statement that changes the truth value of a WHERE clause in a SQL SELECT query, creating a tautology. If a web app performs an authentication check querying a database, this attack will then trick the database into replying in an affirmative way even when no (or wrong) authentication details have been presented by the intruder.

In a data extraction attack, the intruder obtains data from the database. The term "extraction" is used in standard terminology but it can be misleading. With a BB, an intruder exploits the "Boolean behavior" of a web app inferring whether the original query returned some tuples or not. When the intruder understands how the web app behaves when some tuples or no tuples are returned, he can start the "extraction". In this case, the intruder asks whether a certain information is stored in the database and, based on the behavior of the web app, he knows if the information is actually inside the database.

A **Time-Based SQLi (TB)** is quite similar to BB: the only difference is that TB does not need the web app to have a Boolean behavior. The intruder appends a timing function to the validity value of a Boolean clause. Thus, after the submission of the query by the web app, the database waits for a predefined amount of time for a tuple as a response to the query; the intruder can then infer whether the Boolean value of the query was true or false observing a delay in the response. In real case scenarios, a BB is preferable as it is faster than a TB. Timing is not part of our formalization (see Sect. 4), so the abstract attack traces generated by our tool will not distinguish between BB and TB.

When error pages are exposed to the Internet, some error messages of the database could be exposed, thus giving an intruder the possibility of exploiting an **Error-Based SQLi (EB)**. In this type of injection, the intruder tricks the database into performing operations that result in an error and then he extracts information from the error messages produced by the database. EB is generally used to perform a data extraction attack by inducing the generation of an error that contains some information stored in the database.

A UNION **Query-Based SQLi (UQ)** is a technique in which an intruder injects a SQL UNION operator to join the original query with a malicious one. The aim is to overwrite the values of the original query and thus, in order to extract information, UQ requires the web app to print the result of the query within the returned HTML page. This behavior allows the intruder to actually extract information from the database by reading it within the web app itself.

Second-Order SQLi (SO) is an injection that has no direct effect when submitted but that is exploited in a second stage of the attack. In some cases, a web app may correctly handle and store a SQL statement whose value depends on the user input. Afterwards, another part of the web app that doesn't implement a control against SQLi might use the previously stored SQL statement to execute a different query and thus expose the web app to a SQLi. Automated scanners generally fail to detect this type of SQLi (e.g., [33,34]) and may need to be manually instructed to check for evidence that an injection has been attempted.

With a **Stacked Queries SQLi (SQ)**, an intruder can execute an arbitrary query different from the original one. The semicolon character; enables the intruder to concatenate a different SQL query to the original one. By doing so, the intruder can perform data extraction attacks as well as execute whatever operation is allowed by the database. With a SQ, an intruder can perform any of the SQLis described above. Thus, whenever we refer to all the SQLis in our categorization, we exclude SQ as it is already covered by the other ones.

Prevention techniques. Avoiding SQLi attacks is theoretically quite straightforward. In fact, developers can use sanitization functions or prepared statements. Roughly speaking, the general idea is to not evaluate the injected string as a SQL command.

A *sanitization function* takes the input provided by the user and removes (i.e., escapes) all the special characters that could be used to perform a SQLi. Sanitization functions are not the best option when dealing with SQLi because they might not be properly implemented or do not consider some cases.

Prepared statements are the best option for preventing SQLis. They are mainly used to execute the same query repeatedly maintaining efficiency. However, due to their inner execution principle (if properly implemented) they are immune to SQLi attacks. The execution of a prepared statement consists mainly in two steps: preparation and execution. In the preparation step, the query is evaluated and compiled, waiting for the parameters for the instantiation. During the execution step, the parameters are submitted to the prepared statement and handled as data and thus they cannot be interpreted as SQL commands.

4   A Formalization of SQLi

We will now describe how we formally represent a web app that interacts with a database using insecure SQL queries and/or a sanitized (i.e., secure) query. In Sect. 4.1, we propose an extension of the DY model that can deal with SQLi.[2] We formalize the database in Sect. 4.2, the web app in Sect. 4.3, and the goals in Sect. 4.4. For brevity and readability, we omit many details and only give pseudo-code that should be quite intuitive. See [10] for full details and the ASLan++ code of our formalizations and case studies, along with a brief introduction to ASLan++.

4.1   The DY Web Intruder

We extend the standard DY intruder model [11] for security protocol analysis. Suppose that we want to search for an authentication bypass attack via BB (Sect. 3), in which the intruder injects a statement that changes the truth value of a WHERE clause in a SQL SELECT query, creating a tautology. To formalize this, we need to extend the DY intruder by giving him the ability to send a concatenation of Boolean formulas made of conjunctions and disjunctions. This characteristic highlights an important difference between the classical DY intruder and the enhanced version we are proposing: *our web intruder works with abstract payloads rather than messages*. Due to technical details (e.g., implementation constraints and non-termination problems), implementing such a modification is impractical. We have thus allowed the intruder to concatenate the exact payload, *or true*, and defined a Horn clause to model that whenever a formula has *or true* injected by the intruder, it evaluates to true.

We can rephrase the same reasoning in the case of BB for data extraction attacks, in which the intruder tricks the web app into asking to the database if a particular information is present; for example, instead of or.true, the intruder adds or username=admin. The DBMS will reply in an affirmative way only if there is a tuple in the database with admin as username. To allow the intruder to perform all the SQLis described in Sect. 3, we thus extend the DY intruder with one constant sqli that represents any SQLi payload (e.g., or.true).

---

[2] This formal representation is intended to work with tools that perform symbolic analysis. We don't formalize the honest client behavior and we assume the DY intruder to be the only agent able to communicate with the web app. The DY intruder will eventually perform honest interactions if needed to achieve a particular configuration of the system. See [10] for more details.

4.2   The Database

We give a general formalization of a database that can be used in any specification to exploit SQLi when searching for security flaws in a web app. Our
formalization aims to be both *compact*, to avoid state-space explosion problems, and *general enough* not to be tailored to a given technology (e.g., MySQL
or PostgreSQL). Hence, we don't represent the database content, the database
structure, the SQL syntax nor access policies specified by the DBMS. Rather, we
formalize messages sent and received and queries, and a database can be seen as
a network node that interacts only with the web app through a secure channel.[3]

Definition 1. Messages *consist of* variables V, constants c *(sqli, etc.)*, concatenation $M.M$, function application $f(M)$ *of uninterpreted function symbols*
f *to messages M (e.g., $\texttt{tuple}(M)$), and* encryption $\{M\}_M$ *of messages with
public, private or symmetric keys that are themselves messages. We define that
M_1 is a submessage of M_2 as is standard (e.g., M_1 is a submessage of $M_1.M_3$,
of $f(M_1)$ and of $\{M_1\}_{M_4}$) and, abusing notation, write $M_1 \in M_2$.*

Definition 2. *A query is* valid *(respectively,* not valid*) when, evaluated by a
database, it returns one or more (respectively, zero) tuples.*

We formalize the validity of SQL queries by means of the Horn clause:
$\texttt{inDB(M.sqli)} \implies true$, where, in order to represent a SQLi attack, the predicate $\texttt{inDB()}$ holds for a message (which represents a SQL query) whenever it is
of the form $M.\texttt{sqli}$. This states that the intruder has injected a payload $\texttt{sqli}$
into the query parameters (expressed as a variable) M.

Incoming messages. We consider, as incoming messages, only SQL queries via
raw SQL and via sanitized queries. The parameters of queries are represented by
a generic variable $\texttt{SQLquery}$. In case of a raw SQL query, they are wrapped by an
uninterpreted function $\texttt{query()}$; if a sanitized query has been implemented then
we use another uninterpreted function $\texttt{sanitizedQuery()}$. These two uninterpreted functions allow the modeler to "switch on/off" the possibility of a SQLi
in some point of the app.

Database responses. The tuple generated by the database as a response to a
raw SQL query is represented by an uninterpreted function $\texttt{tuple()}$ over a
message representing a SQL query. Given that we do not model the content of
the database, this function represents any (and all) database data.

   Whenever the database receives a SQL query $\texttt{query(SQLquery)}$ from the web
app, the uninterpreted function $\texttt{tuple(SQLquery)}$ is sent back to the web app to
express that a tuple, as a response to the query, has been found. This response is
returned only if $\texttt{inDB()}$ holds; in all other cases, a constant $\texttt{no\_tuple}$ is returned
to represent that no tuples are returned in the responses of the database.

---

[3] Nothing prevents us from relaxing this assumption but this would give the DY
   intruder the possibility of performing attacks (e.g., man-in-the-middle attacks) that
   are rare in web app scenarios.

If the database receives a sanitized query, no injection is possible. Hence, the database does not return any useful information to the web app; instead, a constant no_tuple is returned. Since the intruder cannot perform a SQLi in presence of a sanitized query, we also assume that a sanitized query can be executed only with legitimate parameters, i.e., as a function of tuple() (this is because we are interested in modeling only SQLi scenarios).

The pseudo-code representing the database behavior is given in Listing 1.1, where, here and in the following, we write DB for the database. DB is a network node and we assume it to be always actively listening for incoming messages. It is defined by two main, mutually exclusive, branches of an if-elseif statement: one guard is in line 1 in which DB is waiting (expressed in Alice-and-Bob notation) for a sanitized query and the other in line 3 in which it is waiting for a raw SQL query. If a sanitized query is received, then there is no SQLi. Given that we only consider dishonest interactions, the data sent back to the intruder will not increase his knowledge. In other words, no SQLis are permitted and any permitted query will just give to the intruder the possibility of continuing his execution with the web app but won't add any extra information to his knowledge.

Listing 1.1. Pseudo-code of a DBMS.

```
1  if(WebApp -> DB: sanitizedQuery(SQLquery)){
2    if(SQLquery == tuple(*)) DB -> WebApp: no_tuple;
3  }elseif(WebApp -> DB: query(SQLquery)){
4    if(inDB(SQLquery)) DB -> WebApp: tuple(SQLquery);
5    if(!(inDB(SQLquery))) DB -> WebApp: no_tuple;}
```

One may argue that a valid query should indeed add extra information to the intruder knowledge. However, we do not model the content of the database and any information received by the intruder as a response to a sanitized query is included in the action that the web app performs after this database response. Thus, in our formalization, the query in SQLquery is not valid and then the no_tuple constant is sent back in line 2. We also add a constraint in line 2 that any query received (SQLquery) must be of the form tuple(*), i.e., as a function of the content of the database where * acts as a wildcard character that matches any possible parameter. This is because, in the case of a sanitized query, the intruder cannot perform a SQLi and we exclude the case in which the DY intruder sends a random query just to continue the execution with the web app. Instead, he has to either know a tuple of the database or data as functions of a tuple of the database. In the case the intruder knows tuple(Query), he will just receive no_tuple, i.e., correctly no data has been leaked to the intruder.

The second branch of the initial if-elseif statement (line 3) handles raw queries. If a raw query is submitted, then there are two cases: the raw query is not valid (line 5, where ! formalizes the negation) and then, as in the previous case, no_tuple is sent back (line 5); the raw query is valid (line 4) and a tuple is sent back (line 4). Given that all these queries are sent from the intruder, we can assume they have a malicious intent. One may argue that, in a real case scenario, the database is not actually returning a tuple but, given that an intruder could repeatedly send a SQLi exploiting that injection point, it is fair to assume that the database is sending all the tuples it contains, i.e., tuple(SQLquery).

4.3   The Web App

As for the database, the web app is a node of the network that can send and receive messages. The web app communicates with a client or with the database (it can, potentially, also communicate with other apps but we do not consider that explicitly here). We assume only one database is present because adding other databases would not add any further useful information for finding attacks based on SQLi. The proof is straightforward. Since we do not consider database contents and structures, if we wanted to have two database models, then we would have two exact copies of the formalization given in Sect. 4.2. Since we have assumed that there exists a long-lasting secure relation between the database and the web app, no man-in-the-middle attacks are considered. Therefore, any attack found that involves the communication with one of the two databases could be found by considering the other database only.

A specification of a web app can be seen as a behavioral description of the web app itself (along with its interaction with the database). A modeler can define this specification from the design phase documentation of the engineering process of the web app. A model can also be created in a black box way by just looking at the HTTP messages exchanged from a client and the web app and guessing the communication with the database.

We now consider the main aspects that allow for the modeling of a web app.

Sending and receiving messages. A web app can communicate with a client and the database. We abstract away as many details as possible of the web pages and thus any incoming message will only contain: (i) parameters of forms expressed as variables, e.g., `Client -> WebApp: Username.Password`, and (ii) the web page itself expressed as a constant, e.g., `WebApp -> Client: dashboard` where `dashboard` represents a web page. Note that, in any response of the web app, if the content of the response is linked to a response of the database, i.e., `tuple(Query)` (where the query is either `SELECT`, `UPDATE` or `DELETE`), then `tuple(Query)` must be included in the response. Otherwise, we would end up representing a scenario in which no content of the tuple received by the database is included in, or linked to, the web page and thus no SQLi would be present.

Queries. The web app creates either a sanitized query or a raw query. Then, the web app wraps the variables representing the query parameters with either `sanitizedQuery()` or `query()`, both uninterpreted functions, and afterwards sends the SQL query to the database. Note that we only need to represent the parameters of a SQL query since we do not distinguish between different queries in the database formalization. If the query does not depend on parameters sent from a client, the intruder cannot exploit it to perform a SQLi. The SQL query used to query the database is represented as a constant, resulting in the database always replying with `no_tuple` (as `inDB()`, in this case, is never valid).

If statements. We use them mainly to decide, based on which kind of message has been received, what the web app has to reply. For example, if the database replies with a tuple `tuple(Query)`, then the web app might return a specific page along with `tuple(Query)` or might return a different page.

Assignments. A constant or a message can be assigned to a variable: `Variable := constant|message`. Assignments are, e.g., useful to save incoming messages.

4.4   Goals

Finally, we define the security properties we want the model to satisfy. As we discussed in Sect. 3, we consider two main attacks: authentication bypass and data extraction. We give the formalization in Listing 1.2, where `iknowledge` is a predicate that represents the knowledge of the intruder. By using the LTL "globally" operator `[]`, we can specify an authentication check by stating that the intruder should not have access to a specific page (`dashboard` in Listing 1.2), whereas data extraction is represented by specifying that the intruder should not increase his knowledge with data from the database (i.e., as function of `tuple()`).

Listing 1.2. Authentication bypass and data extraction goals of the BB example.

```
[](!(iknowledge(dashboard))); %authentication bypass
[](!(iknowledge(tuple(*)))); %data extraction
```

5   SQLfast, Case Studies and Results

To show that our formalization can be used effectively to detect security flaws linked to SQLi attacks, we have developed *SQLfast*, a prototype *SQL Formal AnalysiS Tool* [32]. In [32] we also provide a friendly web-based user interface that helps the modeler in creating the web-app model. SQLfast takes in input a specification written in ASLan++, the modeling language of the AVANTSSAR Platform [3], and then calls CL-AtSe (one of the platform's model checkers) and generates an *Abstract Attack Trace (AAT)* as a *Message Sequence Chart (MSC)* if an attack was found. SQLfast automatically detects which type of SQLi was exploited and, in an interactive way, generates the curl or sqlmap commands to concretize the attack.

As a concrete proof-of-concept, we have applied SQLfast to (i) WebGoat [29], (ii) Damn Vulnerable Web Application (DVWA) [13], (iii) Joomla! 3.4.4, and (iv) *Yet Another Vulnerable Web Application (YAVWA)*, an ad-hoc testing environment that we have developed and that also includes a SO SQLi example. (Recall that full details are given in [10].) The case studies provided by WebGoat and DVWA might sound limited but capture all possible scenarios with respect to SQLi attack combinations considered in this paper — recall that our formalization for SQLi attacks does not find SQLi payloads, but focuses on vulnerabilities based on SQLi. We tested SQLfast in order to show all the combinations that could be represented by considering SQLi for (1) authentication bypass, (2) data extraction and (3) data extraction with reuse of the extracted information. Our case studies are quite heterogenous, so it should not be difficult to map other case studies to one of these scenarios we have considered.

We have implemented the case studies in ASLan++ to be able to apply the model checkers of the AVANTSSAR Platform (in particular, CL-AtSe), but other model checkers implementing the Dolev-Yao intruder model could be used as well, provided that their input language is expressive enough. For the sake of brevity, we discuss here only the case studies Joomla!, YAVWA and SO, which show how our formalization can find attacks linked to the logic of a web app that is vulnerable to SQLi attacks. The type of attacks that SQLfast can detect and concretize cannot be detected by state-of-the-art tools for SQLi such as sqlmap.

5.1 Case Study: Authentication Bypass via Data Extraction

We now discuss two scenarios in which our approach detects attacks that state-of-the-art tools, such as sqlmap, are *not* able to detect and exploit. In the first scenario, the intruder exploits a recent SQLi vulnerability found (by manual inspection only) in Joomla! [7]. The second scenario (YAVWA) is a variant of the first and shows a concatenation of different attacks.

Joomla!. A recent assessment has shown that the Content History module of Joomla! suffers from a SQLi vulnerability that allows a remote (non-authenticated) user to execute arbitrary SQL commands [7]. The pseudo-code in Listing 1.3 represents the following behavior: a remote user visits the Content History component (line 1). The web app queries the database with the user supplied data (2). If some tuples are generated (3), the web app sends to the client the history page viewHistory along with the tuple() function (4). The web app then has two possible ways of authenticating the user (5–9): by using credentials or cookies. If username and password are provided (5), the web app applies a non-invertible hash function hash() to the password, and queries the database to verify the credentials (6).[4] If the credentials are correct, the administration panel is sent to the user (7). In case of a cookie session, the user provides a cookie that the web app checks querying the database (8). If the cookie is valid, the administration panel is sent back to the user (9).

Listing 1.3. Pseudo-code representing the Joomla! scenario.

```
1  User -> WebApp: com_contenthistory.history.Listselect;
2  WebApp->DB: query(com_contenthistory.history.Listselect);
3  if(DB -> WebApp: tuple(SQLquery)){
4   WebApp -> User: viewHistory.tuple(SQLquery); }
5  if(User -> WebApp: Username.Password){
6   WebApp -> DB: sanitizedQuery(Username.hash(Password));
7   if(DB -> WebApp: no_tuple){ WebApp -> User: adminPanel; }}
8  if(User -> WebApp: Cookie){ WebApp -> DB: sanitizedQuery(Cookie);
9   if(DB -> WebApp: no_tuple){ WebApp -> User: adminPanel; }}
```

As goal, we check if there exists an execution in which the intruder can access the administration panel represented by the constant adminPanel.

Listing 1.4. Authentication bypass for the Joomla! scenario.
```
[](!(iknowledge(adminPanel)));
```

---

[4] The web app applies a hash function to the password before checking whether credentials are correct because Joomla! stores the passwords hashed into the database.

SQLfast generates the AAT in Listing 1.5, which is an authentication bypass attack where the intruder hijacks a user session by using a cookie instead of login credentials. In fact, the web app applies a hash function to the password before verifying the credentials submitted by the user. The hash function would not allow an intruder to blindly submit a password extracted from the database, the only possibility is using a valid cookie value.[5] The intruder performs a data extraction and retrieves the information to access the administration panel (1–4), and uses it to hijack a user session by submitting a valid cookie value (5–8).

Listing 1.5. Abstract attack trace that extracts data with a SQLi in order to bypass the authentication of the Joomla! scenario.

```
1   i -> WebApp   :  com_contenthistory.history.sqli
2   WebApp -> DB  :  query(com_contenthistory.history.sqli)
3   DB -> WebApp  :  tuple(com_contenthistory.history.sqli)
4   WebApp  -> i  :  viewHistory.tuple(com_contenthistory.history.sqli)
5   i ->WebApp    :  cookie.tuple(com_contenthistory.history.sqli)
6   WebApp -> DB  :  sanitizedQuery(tuple(com_contenthistory.history.sqli))
7   DB -> WebApp  :  no_tuple
8   WebApp  -> i  :  adminPanel
```

YAVWA. We have designed a variant of Joomla! to show that a SQLi can be exploited to compromise a part of a web app that does not directly depend on databases. YAVWA provides an HTTP form login and a login by HTTP basic authentication [18] configured with the .htaccess [2] file. The credentials used for the HTTP basic authentication, which are stored in the .htpasswd file, are the same as the ones employed by the users to login into the web app (i.e., the same as the ones stored in the database). The intruder's goal is to access the area protected by the HTTP basic authentication login. Obviously, he cannot perform a SQLi to bypass HTTP basic authentication since the login procedure doesn't use SQL. Bypassing the login page, without knowing the correct credentials, doesn't allow the intruder to gain access to the secure folder.

We have defined this scenario in the pseudo-code in Listing 1.6. The client sends his personal credentials (**Username.Password**) to the web app (1). The web app creates a query that it sends to the database (2) for verifying the submitted credentials. If tuples are generated from the database (3), a dashboard page is returned to the client along with the function **tuple()** (4), otherwise, the web app redirects the user to the login page (5). At this point, the web app waits to receive correct credentials that will allow the client to access the secure folder **secureFolder** (6). Given that the credentials are the same as the ones stored in the database, and the database content is represented with the function **tuple()**, we can also represent credentials here with the function **tuple()**.[6]

---

[5] We do not consider the possibility of brute forcing the hashed password, in accordance with the perfect cryptography assumption of the DY model.

[6] We recall from Sect. 4.2 that **tuple()** represents an abstraction of any data that can be extracted from the database. This means that whenever a web app requires any data in the domain of the database, we can write them as a function of **tuple()**.

Listing 1.6. Pseudo-code representing the YAVWA scenario.

```
1  User -> WebApp: Username.Password;
2  WebApp -> DB: query(Username.Password);
3  if(DB -> WebApp: tuple(SQLquery)){
4    WebApp -> User: dashboard.tuple(SQLquery);
5  }elseif(DB -> WebApp: no_tuple){ WebApp -> User: login; }
6  if(User -> WebApp: tuple(*)){ WebApp -> User: secureFolder; }
```

As goal, we check if the intruder can reach **secureFolder**. SQLfast generates the AAT given in Listing 1.7, in which the intruder successfully retrieves information from the database and uses such information to access a protected folder. The intruder performs a data extraction attack using SQLi (1–4), which allows him to retrieve information stored in the database, and then (5–6) submits the extracted data and accesses the restricted folder **secureFolder**.

Listing 1.7. Abstract attack trace of the YAVWA case study.

```
1  User -> WebApp: Username(4).sqli
2  WebApp -> DB   : query(Username(4).sqli)
3  DB -> WebApp   : tuple(Username(4).sqli)
4  WebApp -> i    : dashboard.tuple(Username(4).sqli)
5  i   -> WebApp  : tuple(Username(4).sqli)
6  WebApp  -> i   : secureFolder
```

5.2   Case Study: Second-Order SQLi (SO)

We now show that our formalization is flexible enough to represent SOs, which are notoriously very difficult to detect and exploit.

This scenario is part of YAVWA and implements a web app that allows users to register a new account. In the registration process, the web app executes an (INSERT) SQL query that stores the user's credentials into a database. The intruder can create an account submitting malicious credentials that don't result in a SQLi but will trigger an injection later on in the web app. After the registration phase, the user submits a request for accessing an internal page. The web app performs another SQL query using the same parameters previously used in the registration process (i.e., the registration credentials). At this point, a page is showed together with the injection and the intruder can exploit a SO.

We have formalized this scenario in Listing 1.8: a client sends a registration request along with his personal credentials (**Username** and **Password**) to the web app (1). The web app sends a query containing the client's credentials to the database (2). The web app checks if it receives a response from the database containing the data resulting from the execution of the query **tuple(SQLquery)** submitted by the web app (3). The web app sends back to the client the page **registered** (4). Here, the web app does not forward **tuple()** because the registration query is an INSERT (see Sect. 4.2). The client asks for a page (5), which makes the web app use previously submitted values of **Username** and **Password** to execute a new SQL query (6). Here is where the SO takes place; the variables embedded in the query in (6) will trigger a SO. The database executes the query and sends back the results to the web app (7). Finally (8), the web app sends (by using a SELECT query) to the client the requested page and the tuple().[7]

Listing 1.8. Pseudo-code representing a web app vulnerable to a SO attack.

```
1  User -> WebApp: registrationRequest.Username.Password;
2  WebApp -> DB: query(Username.Password);
3  if(DB -> WebApp: tuple(SQLquery)){
4    WebApp -> User: registered;
5    User -> WebApp: requestPage;
6    WebApp -> DB: query(Username.Password);
7    DB -> WebApp: tuple(SQLquery);
8    WebApp -> User: page.tuple(SQLquery); }
```

As goal, we ask if the intruder can interact with the web app until he obtains data from the database, i.e., with a data extraction attack, as in Listing 1.2. SQLfast generates the AAT in Listing 1.9, in which the intruder performs the registration process (1–4) by registering malicious credentials Username(4) and sqli. At the end of the registration process (5), the intruder asks for requestPage that makes the web app send to the database a SQL query with the same parameters the intruder used in the registration (6–7). In (8), the intruder receives the requested page and the result of the execution of the injected SQL query performing a SO.

Listing 1.9. Abstract attack trace for the SO case study.

```
1  User -> WebApp: registrationRequest.Username(4).sqli
2  WebApp -> DB  : query(Username(4).sqli)
3  DB -> WebApp  : tuple(Username(4).sqli)
4  WebApp -> i   : registered
5  i -> WebApp   : requestPage
6  WebApp -> DB  : query(Username(4).sqli)
7  DB -> WebApp  : tuple(Username(4).sqli)
8  WebApp -> i   : page.tuple(Username(4).sqli)
```

5.3 Concretization Phase

We executed SQLfast on all our case studies using a standard laptop (Intel i7 with 8G RAM). The execution time of the model-checking phase of SQLfast ranges from 35 to 45 ms. The overall process (from translation to concretization) takes a few seconds. In all the cases, we generated AATs violating the security property we defined over the model (authentication bypass or data extraction attack). Once the AAT has been generated, SQLfast interactively asks the user to provide information such as the URL of the web app. Finally, if we are concretizing a SQLi that exploits an authentication bypass attack a curl command is showed, whereas sqlmap is used for data extraction SQLi. By executing the traces generated by SQLfast, we exploited all the AATs over the real web app.

6   Conclusions, Related Work, and Future Work

We have presented a formal approach for the representation of SQLi and attacks that exploit SQLi in order to violate security properties of web apps. We have

---

[7] Recall that we don't represent SQL syntax in our models, so we don't explicitly represent the type of the SQL according to the modeling guidelines in Sect. 4.3.

formally defined web apps that interact with a database (that properly replies to queries containing SQLi) and an extended DY intruder able to deal with authentication bypass and data extraction attacks related to SQLi. We have shown the efficiency of our prototype tool SQLfast on four real-world case studies (see also [10]). SQLfast handles SO and detects multi-stage attacks and logical flaws that, to the best of our knowledge, no other tool can handle together, and hardly ever even individually, including the discovery of an attack in Joomla!.

Many works have proposed new SQLi techniques and payloads (e.g., [9, 21, 35]) or formal approaches to detect SQLi (e.g., [16, 23–25]). However, to the best of our knowledge, ours is the first attempt to search for vulnerabilities based on SQLi rather than to detect SQLi. There are, however, a number of works that are closely related to ours and that are thus worth discussing.

SPaCiTE is a model-based security testing tool for web apps that relies on mutation testing [4]. SPaCiTE starts from a secure ASLan++ specification of a web app and automatically introduces flaws by mutating the specification. The strength of this approach is the concretization phase. Starting from an AAT, generated from the mutated specification using a model-checking phase, SPaCiTE concretizes and tests the attack trace on the real web app. The major differences with respect to our approach reside in how we model web apps and in particular those aspects that strictly characterize SQLi aspects. The main goal of the approach in [4] is to find SQLi entry points and concretize them, our main goal is to consider SQLi aspects that can be exploited to attack a web app.

Another formal approach that uses ASLan++ and the DY intruder model for the security analysis of web apps is [31]. In this work, the authors model a web app searching for CSRF and they do not consider databases or extensions to the DY model. However, the idea and the representation of web apps is close to ours and we envision some potentially useful interaction between the two approaches.

In [5], the authors describe the "Chained Attack" approach, which considers multiple attacks to compromise a web app. The idea is close to ours, but: (i) they consider a new kind of web intruder, whereas we stick with the DY intruder; (ii) we analyzed the most common SQLi techniques and proposed a formalization of a vulnerable database, they only consider the behavior of the web app.

In [1], the authors present a model-based method for the security verification of web apps. They propose a methodology for modeling web apps and model 5 case studies in Alloy [20]. Even if the idea is similar to our approach, they have defined three different intruder models that should find web attacks, whereas we have used (and extended) the standard DY one. Their AATs are difficult to interpret because no MSCs are given but state configurations. They have also considered a number of HTTP details that we have instead abstracted away in favor of an easier modeling phase. In contrast, we display AAT as MSCs and we proposed a concretization phase to obtain the concrete payloads of SQLi.

As future work, we plan to extend the database formalization in order to consider SQLi that would modify the database state leading to more complex SQLi exploitations. We also plan to analyze other web app vulnerabilities such as stored/reflected XSS and broken session management, and investigate synergies between our approach and the one of [31] on CSRF. We will extend our approach to detect (i) complex concatenations of vulnerabilities (similar to, and more complex than, [17]) that lead to concatenations of attacks, and (ii) articulated paths to vulnerabilities that would hardly ever be discovered by manual analysis.

References

1. Akhawe, D., Barth, A., Lam, P., Mitchell, J., Song, D.: Towards a formal foundation of web security. In: CSF, pp. 290–304. IEEE (2010)
2. Apache software foundation. Apache HTTP Server Tutorial: .htaccess files. https://httpd.apache.org/docs/current/howto/htaccess.html
3. Armando, A., et al.: The AVANTSSAR platform for the automated validation of trust and security of service-oriented architectures. In: Flanagan, C., König, B. (eds.) TACAS 2012. LNCS, vol. 7214, pp. 267–282. Springer, Heidelberg (2012)
4. Büchler, M., Oudinet, J., Pretschner, A.: Semi-automatic security testing of web applications from a secure model. In: SERE, pp. 253–262 (2012)
5. Calvi, A., Viganò, L.: An automated approach for testing the security of web applications against chained attacks. In: ACM/SIGAPP SAC. ACM Press (2016)
6. Christey, S.: The 2009 CWE/SANS Top 25 Most Dangerous Programming Errors. http://cwe.mitre.org/top25
7. CVE-2015-7857. https://cve.mitre.org/cgi-bin/cvename.cgi?name=CVE-2015-7857
8. CWE. CWE-89: Improper Neutralization of Special Elements used in an SQL Command ('SQL Injection'). https://cwe.mitre.org/data/definitions/89.html
9. Damele, B., Guimarães, A.: Advanced SQL injection to operating system full control. In: BlackHat EU (2009)
10. De Meo, F., Rocchetto, M., Viganò, L.: Formal Analysis of Vulnerabilities of Web Applications Based on SQL Injection (Extended Version) (2016). arXiv:1605.00358
11. Dolev, D., Yao, A.C.: On the security of public key protocols. IEEE Trans. Inf. Theory 29(2), 198–208 (1983)
12. Doupé, A., Cova, M., Vigna, G.: Why Johnny can't pentest: an analysis of black-box web vulnerability scanners. In: Kreibich, C., Jahnke, M. (eds.) DIMVA 2010. LNCS, vol. 6201, pp. 111–131. Springer, Heidelberg (2010)
13. Damn Vulnerable Web Application (DVWA). http://www.dvwa.co.uk
14. Forristal, J.: ODBC and MS SQL server 6.5. Phrack 8(54) (1998). Article 08
15. Halfond, W.G., Viegas, J., Orso, A.: A classification of SQL-injection attacks and countermeasures. In: SIGSOFT 2006/FSE-14 (2006)
16. Halfond, W.G.J., Orso, A.: AMNESIA: analysis and monitoring for NEutralizing SQL–injection attacks. In: ASE, pp. 174–183. IEEE (2005)
17. Homakov, E.: How I hacked Github again (2014). http://homakov.blogspot.it/2014/02/how-i-hacked-github-again.html
18. Internet Engineering Task Force (IETF). HTTP Authentication: Basic and Digest Access Authentication (1999). https://www.ietf.org/rfc/rfc2617.txt
19. iSpiderLabs. Joomla SQL Injection Vulnerability Exploit Results in Full Administrative (2015). https://www.trustwave.com/Resources/SpiderLabs-Blog/Joomla-SQL-Injection-Vulnerability-Exploit-Results-in-Full-Administrative-Access/?page=1&year=0&month=0. Accessed
20. Jackson, D., Abstractions, S.: Logic, Language, and Analysis. MIT Press, Cambridge (2012)

21. Jayathissa, O.M.: SQL Injection in Insert, Update and Delete Statements
22. Joomla! https://www.joomla.org
23. Kieżun, A., Guo, P.J., Jayaraman, K., Ernst, M.D.: Automatic creation of SQL injection and cross-site scripting attacks. In: ICSE, pp. 199–209. IEEE (2009)
24. Livshits, V.B., Lam, M.S.: Finding security vulnerabilities in Java applications with static analysis. In: USENIX, p. 18 (2005)
25. Martin, M., Lam, M.S.: Automatic generation of XSS and SQL injection attacks with goal-directed model checking. In: USENIX, pp. 31–43 (2008)
26. MySQL. https://www.mysql.com
27. OWASP. Owasp top 10 for 2013. https://www.owasp.org/index.php/Category:OWASP_Top_Ten_Project
28. OWASP. SQL Injection. https://www.owasp.org/index.php/SQL_Injection
29. OWASP. WebGoat Project. https://www.owasp.org/index.php/Category:OWASP_WebGoat_Project
30. PostgreSQL. http://www.postgresql.org
31. Rocchetto, M., Ochoa, M., Torabi Dashti, M.: Model-based detection of CSRF. In: Cuppens-Boulahia, N., Cuppens, F., Jajodia, S., Abou El Kalam, A., Sans, T. (eds.) SEC 2014. IFIP AICT, vol. 428, pp. 30–43. Springer, Heidelberg (2014)
32. SQLfast: SQL Formal AnalisyS Tool (2015). http://regis.di.univr.it/sqlfast/
33. sqlmap: Automatic SQL injection and database takeover tool (2013). http://sqlmap.org
34. sqlninja: a SQL Server injection & takeover tool (2013). http://sqlninja.sourceforge.net
35. Stampar, M.: Data Retrieval over DNS in SQL Injection Attacks (2013). http://arxiv.org/abs/1303.3047
36. Viganò, L.: The SPaCIoS project: secure provision and consumption in the internet of services. In: ICST, pp. 497–498 (2013)

MalloryWorker: Stealthy Computation and Covert Channels Using Web Workers

Michael Rushanan[✉], David Russell, and Aviel D. Rubin

Department of Computer Science, Johns Hopkins University, Baltimore, MD, USA
{micharu1,drusse19,rubin}@cs.jhu.edu

Abstract. JavaScript execution and UI rendering are typically single-threaded; thus, the execution of some scripts can block the display of requested content to the browser screen. Web Workers is an API that enables web applications to spawn background workers in parallel to the main page. Despite the usefulness of concurrency, users are unaware of worker execution, intent, and impact on system resources. We show that workers can be used to abuse system resources by implementing a unique denial-of-service attack and resource depletion attack. We also show that workers can be used to perform stealthy computation and create covert channels. We discuss potential mitigations and implement a preliminary solution to increase user awareness of worker execution.

Keywords: Web security · Stealthy computation · Covert channel

1 Introduction

Adobe Flash is an example third-party plugin that extends functionality like video streaming to web applications. HTML5 eliminates this necessity by providing new APIs that improve core functionality of the web browser (herein browser). Web Workers is one such API specified by the World Wide Web Consortium (W3C) [11] and Web Hypertext Application Technology Working Group (WHATWG) [10]. Web Workers enable web applications to spawn background *workers* (i.e., threads) in parallel to the main page. Workers are intended for long-lived and computationally intensive operations that would otherwise block the UI.

Encryption, motion detection, and simulated annealing are use cases for workers. Any application that has to have its execution broken up to avoid being prematurely terminated by the browser is a candidate for workers.

Despite the usefulness of concurrency in JavaScript, permissive execution of workers enables stealthy computation. Workers are instantiated unbeknownst to the user of a web application and can perform any number of computations. An attacker can cause a user to perform work for her by exploiting a cross-site scripting (XSS) vulnerability on a legitimate website or by placing an advertisement that hides the work in a worker.

© Springer International Publishing AG 2016
G. Barthe et al. (Eds.): STM 2016, LNCS 9871, pp. 196–211, 2016.
DOI: 10.1007/978-3-319-46598-2_14

We demonstrate the feasibility of stealthy computation using workers by implementing a distributed password cracker that uses the Web Workers API. We can compute 500,000 MD5 hashes per second using the Chrome 50.0.2661.94 browser on a Mid-2013 MacBook Air. We also implement a denial-of-service (DoS) attack that is unique to how OS X manages virtual memory. We define *wasteful* stealthy computation that exploits garbage collection mechanisms in Chrome, Firefox 46.0.1, and Safari 9.1. The execution of this computation results in high CPU and memory utilization that eventually fills the swap partition and causes a deadlock.

We target the Android browser and Android Chrome browser to perform wasteful stealthy computation on a mobile platform. We find exploiting garbage collection results in a resource depletion attack against the browsers. In fact, 55 % of CPU load, 45 % of memory usage, and an approximate 4°F increase in temperature was the direct result of five minutes of stealthy computation. We did not attempt this on the mobile Safari browser for iOS but believe that it is also susceptible because its operating system counterpart is. The mobile Safari browser is not susceptible to the DoS attack because it manages virtual memory differently than OS X.

A natural criticism to stealthy computation using workers is that a worker is *unnecessary* to perform attacker-controlled computation such as the DoS attack mentioned above. While the UI thread can carry out this type of computation, the thread becomes unresponsive and is later terminated by the browser. JavaScript Window Timers like setTimeOut avoid blocking the UI thread by executing code at specified time intervals. However, we find that our stealthy computation still results in unresponsiveness and later termination when using setTimeOut.

Lampson, when defining the confinement problem, first introduces covert channels as information leakage between processes that facilitate communication [14]. Covert channels are difficult to identify because other processes often obscure them. For example, CPU cycles can be used as a covert channel and it is affected by every single process on a system. Further, application firewalls and anti-virus software typically block non-whitelisted ports and anomalous behavior, not profile software system resource utilization.

We describe and implement a covert channel that is not unique to workers but is easily implemented using them. Our covert channel uses CPU and memory throttling to transmit bits to an unauthorized application. We find that CPU throttling is noisier than memory throttling because other processes can obscure our covertly transmitted bits (i.e., a random peak can corrupt bits or semantic structures such as a preamble). We throttle memory by exploiting garbage collection to create a peak and then terminating the web worker to force garbage collection.

This covert channel enables an attacker to transmit data from a website to an application on the user's system. This application may be untrusted or malicious. The attacker can send command-and-control instructions, binary updates, and sensitive data about the user's browsing without detection as browsers typically use a range of system resources depending on viewed content.

We scanned 7000 websites from Alexa's top sites to determine the prevalence of worker use. We found that 1.2 % of them use workers to perform some computation. Websites such as yahoo.com, usbank.com, and mediafire.com use workers for various reasons. For example, usbank.com uses a worker defined in `foresee-worker.js` to compress session event logs.

In this paper, we are concerned with using the Web Workers API to create workers that enable stealthy computation and covert channels. We demonstrate the feasibility of these by implementing our own distributed password cracker using workers, a DoS attack against OS X, a resource depletion attack against Android, and a covert channel using memory throttling. We provide the necessary background for JavaScript code execution and Web Workers, discuss related work focused on HTML5 vulnerabilities, and we give the first mitigation strategy for the misuse of workers.

2 Background

Browsers typically have one thread that JavaScript and the UI share. Therefore, UI updates are blocked while the JavaScript interpreter executes code and vice versa. A shared task queue enables asynchronous execution of JavaScript and UI updates, allowing either to execute when the thread is available. Asynchronous execution does not solve the problem of an arbitrary script taking unusually long. The browser attempts to terminate any script that takes longer than some threshold regardless of its purpose or importance. The user is aware of this when the UI freezes. Not much later, the browser presents a status (i.e., terminate or continue) or crash message.

The browser's approach to ending long-running scripts is undesirable because it provides no context per the scripts execution. The user is unaware of what the script is meant to do and how long it has been running. Web application developers approach this issue by leveraging asynchronous execution and dividing their scripts into logical chunks that execute on some period. This method does not benefit from parallel execution where a computation is uninterrupted until it finishes.

HTML5 addresses these limitations with the Web Workers API. This API enables web applications to spawn background workers in parallel to the main page. Workers are unable to access the Dynamic Object Model (DOM) or the callers (i.e., parent object) variables and functions. Workers are instantiated as one of two types: shared or dedicated.

Shared workers can be accessed by multiple web applications but dedicated workers cannot. Web applications instantiate both shared and dedicated workers by providing a script object to the `Worker` constructor. The script object is either an externally loaded file or defined *inline* as a string description of the worker.

The string description is provided as input to the `blob` constructor, a file-like object, and is referenced by an output URL handle. This URL handle is provided to the `Worker` constructor. Listing 1.1 is an example inline instantiation. We note that inline instantiation is important to our threat model because attackers that inject malicious scripts must be able to inject a worker.

```
<script id="mw" type="javascript/worker">
  self.onmessage = function(event) {
    self.postMessage({'msg': 'hello.',});
  }
</script>
<script language="javascript">
  var blob = new Blob([document.querySelector('#mw').
    textContext]);
  var m_worker = new Worker(window.URL.createObjectURL(
    blob));
</script>
```

Listing 1.1. Instantiate worker using blob.

Workers support communication with each other and their parent object via message passing. The `onMessage` method listens for messages and upon receiving one it will call the `postMessage` method to send a message. Workers continue to listen for messages until the user navigates away from the web application, or the parent object calls the `terminate` method on the worker. Terminating a web worker causes garbage collection on all allocated memory.

3 Threat Model

We use the definition of a *web attacker* and *gadget attacker* by Akhawe et al. [4] to define an attacker that maliciously misuses workers. A web attacker operates a malicious web application but has no visibility into the network beyond the requests directed to her application. A gadget attacker can inject content into otherwise legitimate web applications.

A web attacker that misuses workers hosts a web application with a mechanism for generating traffic (e.g., misleading domain name or social engineering). Every time a user visits the web application, stealthy computation is performed via a worker or workers. A gadget attacker that misuses workers exploits web vulnerabilities such as cross-site scripting to inject her workers. She may also purchase a web advertisement and bundle her workers in the ad. A user that visits a legitimate site will now perform some stealthy computation.

A web attacker is considered an insider threat; for example, a web application administrator. A gadget attacker is an outside threat. She is simply a web application user. We consider both attackers to be unsophisticated as neither has visibility or control of the network. Also, both attackers rely on generally accessible tools such as a laptop, internet access, and at most a web server.

The goals of both a web attacker and gadget attacker that misuse workers include: performing stealthy computation, mounting a DoS or resource depletion attack, and establishing a covert channel with an untrusted or malicious application. While we do not describe how to install such an application, we consider all typical malware delivery methods (e.g., flash drives, e-mail, etc.).

4   Web Worker Primitives

While creating stealthy computation is as simple as writing function x, a wasteful computation needs to exploit garbage collection mechanisms for multiple browsers. Covert channels also require a mechanism for throttling a system's CPU and Memory. We introduce three primitives to achieve wasteful stealthy computation: infinite loop sequences, CPU throttling, and memory throttling.

```
var cpu_work = function() {
  var scratch = [];

  // Fill the ArrayBuffer with random values.
  for(var j = 0; j < 1024; j++) {
      scratch.push(Math.random());
  }

  var firstArr = new Uint8Array(scratch);
  var secondArr = new Uint8Array(scratch);

  // ArrayBuffer concatenation.
  var concatBuf = new Uint8Array(firstArr.byteLength +
      secondArr.byteLength);
  concatBuf.set(new Uint8Array(firstArr), 0);
  concatBuf.set(new Uint8Array(secondArr), firstArr.length
      );
}
```

Listing 1.2. Browser CPU throttling.

Infinite Loop Sequences. An infinite loop is a sequence of instructions which loops endlessly because the boolean condition never changes (e.g., it always evaluates true). If an infinite loop is executed by the JavaScript interpreter, the browser UI will freeze due to blocking on the shared thread. However, blocking does not occur if this loop is executed in a worker.

We use an infinite loop such as `while(true){}` to perform a wasteful stealthy computation. This type of computation enables CPU and memory throttling. Again, the execution of this loop is undetected by the user because it does not block the UI thread.

CPU Throttling. Executing an empty infinite loop alone will throttle a modern CPU. We achieve throttling by looping on intensive operations such as recursive function calls and large data manipulation to quickly achieve maximum CPU utilization. Listing 1.2 implements a data manipulation loop that randomly fills two 1024-byte arrays and then concatenates them.

Memory Throttling. Throttling memory is browser specific as it exploits corner-cases not yet handled by the browser's garbage collection. We note that the browser does, in fact, do garbage collection correctly; however, the process is approximate as deciding whether memory can be freed is *undecidable*. We use this knowledge to our advantage to discover browser-specific memory leaks and use them to throttle system memory.

In Listing 1.3 we use a technique outlined by Glasser [9] to demonstrate a memory leak in Firefox. This technique relies on JavaScript closures. Specifically, both unused and bucket are both defined inside of RD_ATTACK_FIREFOX_SAFARI scope, and if both functions access the variable leak it's imperative that both get the same object. So leak is never garbage collected.

In our experimentation with these primitives, we crashed Firefox and Chrome when throttling CPU and memory. We mitigate this by using the worker method terminate(). This method helps us avoid crashing the browser and completes our throttling primitives by exposing a mechanism for quickly freeing system resources.

```
var bucket = null;
var RD_ATTACK_FIREFOX_SAFARI = function () {
  var leak = bucket;
  var unused = function () {
    if (leak) {
      var hole_in_bucket = 1;
    }
  };
  bucket = {
    longStr: new Array(10000000).join(Math.random()),
    someMethod: function () {
      var hole_in_bucket = 2;
    }
  };
  // Placeholder for doing some repetitive operation.
  cpu_work();
};
```

Listing 1.3. Firefox memory throttling.

5   Stealthy Computation

We demonstrate the feasibility of stealthy computation using workers by implementing a distributed password cracker that uses the Web Workers API. We implement the main HTML page to define a target MD5 password hash, a worker instantiation, and an event listener to receive the result of password cracking (i.e., an MD5 collision was found).

The worker instantiation is on input md5cracker.js. This worker script defines the MD5 hashing algorithm, a dictionary download method, and the event listeners start and stop.

The start listener waits to receive the onMessage start string. When it receives the string, it downloads an array of passwords using the method importScripts(). This method synchronously imports a script into the worker's scope. We use it to import an array of passwords because we want the worker

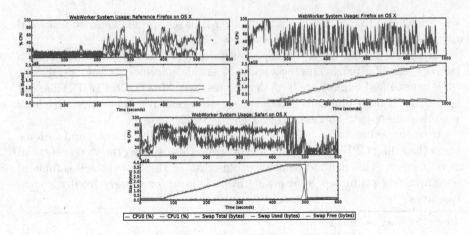

Fig. 1. OS X DoS attack.

to be self-contained. Specifically, if an attacker should inject a worker or upload an advertisement with a worker, she can not rely on the calling parent object to pass in any data such as an array of passwords.

After downloading the array, the worker selects a random index into the array and begins to hash each password and compares it to the target hash. If it finds a collision, it returns the result to the parent object, or it could use a web socket to send it elsewhere (e.g., the attacker's server).

The stop listener simply kills the worker once it is no longer useful.

We send 1 million passwords to the worker using `importScripts` which is approximately 13 MB. This step adds approximately 50 % latency on the dataset and takes 3 s to download. We can minimize this time by compressing the password array and partitioning it into multiple arrays. The password cracker performs 500 K hashes per second on a Mid-2013 MacBook Air.

The average user visits a website for no longer than 15 s. Thus, one might think that workers that perform stealthy computation do not have much time to carry out any worthwhile computation. We find that media streaming sites such as Youtube or SoundCloud are ideal web applications for stealthy computation because users will remain on the page for a time much greater than 15 s. In addition, this technique has been proven via projects that unintentionally do stealthy computation using workers such as bitcoin mining [6]. We are the first, that we know, to point out the scope (i.e., all modern browsers) and potential of this type of computation.

5.1   Denial-of-Service

We use our loop and memory throttle primitives to mount a DoS attack against any 64-bit OS X device. This DoS is unique to OS X because of how virtual memory is handled. Specifically, OS X can grow its swap to the maximum available size of the backing store – the portion of hard disk responsible for storing

virtual memory pages. On 32-bit systems the backing store is limited to 4 giga-
bytes, whereas 64-bit OS X systems can use up to 18 exabytes. Therefore, if we
exploit garbage collection for an extended period, OS X will continually write
out memory pages until deadlock. The period required for deadlock depends on
the amount of memory leaked and the available space on disk.

In one test on a Mid-2013 MacBook Air with 50 GB free, 10 MB was leaked
each loop iteration and deadlock occurred after 15 min. We can adjust the memory throttle primitive to allocate more memory each iteration and speed up
deadlock.

This attack is successfully executed on Firefox and Safari only (specifically,
versions Firefox 46.0.1 and Safari 9.1 (11601.5.17.1)). In Firefox, deadlock is
always achieved since the upper-bound on paged memory is the full 18 exabytes.
Deadlock is only achieved in Safari if the user has less than 32 GB available on
disk. Otherwise, the browser kills the process.

We note that running the attack in a worker results in no UI indication; the
user is unaware of the DoS attack. This is especially poignant in Firefox and
Chrome, where running the attack *without* a worker results in an 'Unresponsive
Script' notification. In Safari, no indication is given regardless of the payload's
delivery (via UI thread or web worker). We therefore find that Safari and Firefox are susceptible to this attack, with Firefox's viability being dependent on
workers.

The steadily growing swap in Fig. 1 depicts our exploitation of garbage collection in Firefox and Safari. In the upper-left we have a normal profile of the
browser's swap and CPU loads. The low-CPU section corresponds to no browser
interaction on a static page. In the upper right and central figures, the scale for
swap usage is now 10 GB. In the upper-right, swap is filled until deadlock occurs
around 24 GB (the max available on the test system). In the central figure, swap
is filled until it hits the 32 GB threshold, at which point Safari kills the process.
In both cases, when deadlock occurs, OS X needs to be hard rebooted in order to
recover. Fortunately, disk space is recovered and the swap returns to its original
size.

5.2   Resource Depletion

The mobile Chrome browser also supports the Web Workers API. Figure 2
depicts user memory usage as it steadily increases from the stealthy computation. The over usage of memory results in I/O waiting toward the end of our
experiment. Stealthy computation can exacerbate resource depletion as it uses
system resources to perform wasteful work. Figure 3 illustrates resource depletion
in terms of its effects on the battery. When the attack is initiated, battery temperature immediately spikes more than 8° F (in orange). Furthermore, projected
battery lifetime drops significantly.

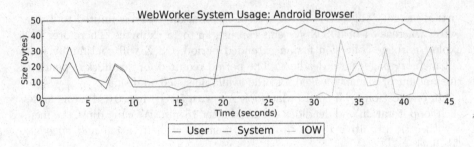

Fig. 2. Android Chrome resource depletion attack.

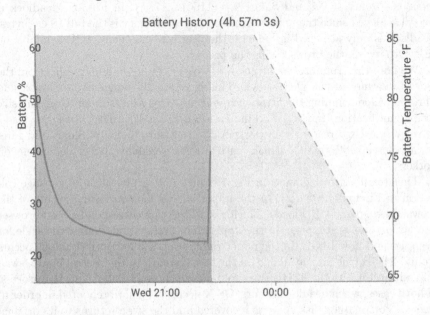

Fig. 3. Android Chrome resource depletion attack. (Color figure online)

6   Covert Channel

A covert channel is a communication mechanism for two processes that are not supposed to be able or allowed to communicate. For example, Lampson first described a covert channel based on a program's effect on system resources [14]. The program attempting to transmit information can vary resources such as I/O or memory, and the receiver will observe the change. While this is a noisy channel, it can be corrected given a message encoding. Other covert channels include cache-memory bus interactions [19], CPU scheduling [12], and network packets and protocols [7,15]. These covert channels are timing channels because they transmit information by modulating system resources. Storage channels require access to storage locations whereby the transmission of information is written and read from the filesystem.

We use. our CPU and memory throttling primitives to create a covert channel between a web application and some untrusted or malicious application on the user's system. The application is a desktop or mobile application that only requires access to monitor system resources, which is an unprivileged operation.

Application firewalls and anti-virus software can block TCP connections to non-whitelisted ports and anomalous behavior. Our covert channel circumvents these technologies by not using a standard channel like TCP. Further, if the covert channel could be identified, the result would be to block the entire browser. An attacker can use this channel to deliver command-and-control instructions, binary updates, and sensitive data about the user's browsing.

The use of both CPU and memory throttling primitives and the unauthorized application constitutes a timing channel. The web application, or injected script, transmits information about the user's browsing to the unauthorized application. Like other timing-based covert channels, this is difficult to detect. However, the covert channel cannot transmit information to other JavaScript scripts because the browser isolates execution and disallows access to system resources with sandboxing.

We first try CPU throttling to observe messages with a simple structure. Specifically, we do not define a pre or postamble; rather, we define a period in which to observe a bit based upon a CPU usage spike. We find that the CPU channel is noisy, as seen in Fig. 4, and we can only achieve good accuracy by employing a high sampling rate. Unfortunately, we use PSUTIL to get current CPU usage and it imposes a sampling rate with a minimum bound of 100 milliseconds. Also due to JavaScript runtime limitations, anything less than one millisecond isn't feasible.

We attempt to minimize CPU noise by increasing the length between CPU spikes to 500 milliseconds and 1 s. We can obtain bits in the covert channel but under ideal conditions. For example, if any other work is done in the browser it significantly impacts our ability to discern relevant CPU spikes.

Next, we try our memory throttling primitive. Memory usage is a more deterministic channel and thus less noisy than CPU usage. This makes it more viable as a covert channel. We use our memory throttling primitive to fill a 40MB array and then clear the memory with a **terminate** worker method call. We can successfully send 1 bit per 5 s. We send the bits for "hello world" in Fig. 4. Unlike the CPU covert channel, the memory covert channel is usable when the user browses the internet or streams videos. This finding is a consequence of the amount of memory used which far exceeds the memory needed to buffer a video in our tests.

We note that our covert channel does not require a web worker. However, when executing the covert channel in the UI thread, the browser is noticeably less responsive due to the looping execution of the memory primitive. Moreover, we find that, unlike workers, we do not have a mechanism to force garbage collection and thus create a clean signal (i.e., discernible peaks in memory). We also implement the covert channel with **setTimeout** and find it to be intractable. Web workers are unaffected by these limitations. Our ability to force garbage

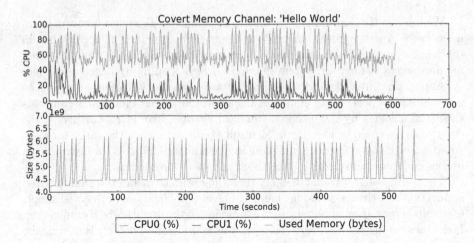

Fig. 4. Memory covert channel sending hello world.

collection by terminating the worker allows for distinct, deterministic memory peaks, as shown in Fig. 4.

We implement and test this covert channel on OS X 10.11.4 using the Firefox 46.0.1 and Chrome 50.0.2661.94 browsers. The covert channel is inefficient regarding channel bandwidth; we can send approximately 1 bit per 5 s. We can speed this up by reducing the amount of memory throttled (e.g., less than 2 GB peaks), by increasing the size of the leak to fill memory faster, and by using multiple workers to concurrently fill swap.

7   Potential Mitigations

The challenge for the Web Workers API is how to inform users a worker is executing, what the intent of the execution is, and how the execution is impacting system resources. We assert that the most effective solution is to provide fine-grained controls for workers similar to browser pop-up controls, and to restrict the Web Workers API in the ECMAScript specification. We envision a system administrator or user with an understanding of computer processes interacting with a dialog box that lists the options: Do not allow any site to execute computationally intensive scripts, Inform me when any site executes computationally intensive scripts (Recommended), Allow all sites to execute computationally intensive scripts.

In the interim, we implement a browser extension to mitigate worker stealthy computations partially. This mitigation is partial because the browser extension only informs the user of when a worker has executed. If the worker is named appropriately, the user is provided with some context of the workers intent, but name mangling and poor coding practices will undo this. We call our browser extension *wAudit*.

wAudit is a Google Chrome content script. Content scripts use the Document Object Model (DOM) to read and modify details of a visited web page. These scripts, however, cannot use or modify variables or functions defined by the visited web page. For wAudit to determine whether a worker exists it must be able to the later.

We programatically inject wAudit as a script into visited web pages using `document.createElement`. This function creates an HTML script element that we append to the document object's root element using the function `document.documentElement.appendChild`. The injected script recursively searches all DOM objects and identifies object types of `[object Worker]`.

The script alerts the user if it finds a worker or workers by drawing a banner at the bottom of the browser window. This banner includes the name of the worker and a UI button for terminating a selected worker. We implement the terminate function by crafting the string `"workers[i]+".terminate()"`. This string contains the worker name and the method call to terminate. We call `eval` on the string input to execute.

8 Related Work

Security researchers have found numerous vulnerabilities in the HTML5 APIs that enable traditional web application attacks such as CSRF and clickjacking, and HTML5-specific attacks such as cache poisoning and botnets.

Tian et al. [18] show that the HTML5 screen-sharing API can allow for cross-site request forgery (CSRF) attacks, even if the target website utilizes CSRF defenses such SSL and secure random tokens. The authors are also able to sniff user account, autocomplete, and browsing history data because it can be viewed directly on the user's screen.

The HTML5 FullScreen API displays web content that fills the user's entire screen. Aboukhadijeh [3] describes how a malicious website can trick users into clicking a link to a legitimate website (e.g., https://www.bankofamerica.com/), and then display a malicious website in fullscreen.

Kuppan [13] overviews multiple HTML5-specific attacks. For example, an attacker can use the HTML5 Drag and Drop API to trick users into setting target form fields with attacker controlled data, a clickjacking attack. An attacker can poison HTML5 caches designed to enable offline browsing with her own pages that recover user supplied data. Specific to our work, workers enable HTML5 botnets. These botnets can mount distributed denial-of-service (DDoS) attacks by sending cross-domain XMLHttpRequests.

Anibal Sacco et al. [16] use workers to optimize heap-spray attacks. By employing multiple workers, the authors show that they can populate the target systems' memory faster than conventional heap-spray attacks. They leverage HTML5 canvas objects to obtain both full control over consecutive heap pages and to provide byte-level access to pixel information. This gives four bytes per pixel for use in spray contents – typically a use-after-free exploit, heap-based buffer overflow, or ROP chain. Also, due to the increasing prevalence of browser-based devices with HTML5 support (smartphones, TVs, consoles, etc.) the use of workers as an attack vector are largely platform and browser agnostic.

The Open Web Application Security Project (OWASP) blog [2] mentions the use of workers to perform DoS attacks. The post gives a cursory treatment of these vulnerabilities and does not provide any concrete details regarding implementation, measurement, or countermeasures.

In general, defenses for HTML5 API vulnerabilities include modifications to the APIs. Son and Shmatikov [17] find that many web applications perform origin checks incorrectly, if at all. The lack of stringent checking allows for cross-site scripting (XSS) attacks, as well as data injection into local storage. The authors propose accepting only messages from the origin of the page that loaded a frame and the parent of that frame.

Akhawe et al. [5] find that HTML5 web applications need better privilege separation. Rather than advocate for browser redesign or artificial limits on partitions, the authors propose a way for HTML5 applications to create an arbitrary number of unprivileged components. Each component executes with its own temporary origin, isolated from the rest of the components.

9 Conclusions

We described how the Web Workers API can be used to create workers that enable stealthy computation and covert channels. We demonstrated the feasibility of stealthy computation by implementing a distributed password cracker using workers, a DoS attack against OS X, and a resource depletion attack against Android. We evaluated the feasibility of a covert channel using CPU and memory throttling, and implemented the latter. Lastly, we gave the first mitigation strategy for the misuse of workers.

Acknowledgments. This research was funded by the National Science Foundation under award number CNS-1329737. The views and conclusions contained in this document are those of the authors and should not be interpreted as necessarily representing the official policies, either expressed or implied, of the sponsors.

Appendix: Health and Medical Systems

Health and medical systems are increasingly becoming networked. An industry report by Parks Associates predicts that networked medical systems will exceed 14 million sales in 2018 [1]. These medical systems often employ commodity operating systems such as Windows Embedded and can access and be accessed over the internet.

We investigate the effects of running stealthy computation on Baxa ExactaMix. The Baxa ExactaMix is an embedded health and medical system that mixes total parenteral nutrition and other multi-ingredient solutions. The compounder runs Windows XP Embedded 2002 Service Pack 2 and has a 664 MHz

VIA C5 × 86 CPU with 496 MB of memory [8]. It also has Internet Explorer version 6.0, which does not support HTML5 APIs. However, since the Baxa ExactaMix can access the internet, we can install a modern browser. We installed Firefox 29 at the time of this experiment. We note that modern medical systems use more recent operating systems and thus support Web Workers without installing a third-party browser.

In our experiment, we first start the Baxa ExactaMix and wait for it to run its clinical software. We then begin measuring the CPU, memory, and swap usage of the device to establish a baseline of activity. Next, we launch Firefox and navigate to a website that we control. This website uses a worker to perform our stealthy computation, specifically, the DoS attack we describe earlier in Sect. 5. We continue our measurements for 3 min.

Results. We note a clear delineation between pre- and post-worker computation in Fig. 5. Memory and swap usage are at 60 % and 20 %, respectively, when the Baxa ExactaMix first starts. As this is a single-core device, the CPU utilization remains high for the entire experiment because all processes are scheduled to execute on the same core. We note linearly increasing memory usage and a near-instantaneous spike in swap usage to 60 % when we visit our website that performs the stealthy computation.

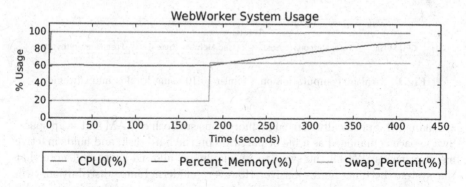

Fig. 5. Stealthy computation on Baxa ExactaMix.

Appendix: Linux Stealthy Computation

We experiment with stealthy computation on other operating systems. We find that Chrome 48.0.2564.103 and Firefox 41.0.2 in Ubuntu 15.10 both allow stealthy computation using web workers. Figure 6 illustrates CPU and memory throttling in Chrome and Firefox. We can use these primitives to implement our covert channel as described in Sect. 6.

We also test our DoS attack described in Sect. 5.1. This attack does not work in Ubuntu, and Linux in general, because of how virtual memory and processes

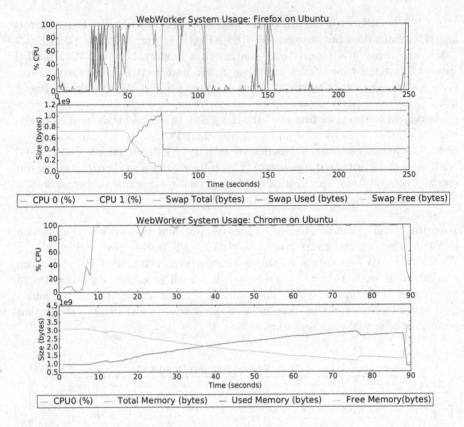

Fig. 6. Stealthy computation on Ubuntu 15.10 using Firefox and Chrome.

are managed. Specifically, virtual memory consists both of RAM and swap space. Swap space is managed as a file or partition on the hard disk, and holds inactive memory pages. We fill the swap to its maximum allowed space and note that the system becomes unresponsive. However, modern Linux distributions will terminate processes that consume resources, thus, we notice that free memory decreases and then rapidly increases when the process is killed in Fig. 6.

References

1. Networked medical devices to exceed 14 million unit sales in 2018, December 2013. https://www.parksassociates.com/blog/article/dec2013-medical-devices
2. Html5 security cheat sheet, April 2014. https://www.owasp.org/index.php/HTML5_Security_Cheat_Sheet#Web_Workers/
3. Aboukhadijeh, F.: Using the HTML5 fullscreen api for phishing attacks, October 2012. http://feross.org/html5-fullscreen-api-attack/. Accessed 27 May 2014

4. Akhawe, D., Barth, A., Lam, P.E., Mitchell, J., Song, D.: Towards a formal foundation of web security. In: Proceedings of the 2010 23rd IEEE Computer Security Foundations Symposium, pp. 290–304. IEEE Computer Society (2010). http://dx. doi.org/10.1109/CSF.2010.27

5. Akhawe, D., Saxena, P., Song, D.: Privilege separation in html5 applications. In: Proceedings of the 21st USENIX Conference on Security Symposium, p. 23, August 2012. http://dl.acm.org/citation.cfm?id=2362793.2362816

6. Biniok, J.: Hash me if you can - a bitcoin miner that supports pure javscript, webworker and webgl mining (2015). https://github.com/derjanb/hamiyoca

7. Cabuk, S., Brodley, C.E., Shields, C.: Ip covert timing channels: Design and detection. In: Proceedings of the 11th ACM Conference on Computer and Communications Security, CCS 04, pp. 178–187. ACM, New York (2004). http://doi.acm.org/ 10.1145/1030083.1030108

8. Clark, S.S., Ransford, B., Rahmati, A., Guineau, S., Sorber, J., Xu, W., Fu, K.: Wattsupdoc: power side channels to nonintrusively discover untargeted malware on embedded medical devices. In: Presented as part of the 2013 USENIX Workshop on Health Information Technologies, USENIX (2013)

9. Glasser, D.: An interesting kind of javascript memory leak (2014). http://info. meteor.com/blog/an-interesting-kind-of-javascript-memory-leak

10. Group, W.H.A.T.W.: Web workers, July 2014. http://www.whatwg.org/specs/ web-apps/current-work/multipage/workers.html

11. Hickson, I.: Web workers editor's draft, 19 May 2014. http://www.w3.org/TR/ workers/

12. Huskamp, J.C.: Covert communication channels in timesharing systems. Ph.D. thesis, California Univ., Berkeley (1978)

13. Kuppan, L.: Attacking with HTML5. In: Black Hat Abu Dhabi, October 2010. https://www.usenix.org/conference/healthsec12/workshop-program/presentation/ Chang

14. Lampson, B.W.: A note on the confinement problem. Commun. ACM **16**(10), 613–615 (1973). http://doi.acm.org/10.1145/362375.362389

15. Rowland, C.H.: Covert channels in the tcp/ip protocol suite. First Monday B(5) (1997). http://firstmonday.org/ojs/index.php/fm/article/view/528

16. Sacco, A., Muttis, F.: Html5 heap sprays, pwn all the things (2012). https:// eusecwest.com/speakers.html, eUSecWest

17. Son, S., Shmatikov, V.: The postman always rings twice: Attacking and defending postmessage in html5 websites. In: Proceedings of the 20th Annual Network and Distributed System Security Symposium (NDSS). The Internet Society (2013). http://dblp.uni-trier.de/db/conf/ndss/ndss2013.html#SonS13

18. Tian, Y., Liu, Y.C., Bhosale, A., Huang, L.S., Tague, P., Jackson, C.: All your screens are belong to us: Attacks exploiting the HTML5 screen sharing api. In: Proceedings of the 35th Annual IEEE Symposium on Security and Privacy (SP 2014), May 2014

19. Wu, Z., Xu, Z., Wang, H.: Whispers in the hyper-space: high-speed covert channel attacks in the cloud. In: Proceedings of the 21st USENIX Conference on Security Symposium, Security 2012, p. 9. USENIX Association, Berkeley (2012). http://dl. acm.org/citation.cfm?id=2362793.2362802

PSHAPE: Automatically Combining Gadgets for Arbitrary Method Execution

Andreas Follner[1]([✉]), Alexandre Bartel[1], Hui Peng[2], Yu-Chen Chang[2],
Kyriakos Ispoglou[2], Mathias Payer[2], and Eric Bodden[3]

[1] Technische Universität Darmstadt, Darmstadt, Germany
{andreas.follner,alexandre.bartel}@cased.de
[2] Purdue University, West Lafayette, USA
{peng124,chang397,kispoglo}@purdue.edu, mathias.payer@nebelwelt.net
[3] Paderborn University & Fraunhofer IEM, Paderborn, Germany
bodden@acm.org

Abstract. Return-Oriented Programming (ROP) is the cornerstone of today's exploits. Yet, building ROP chains is predominantly a manual task, enjoying limited tool support. Many of the available tools contain bugs, are not tailored to the needs of exploit development in the real world and do not offer practical support to analysts, which is why they are seldom used for any tasks beyond gadget discovery. We present PSHAPE (*P*ractical *S*upport for *H*alf-*A*utomated *P*rogram *E*xploitation), a tool which assists analysts in exploit development. It discovers gadgets, chains gadgets together, and ensures that side effects such as register dereferences do not crash the program. Furthermore, we introduce the notion of *gadget summaries*, a compact representation of the effects a gadget or a chain of gadgets has on memory and registers. These semantic summaries enable analysts to quickly determine the usefulness of long, complex gadgets that use a lot of aliasing or involve memory accesses. Case studies on nine real binaries representing 147 MiB of code show PSHAPE's usefulness: it automatically builds usable ROP chains for nine out of eleven scenarios.

1 Introduction

Exploiting software vulnerabilities was simple and straightforward up until the early 2000s, when mitigation techniques were scarce and seldom applied. In contrast, contemporary systems deploy a multitude of defense mechanisms such as stack canaries [5], data execution prevention (DEP) [1], and address space layout randomization (ASLR) [18], each of which presents an obstacle to exploitation that needs to be bypassed. This has largely restricted exploit development to manual effort with only basic tool support.

While the circumvention of mitigations has been studied in detail, there is no comprehensive and automatic approach to bypassing all mitigations at once. Different mitigations must be defeated using different attacks. For example, DEP is bypassed using ROP or other code-reuse attacks [4,6,17,26,32]. Although

© Springer International Publishing AG 2016
G. Barthe et al. (Eds.): STM 2016, LNCS 9871, pp. 212–228, 2016.
DOI: 10.1007/978-3-319-46598-2_15

DEP exploits may share some commonality amongst themselves, this does not carry over to exploits targeting ASLR and stack canaries, which tend to be very scenario-specific and often rely on another vulnerability in addition to the one that allows a code pointer to be overwritten. In general, information leaks [2,7, 31] are the preferred way of learning a program's memory layout and contents. However, these often require either another vulnerability like a format string vulnerability, or a scriptable environment under the analyst's control such as Javascript or Actionscript. More sophisticated attacks must operate with stricter constraints or are limited to a specific use case [3,12,19,29,33].

Current exploits consist of three stages: (i) information collection to bypass ASLR, (ii) ROP to bypass DEP, and (iii) executing the desired payload. The first stage uses an information leak to discover all required information to get around ASLR. The second stage uses ROP to initialize a memory area and remap it as executable. Then, in the third stage, the exploit runs classic shellcode within the newly mapped region. Exploits are split into three stages because (i) information leaks are program specific and (ii) ROP programming is cumbersome, complicated, and hard to control. Attackers prefer short ROP chains and inject and execute binary code as soon as possible.

The plurality of mitigations complicates the automation of exploit generation, yet certain mundane tasks, particularly those in later stages of ROP chain creation, are good targets for automation. These tasks include finding gadgets, assessing gadgets' usefulness, and combining gadgets to achieve useful behavior. These tasks require the analyst to (i) decompose the code she wants to execute into analogues of individual assembly instructions (e.g., write a certain value in a register), then (ii) manually find individual gadgets whose semantics correspond to all the individual assembly instructions, (iii) undo any unintended side effects of executed gadgets, and (iv) ensure that preconditions, such as that a register has to point to writeable memory, are satisfied. While many tools have been proposed to automate these steps, every single one appears to show at least some serious limitation when it comes to practical application scenarios.

This work presents and evaluates PSHAPE, a novel approach to automatically perform steps (i) through (iv) through a semantic gadget search and gadget summaries. We assume that the analyst wants to execute a function to make her payload executable, following the idea of three-stage exploit development. First, PSHAPE discovers all gadgets in a given binary and computes their pre- and postconditions. Afterwards, PSHAPE selects the best suited gadgets for loading or modifying values in registers used for passing arguments to functions. Second, PSHAPE combines these gadgets into chains to create a chain of non-interfering gadgets. Finally, in the third step, gadgets may be added to the chain to make sure that the analyst can initialize all registers the chain dereferences, as its execution may otherwise lead to a crash.

This work compares PSHAPE to twelve other tools. Since no other tool offers gadget summaries, one can only compare the number of gadgets found and how well the gadget chaining mechanisms work. For the latter, we use four Linux and five Windows binaries, a total of 147 MiB of executable data. Then, we use the tools to create gadget chains that initialize between three and six registers with analyst-controlled data, allowing the analyst to invoke functions often used in ROP exploits, such as `mprotect`, `mmap`, or `VirtualProtect`. This results in eleven scenarios, for which a gadget chain can be created.

To summarize, the work presents the following original contributions:

– gadget summaries, a compact view on a gadget's semantics, greatly enhancing the search for useful gadgets,
– a mechanism to automatically generate a gadget chain that initializes registers used for passing parameters to execute an arbitrary method, making sure that all preconditions are satisfied,
– PSHAPE, an open-source implementation of the approach, and an evaluation of PSHAPE comparing it to other ROP tools. We show that it can automatically produce chains for nine out of eleven scenarios (81 %), passing up to six parameters to function calls, while other tools can create a chain only in one scenario.

2   Motivating Example

In this section we show how PSHAPE helps building exploits for real-world vulnerabilities. The example we use is CVE-2013-2028, a typical buffer overflow vulnerability, which was found in the *nginx* web engine[1].

For our running example, the goal is to inject arbitrary shellcode, make it executable, and then overwrite the return address with the beginning of the shellcode. To bypass DEP, `mprotect` needs to be called using a ROP chain to make the shellcode page executable. This includes performing the following tasks: (1) information leaking, to discover the address of `mprotect` and the stack frame where the vulnerable buffer is allocated, (2) building the ROP payload for calling `mprotect`, and (3) constructing the shell code.

Problem Definition. While all the tasks mentioned above are difficult, the second task can become increasingly complex due to the huge number of gadgets and constraints that need to be tracked along the gadget chain. Manually crafting the payload is both time-consuming and tedious. To execute a system call or call any other function, an attacker must (i) identify all the registers needed to be initialized, e.g., setting up the syscall number in `rax` and preparing arguments in other registers; (ii) for each register to be initialized, search all the relevant gadgets in the binary using a gadget finding tool; (iii) analyze each gadget to find out how it affects registers and memory; (iv) choose a subset of the identified gadgets and chain them into a coherent exploit.

The task of finding appropriate gadgets for initializing a register in steps (ii) and (iii) is complex and takes a very long time for the analyst. For example, running ROPgadget [27] on nginx with a `grep` filter to identify gadgets for

---

[1] http://www.vnsecurity.net/research/2013/05/21/analysis-of-nginx-cve-2013-2028.html.

touching `rax` produces a list with thousands of candidates. Since ROP gadgets often have unwanted side effects on other memory locations and/or registers (e.g., writing to invalid addresses and causing a crash), only a few gadgets remain viable. This makes the identification of usable gadgets a slow process, even for an experienced analyst. Moreover, chaining gadgets in step (iv) is a repetitive task whose complexity entails a lot of work. To execute a system call using ROP, all arguments need to be passed beforehand, involving memory writes, register initialization and typically cannot be done with only a single gadget. Thus, finding gadgets for different operations is crucial for building the payload. Since finding different gadgets requires iterating through the process of gathering and filtering the viable gadgets, the more gadgets a ROP chain needs, the more heavy manual workload is required.

Our Approach. The automation provided by PSHAPE can simplify the last three steps significantly, saving the analyst from large volumes of repetitive work. For steps (ii) and (iii), PSHAPE can assist in two ways. First, it reduces the result set size of a gadget search by filtering out incompatible gadgets, such as arithmetic gadgets. Second, it produces gadget summaries that speed up the process of gadget analysis. PSHAPE greatly reduces the amount of manual work required in step (iv) by chaining gadgets into an exploit completely automatically, whilst also satisfying any preconditions of the constituent gadgets.

3 Automating Exploit Generation

PSHAPE assists an analyst during exploit development by offering two distinct features which set it apart from existing tools that are publicly available, namely it (i) provides summaries based on gadget semantics, making it straightforward for an analyst to assess and select gadgets, and (ii) chains gadgets together so that they load registers used to pass parameters to functions with analyst-controlled data. This allows the invocation of arbitrary functions. PSHAPE also ensures that any preconditions of a gadget (such as that a register has to point to readable memory) are satisfied.

We first define what gadget summaries are and how they are computed in Sect. 3.1 and then describe our approach to generate gadget chains in Sect. 3.2.

3.1 Gadget Summaries

Overview. ROP mitigations that (i) monitor program executions and detect short code sequences [8,9,14,25] or (ii) require all `return` operations to return to an instruction following a call instruction [25,39] force developers into using long gadgets or even entire functions [29]. The increasing length of gadgets makes manual analysis and reasoning increasingly difficult. We thus propose *gadget summaries*, which reflect a gadget's semantics in a compact specification that allows analysts to understand a gadget's behavior at a glance. Figure 1 shows an example of a gadget summary, with the gadget on the left, and its summary

```
mov rax, rsp
mov [rax+20h], r9
mov [rax+18h], r8
mov [rax+10h], rdx
mov [rax+8], rcx
mov rcx, r9
mov rax, [rcx]
inc rax
mov [rcx+8], rax          PRE:  [r9] <-> [r9 + 0xC]
mov rax, [rcx+4]          PRE:  [rsp] <-> [rsp + 0x20]
inc rax                   POST: rsp = rsp + 8
mov [rcx+0Ch], rax        POST: rax = [r9 + 4] + 1
ret                       POST: rcx = r9
```

(a) A candidate gadget.   (b) Corresponding gadget summary.

Fig. 1. Despite this being a relatively short gadget in `mshtml.dll` which contains only 13 instructions (a), analyzing it manually is still a cumbersome and error-prone task. PSHAPE automates this process by creating a simple summary (b). Note that by default PSHAPE does not display memory write postconditions as they are seldom of interest, and make the summary harder to read.

on the right. This gadget has two preconditions, because `r9` and `rsp` are dereferenced. The actual effects on the program state are that `rsp` is increased by 8, `rax` receives the value of 1 + `[r9 + 4]`, and `rcx` is assigned the value of `r9`.

Method. First, gadgets are identified by finding `return` opcodes and backward disassembly. These gadgets are then converted into an *intermediate representation* (IR) to simplify analysis. Our current prototype uses VEX IR, see Sect. 3.3. Based on this IR, PSHAPE propagates all assignments, such as to temporary or real registers, or memory locations forwards, resulting in a single statement for each real register and memory location. This single statement (referred to as *postcondition*) contains all operations on this register or location, i.e., an abstraction of the new value after a gadget has executed. Of course our analysis models memory locations so it is able to correctly determine postconditions of gadgets that use the stack to pass data. E.g., it detects that after a `push rax ; pop rbx ; ret` gadget, `rbx` contains the value of `rax`. This analysis also allows us to readily extract *preconditions*, such as register or memory dereferences. Post- and preconditions combined result in a *gadget summary*, a compact representation of the state of memory and registers after a gadget has executed along with a list of dereferenced registers and offsets. Our syntax for pre- and postconditions is similar to assembly syntax, and should be intuitive for binary analysts. The current prototype excludes instructions such as jumps, loops, or bit manipulation in the summaries to reduce the explosion in state and complexity, see Sect. 6. We leave more involved search strategies for future work.

As memory is often accessed sequentially using offsets from a register, one can compress summaries by merging such accesses into a range. For example, preconditions `[rax]`, `[rax + 8]`, `[rax + 0x10]` and `[rax + 0x20]` can be compressed to: `[rax] <-> [rax + 0x20]`. This denotes that all memory between `[rax]` and [rax + 0x20] has to be read/writeable. This heuristic sacrifices precision, as not every single byte must be accessed, but makes summaries concise.

Gadget summaries aid the analyst in the process of understanding how a gadget affects the state of registers and memory and are increasingly helpful, the more instructions and aliasing a gadget contains. They also allow for a more efficient gadget search, as expressing postconditions when searching for a gadget is much more intuitive and flexible than specifying a certain instruction. Lastly, gadget summaries are useful for selecting gadgets for automated gadget chain generation, which we describe in the next section.

3.2 Gadget Chaining

Our approach aims at finding a valid and short gadget chain which loads analyst-controlled data, i.e., relative to rsp, into registers. This allows invoking an arbitrary function with analyst-specified parameters. It consists of three steps, as shown in Fig. 2. In the first step, the gadgets are extracted from the target binary and summaries are computed. Then, based on the summaries, the list of gadgets are filtered to keep only the ones related to initializing registers that are used for passing function parameters. The second step combines these gadgets into chains. For a chain, pre- and postconditions are computed, and if the chain has the desired postconditions, the third step analyzes the validity of each chain and adds gadgets to satisfy any preconditions.

Step 1: Gadget Extraction and Summary Computation. First, gadgets are extracted from a given binary, delivering a list of gadgets for which we then compute gadget summaries. The results are stored, making them available for the analyst. Next, the gadgets are filtered to keep only the ones related to initializing registers used for passing parameters to functions. On 64-bit Windows those are rcx, rdx, r8, and r9, in that order. On 64-bit Linux the registers used for parameter passing to functions are rdi, rsi, rdx, rcx, r8, and r9, in that order. Additional parameters are passed on the stack in both cases. Our summaries simplify filtering because gadgets that do not set the registers stated above to a value that can be controlled by the analyst, are discarded automatically.

We divide these gadgets into two categories, *load* and *mod*. Gadgets in the load category overwrite a given register, e.g., a pop instruction, while gadgets in the mod category modify it, e.g., an add instruction. Gadgets in the load category are favored, and within this category, gadgets that use rsp-relative memory dereferences are preferred, as rsp needs to be under the control of the analyst anyway when using ROP. For example, a pop rcx gadget is preferred over a mov rcx, [rax] gadget. If no suitable *load* gadgets exist, *mod* gadgets such as add rcx, rax are used. Based on this ranking and the number and severity of pre-, and postconditions, the n most suitable gadgets for loading each parameter register with arbitrary data are selected and passed to Step 2. The step of assessing the severity of pre- and postconditions reuses some ideas presented in GaLity [13].

Step 2: Combining Gadgets into Chains. In the second step, the gadgets from Step 1 are combined and all possible permutations of a chain are computed. Remember that in Step 1, the n most suitable gadgets are selected for every parameter register. E.g., invoking a function with four parameters results in $n^4 \times 4!$ possible chains. For each permutation of a chain, pre- and postconditions of the whole chain are computed. If a chain's postconditions are not the expected result, i.e., the registers used to pass parameters do not contain analyst-controlled data, it is discarded. Instead of exhausting the search space, we stop the exploration after the first viable combination is found.

Step 3: Solving Pre-Conditions. It may happen that a chain generated in Step 2 contains preconditions such as register dereferences. The analyst needs to have the possibility to initialize the dereferenced registers, so they contain the address of a valid memory area. In Step 3, PSHAPE attempts to build a gadget chain that allows loading analyst-controlled data into an arbitrary register. Once such a gadget is found it is prepended to the incoming chain, forming a new chain. The new chain is then checked for pre- and postconditions again to make sure it does indeed initialize dereferenced registers and does not interfere with the original chain. Note that the number of iterations is limited (four in our prototype), so the chain does not grow forever.

Our gadget chaining fully automates the process of stitching gadgets together to initialize registers used for passing parameters to functions with data the analyst controls. It also adds gadgets to the chain to ensure any dereferenced registers are also initialized with data the analyst controls. This approach simplifies exploit development, especially if functions taking many parameters are called or if the available gadgets consist of many instructions.

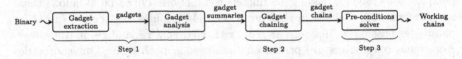

Fig. 2. Overview of our approach to generate gadget chains. In Step 1, we extract gadgets up to a certain size and create summaries. In Step 2 we select a set of n gadgets for the individual parameters to constrain the search space and then create gadget chains. In Step 3 we analyze the chains and prepend gadgets to make any dereferences analyst-controlled.

3.3 Implementation

PSHAPE uses a standard technique to discover gadgets: first, using pyelftools[2] and pefile[3], it finds executable sections in an input binary. Afterwards it scans these sections forwards bytewise until a return opcode is found, storing these

---

[2] https://github.com/eliben/pyelftools.
[3] https://github.com/erocarrera/pefile.

offsets in a list. Then, using several threads, it disassembles backwards from these offsets using the Capstone framework [22]. To limit the number and complexity of gadgets and speed up the discovery process, the analyst can specify the minimum and maximum size, i.e., number of instructions, of a gadget.

If the disassembly yields only legal instructions, we convert this gadget to Valgrind's VEX IR [21] using PyVEX [34]. Lifting the original assembly code to VEX has the advantage that it is much simpler to analyze because there are fewer instructions and side effects are made explicit. After this conversion, VEX assignments are propagated forward, resulting in a single statement for each real register and memory location, which contains all operations on this register or location, i.e., an abstraction of the new value after a gadget has executed.

4   Evaluation

We first compare PSHAPE with existing tools regarding their ability to extract gadgets from binaries as well as their ability to construct gadget chains to initialize registers for function calls in Sect. 4.1. Then, in Sect. 4.2, we qualitatively evaluate gadget chains that PSHAPE creates for various binaries, and discuss optimizations.

4.1   Comparison with Existing Tools

In Table 1 we have listed the tools designed to help an analyst to create ROP exploits. Generally, we have found that there is a big gap between the theoretical state of the art and what actually exists and works well in practice. Many of the tools we evaluate contain bugs and other quirks that limit their usefulness in real scenarios, the main focus of PSHAPE.

OptiROP and Q are not publicly available and also were not made available to us upon request. We also excluded nrop due to its scope (see Sect. 5). We managed to compile ROPC although it has been unmaintained for years, and GitHub issue reports are not answered. Unfortunately, it could not extract gadgets from any of the binaries we use in the evaluation, which is why we exclude it.

For the evaluation we use five Windows binaries: firefox.exe, iexplore.exe, chrome.exe, mshtml.dll, and jfxwebkit.dll, and four Linux binaries: chromium, apache2, openssl, and nginx, representing a total of 147 MiB of executable data. Detailed information about the binaries and PSHAPE are available on the companion website: https://sites.google.com/site/exploitdevpshape/.

Gadget Discovery. In this section, we compare the different gadget discovery routines. For a tool to be considered in these experiments, we require that it can read ELF or PE binaries and find gadgets in 64-bit binaries. DEPlib, Agafi, mona.py, Ropeme, and MSFrop do not fulfill these requirements and were therefore discarded, leaving us with the following tools to compare to: ROPgadget, rp++ and ropper. We configured them to look for gadgets up to a maximum length of 35 instructions. Table 2a summarizes the results.

Table 1. Summary of ROP tools. Note that many tools have limitations, bugs, or do not work as expected, which we discuss in Sects. 4.1 and 5

Tool	Syntactic Search	Semantic search	Gadget Chaining	Turing Complete	Open-Source	Binary available	PE	ELF	64-bit
PSHAPE	✓	✓	✓	×	✓	✓	✓	✓	✓
OptiROP [23]	✓	✓	✓	×	×	×	✓	✓	✓
nrop [38]	✓	✓	×	×	×	×	✓	✓	✓
Q [30]	✓	✓	✓	×	×	×	✓	✓	✓
ROPC [24]	✓	✓	✓	✓	✓	✓	✓	✓	✓
DEPLib [35]	✓	✓	✓	×	✓	✓	✓	×	×
Agafi 1.1 [16]	✓	×	✓	×	✓	✓	✓	×	×
mona.py 2.0 (rev566) [11]	✓	×	✓	×	✓	✓	✓	×	×
ROPgadget 5.4 [27]	✓	×	✓	×	✓	✓	✓	✓	✓
rp++ 0.4 [36]	✓	×	×	×	✓	✓	✓	✓	✓
Ropeme [10]	✓	×	×	×	✓	✓	×	✓	×
ropper 1.8.7 [28]	✓	×	✓	×	✓	✓	✓	✓	✓
MSFrop [20]	✓	×	×	×	✓	✓	✓	✓	×

ROPgadget lists duplicates, i.e., the same gadget at the same address is listed more than once. We informed the developer about this bug. ROPgadget does not have an option to define the maximum number of instructions in a gadget. Only the maximum number of byte per gadget can be set. We ran our experiments using 110 bytes for the maximum length, leading to an average opcode size of about 3 bytes per instruction. Originally, we planned to use a much larger number to make sure we do not miss any gadgets. However, even with a depth of 110 bytes the evaluation of ROPgadget on Chromium took over 6 h, consuming 160 GB of RAM. Afterwards, we used a script to go through the results and remove any gadgets that contained more than 35 instructions. Therefore, we miss gadgets that contain 35 or fewer instructions but are longer than 110 byte.

rp++ originally comes with a fixed maximum gadget length of 20 instructions. We modified the source code, changing this upper limit to 35 and recompiled it, so it correctly discovers longer gadgets, too.

ropper ropper does not find some simple and short gadgets and keeps gadgets that contain conditional jumps. Such gadgets are difficult to use, especially since no information is given about which paths are taken under which circumstances.

Since all four tools use slightly different filters or sometimes contain bugs, it is difficult to compare their results. For example, ROPgadget and rp++ keep gadgets that contain privileged instructions (e.g., in, out, or hlt), which terminate the process. ROPgadget's output contains duplicate gadgets, and ropper keeps gadgets that contain conditional jumps, which the other tools do not.

Table 2. (a) Number of gadgets found by each tool on the given binaries, as determined by our evaluation. (b) It is possible to build chains to mprotect for all four Linux binaries, line mprotect shows how many of those chains each tool creates. For mmap, only three of the Linux binaries have the necessary gadgets to build a chain and this line shows how many of those each tool can create. Chains to VirtualProtect exist in four out of the five Windows binaries, this line shows how many of them each tool creates. A dash indicates that the tool does not support calling a function that requires the tool to initialize the required number of arguments. In (a) and (b), L denotes Linux and W, Windows.

Binary	PSHAPE	rp++	ropper	ROPgadget
firefox$_W$	6,709	6,182	5,445	6,259
iexplore$_W$	928	888	836	888
chrome$_W$	64,372	58,890	52,991	59,969
mshtml$_W$	1,329,705	1,239,403	1,099,466	1,242,616
jfxwebkit$_W$	1,172,718	1,076,350	960,091	1,086,061
chromium$_L$	5,358,283	5,159,712	4,579,388	5,130,856
apache2$_L$	24,164	22,722	18,061	22,875
openssl$_L$	6,978	6,829	5,377	6,845
nginx$_L$	26,314	25,700	21,081	25,245

(a) Number of extracted gadgets

Function	PSHAPE	ropper	ROPgadget
$W_{VirtualProtect}$	2/4	-	-
$L_{mprotect}$	4/4	1/4	1/4
L_{mmap}	3/3	-	-

(b) Number of gadget chains

We filter and clean the output of all tools, removing any duplicates and privileged instructions as well as jumps. As Table 2 shows, eventually all tools find a similar number of gadgets.

Gadget Chaining. Here, we evaluate the tools in regards to their ability to create gadget chains. The minimal requirement for a tool to be considered in the experiments is that it can build ROP chains for 64-bit Windows or 64-bit Linux, correctly initializing the registers used for passing parameters to functions. Since most 32-bit calling conventions pass parameters on the stack, ROP chains have to be constructed differently, making a comparison difficult. We use functions that are regularly used in ROP exploits. For Linux, the goal is to create two chains, one that loads registers with analyst-controlled data for invoking a function that takes three arguments (e.g., mprotect or execve) and one chain that loads registers with analyst-controlled data for invoking a function that takes six arguments (e.g., mmap). For Windows, the goal is to create a chain that loads registers with user-controlled data for invoking a function that takes four arguments (e.g., VirtualProtect or VirtualAlloc). From this point on, we refer to these goals by the function's names but keep in mind that any function using the same number of parameters or fewer can be invoked, too.

From the list of available tools, only ROPgadget and ropper satisfy our requirements. The results of the experiments have been summarized in Table 2b.

ROPgadget cannot create chains for Windows, does not offer any targets for a ROP chain and instead always tries to build a chain to create a shell using execve. However, this function requires initializing three arguments, allowing us to evaluate at least one goal for Linux. ROPgadget successfully created a chain for chromium, but it did not succeed on any of the remaining binaries.

ropper cannot create chains for 64-bit Windows, but offers two targets for ROP chain creation on 64-bit Linux, mprotect and execve, which both take three arguments. Again, this allowed us to evaluate at least one of the goals we specified previously. However, for openssl and nginx, ropper was able to initialize only rdi, despite discovering several useful and simple gadgets that load the other registers. For apache2, ropper successfully initialized rdi and rdx. Ropper successfully created a ROP chain for chromium, initializing all three registers used for passing parameters to mprotect or execve. All gadgets used in the chains are without side-effects and without preconditions. Thus, no additional work to satisfy preconditions is necessary.

PSHAPE successfully created fully functional chains for both mprotect and mmap for the following Linux binaries: chromium, apache2, and nginx. We present and discuss the chains for apache2 and nginx in Sect. 4.2. For openssl it was only possible to create a chain to mprotect. This was due to the fact that no gadget was found to initialize r9, which we confirmed manually using both PSHAPE and ROPgadget. On Windows binaries, PSHAPE failed to build chains for firefox.exe and iexplore.exe, and we confirmed, again using both PSHAPE and ROPgadget, that, in fact, the necessary gadgets are not present in the respective binaries. For mshtml.dll and jfxwebkit.dll, PSHAPE successfully built a chain. It also created a chain for chrome.exe, however, it required another gadget to be prepended manually. Hence, we did not count it towards successful chain creations in Table 2b. We discuss this chain and its shortcomings in Sect. 4.2.

In cases where PSHAPE failed to build a chain, we evaluated whether a human analyst could succeed. In other words, we assessed if it was in fact not possible to build a chain, due to a lack of useful gadgets, or if our tool's limitations (see Sect. 6) were to blame. In the case of openssl and iexplore.exe, the former is the case. While there are gadgets that initialize the registers, they are often initialized to a constant value. Other times we found a gadget that does initialize a register to an analyst-controlled value, however, unless that value is a specific constant, a jump is taken in the same gadget, effectively forcing the analyst to initialize the register with that specific value. For firefox.exe, an analyst can create a ROP chain. The gadgets that have to be used are complex, requiring initialization of several gadgets and memory locations to ensure that jumps are not taken. Since PSHAPE is unable to utilize such gadgets, it was unable to automatically generate a chain in this case.

4.2   PSHAPE in Practice

Next we qualitatively evaluate three automatically created chains. Note that any padding required between gadgets is added automatically but omitted here to increase readability and due to size constraints.

Chain for apache2. The chain is presented in Fig. 3a. Gadgets 2 to 7 are used to initialize the registers used for passing parameters. PSHAPE detects that `rax` is dereferenced by gadget 6 and before that, aliased with `ebp` (gadget 4). Therefore, another gadget is added that initializes `rbp`. An even shorter chain could have been created by arranging the gadgets in such a way, that gadgets 7 and 4 execute before gadget 6. In this case, gadget 7 initializes `rbp`, gadget 4 copies it to `rax`, which is then dereferenced by gadget 6. This would make the first gadget unnecessary. However, PSHAPE does not detect that, as it uses the first permutation whose postconditions are correct (see Sect. 3.2).

Chain for nginx. The chain is presented in Fig. 3b. In the first iteration, the chain consists of gadgets 3 to 8, which are used to initialize the registers used for passing parameters. Gadget 6 dereferences `rax` and `rbx`, which is why PSHAPE initializes these two registers by adding gadgets 1 and 2 to the chain. Gadget 8 dereferences `rbx`, which is initialized by gadget 6.

Chain for chrome.exe. The chain is presented in Fig. 3c. Gadgets 2 to 5 are used to initialize the registers used for passing parameters. PSHAPE correctly detected that there are no better-suited gadgets for initializing `r9` and resorts to using gadget 2, prepended by gadget 1 to make `r15` analyst-controlled. Unfortunately, PSHAPE cannot automatically satisfy the precondition of the `cmovns` instruction, because this conditional `mov` instruction checks the `sign` flag, and currently, PSHAPE ignores flags (see Sect. 6). Therefore, to make sure the chain executes correctly, the analyst has to prepend, e.g., a simple `xor rax, rax` instruction to the chain.

5   Related Work

Here we discuss related work that was not yet covered in Sect. 4.1.

Q [30] takes an existing exploit which does not bypass DEP or ASLR, and attempts to harden it, i.e., rewrite it so it bypasses these mitigation techniques. To bypass ASLR it relies on unrandomized code sections and then uses gadgets from those sections to construct a ROP payload to bypass DEP. The payload is written by the attacker using QooL, Q's own exploit language. In their evaluation, the authors show how Q hardens nine simple stack buffer overflow exploits for Windows and Linux, with a payload that invokes a linked function or `system/WinExec`. Q cannot handle gadgets containing pointer dereferences, which our approach not only handles, but also ensures they are safe to use.

ROPC [24] is based on Q, but publicly available. Its main feature is a gadget compiler which takes an input binary and a program written in their own language called ROPL. Then, ROPC creates this program using only gadgets

1	0x3ebe8	**pop** rbp ; **ret** ;
2	0x46774	**pop** rdi ; **ret** ;
3	0x57abd	**pop** rsi ; **ret** ;
4	0x7800d	**pop** rcx ; **mov** eax, ebp ; **add** rsp, 8 ; **pop** rbx ; **pop** rbp ; **ret** ;
5	0x41200	**pop** rdx ; **pop** rbx ; **ret** ;
6	0x4d552	**pop** r8 ; **mov** rax, qword ptr [rax] ; **ret** ;
7	0x7800c	**pop** r9 ; **mov** eax, ebp ; **add** rsp, 8 ; **pop** rbx ; **pop** rbp ; **ret** ;

(a) Gadget Chain for apache2

1	0x412dab	**pop** rax ; **add** rsp, 8 ; **ret** ;
2	0x45d594	**pop** rbx ; **ret** ;
3	0x406c20	**pop** rdi ; **ret** ;
4	0x42892b	**pop** rsi ; **ret** ;
5	0x425242	**pop** rcx ; **ret** ;
6	0x444965	**pop** r8 ; **mov** qword ptr [rax], rbx ; **mov** rax, qword ptr [rsp + 8] ; **mov** qword ptr [rbx + 0x28], rax ; **mov** rax, qword ptr [rsp + 0x18] ; **mov** qword ptr [rbx + 0x18], rax ; **mov** edx, 0 ; **mov** rax, rdx ; **add** rsp, 0x58 ; **pop** rbx ; **pop** rbp ; **pop** r12 ; **pop** r13 ; **pop** r14 ; **pop** r15 ; **ret** ;
7	0x45a8c4	**pop** rdx ; **ret** ;
8	0x424219	**mov** r9, qword ptr [rsp + 0x28] ; **mov** qword ptr [rbx + 0x48], r9 ; **mov** r10, qword ptr [rsp + 0x30] ; **mov** qword ptr [rbx + 0x50], r10 ; **mov** r11, qword ptr [rsp + 0x38] ; **mov** qword ptr [rbx + 0x58], r11 ; **add** rsp, 0x48 ; **pop** rbx ; **pop** rbp ; **pop** r12 ; **pop** r13 ; **pop** r14 ; **pop** r15 ; **ret** ;

(b) Gadget Chain for nginx

1	0x56c63	**pop** r15 ; **ret** ;
2	0x25272	**cmovns** r9d, dword ptr [r15] ; **ret** 0x2b48 ;
3	0x9fec6	**pop** r8 ; **ret** ;
4	0x385da	**pop** rdx ; **ret** ;
5	0xa15d3	**pop** rcx ; **ret** 0x6e9 ;

(c) Gadget Chain for chrome.exe

Fig. 3. Three chains created by PSHAPE

from the input binary. While it looks favourable to our tool on paper, because it is Turing-complete, only a proof of concept prototype, dating back to June 2013, is available. This prototype only works on one included, synthetic example, but did not succeed on the real binaries we use in the evaluation.

BARFgadgets [37] is based on Q and its main focus is classifying and verifying gadgets into various types such as *load register* or *store memory*. It provides very basic summaries that only contain what the first instruction of a gadget does, and which other registers are clobbered.

nrop [38] finds semantically equivalent gadgets to a given instruction. Our tool could be used for a similar purpose, as semantically equivalent gadgets have the same summary. Until early 2016, nrop's website was online and stated that automatic gadget chaining would be coming soon, however, the tool has not received any updates since then.

ROPER [15] is currently in the early stages of development and will use a genetic component: after gadgets have been found, they will be put together randomly. From this pool, four chains will be selected, executed, their fitness assessed, the two least fit chains killed, the other two chains mated and their children will be added back to the pool. This process will be repeated until it converges on a set of viable chains.

6   Limitations and Future Work

Our prototype implementation currently cannot summarize gadgets that include instructions that check CPU flags (e.g., cmov) and filters out gadgets that contain instructions changing the program flow (e.g., jne). We plan do address this in future work, as it will enable PSHAPE to successfully build chains for more binaries. In our evaluation it was in all but one cases possible to build a ROP chain without having to incorporate gadgets that contain jumps, however, with mitigation techniques that drastically reduce the number of available gadgets (e.g., Control-Flow Integrity), it will be important to utilize all available gadgets.

Further optimizations are possible, e.g., when combining gadgets we can continue to check for a permutation that has fewer preconditions instead of taking the first permutation that has the correct postconditions.

We plan to add features which help the analyst to find gadgets that are useful for bypassing certain mitigation techniques. E.g., we consider adding a filter to use only call-preceded gadgets, which helps bypass some CFI solutions [25,39].

7   Conclusion

ROP is the cornerstone of today's low-level exploits, yet tool-support is lacking. Current ROP chain creation requires significant manual work. Here we present PSHAPE, a tool that supports analysts during exploit development. It offers gadget summaries, a compact representation of the effects a gadget has on registers and memory. Furthermore, it automates gadget chaining, loading registers used for passing parameters with analyst-controlled data, and making sure that any preconditions are satisfied.

We compare PSHAPE to twelve other tools in terms of their gadget finding and autochaining abilities. Most of those tools, however, do not work properly in realistic scenarios, contain bugs, or are not available. This left us with three tools to compare to empirically. We applied these tools and PSHAPE to nine widely used binaries, a total of 147 MiB of code, and eleven realistic exploit scenarios. Our tool is the only one that successfully creates ROP chains fully-automated and succeeds in nine out of eleven scenarios. Other tools only create a chain for a single scenario, showing that there is a big gap between the theoretical capabilities of current state of the art tools and their usefulness in practice.

Acknowledgments. We would like to thank the anonymous reviewers for their feedback and suggestions on improving the paper. This work was supported, in part, by NSF CNS-1513783, by the German Federal Ministry of Education and Research (BMBF) and by the Hessian Ministry of Science and the Arts within CRISP (www.crisp-da.de), as well as by the Heinz Nixdorf Foundation.

References

1. Andersen, S., Abella, V.: Memory protection technologies. https://technet.microsoft.com/en-us/library/bb457155.aspx, August 2004
2. Athanasakis, M., Athanasopoulos, E., Polychronakis, M., Portokalidis, G., Ioannidis, S.: The devil is in the constants: Bypassing defenses in browser JIT engines. In: 22nd Annual Network and Distributed System Security Symposium, NDSS 2015, San Diego, California, USA, February 8–11, 2014 (2015)
3. Bittau, A., Belay, A., Mashtizadeh, A., Mazières, D., Boneh, D.: Hacking blind. In: Proceedings of the IEEE Symposium on Security and Privacy, SP 2014, pp. 227–242. IEEE Computer Society, Washington, DC (2014)
4. Bletsch, T., Jiang, X., Freeh, V.W., Liang, Z.: Jump-oriented programming: a new class of code-reuse attack. In: Proceedings of the 6th ACM Symposium on Information, Computer and Communications Security, ASIACCS 2011, pp. 30–40. ACM, New York (2011)
5. Bray, B.: Compiler security checks in depth, February 2002. http://msdn.microsoft.com/en-us/library/aa290051(v=vs.71).aspx
6. Checkoway, S., Davi, L., Dmitrienko, A., Sadeghi, A.-R., Shacham, H., Winandy, M.: Return-oriented programming without returns. In: Proceedings of the 17th ACM Conference on Computer and Communications Security (USA, 2010), CCS 2010, pp. 559–572. ACM, New York, NY (2010)
7. Chen, X.: Aslr bypass apocalypse in recent zero-day exploits. https://www.fireeye.com/blog/threat-research/2013/10/aslr-bypass-apocalypse-in-lately-zero-day-exploits.html
8. Cheng, Y., Zhou, Z., Yu, M., Ding, X., Deng, R.H.: Ropecker: A generic and practical approach for defending against ROP attacks. In: NDSS (2014)
9. Davi, L., Sadeghi, A.-R., Winandy, M.: Ropdefender: a detection tool to defend against return-oriented programming attacks. In: Proceedings of the 6th ACM Symposium on Information, Computer and Communications Security, ASIACCS 2011, pp. 40–51. ACM, New York (2011)
10. Dinh, L.L.: Ropeme - rop exploit made easy. https://github.com/packz/ropeme
11. Eeckhoutte, P. V. mona.py. https://github.com/corelan/mona
12. Federico, A.D., Cama, A., Shoshitaishvili, Y., Kruegel, C., Vigna, G.: How the elf ruined christmas. In 24th USENIX Security Symposium (USENIX Security 15), pp. 643–658. USENIX Association, Washington, D.C. (2015)
13. Follner, A., Bartel, A., Bodden, E.: Analyzing the gadgets. In: Caballero, J., et al. (eds.) ESSoS 2016. LNCS, vol. 9639, pp. 155–172. Springer, Heidelberg (2016). doi:10.1007/978-3-319-30806-7_10
14. Follner, A., Bodden, E.: Ropocop - dynamic mitigation of code-reuse attacks. J. Inf. Secur. Appl. **82**, 3–22 (2016)

15. Fraser, L.: Roper. https://github.com/oblivia-simplex/roper
16. Gallo, M.: Agafi. https://github.com/CoreSecurity/Agafi
17. Göktas, E., Athanasopoulos, E., Bos, H., Portokalidis, G.: Out of control: Overcoming control-flow integrity. In: Proceedings of the IEEE Symposium on Security and Privacy SP 2014, pp. 575–589. IEEE Computer Society, Washington, DC (2014)
18. Howard, M., Miller, M., Lambert, J., Thomlinson, M.: Windows isv software security defenses, December 2010. http://msdn.microsoft.com/en-us/library/bb430720.aspx
19. Hund, R., Willems, C., Holz, T.: Practical timing side channel attacks against kernel space aslr. In: Proceeding of the IEEE Symposium on Security and Privacy SP 2013, pp. 191–205. IEEE Computer Society, Washington, DC (2013)
20. Metasploit. Msfrop. http://www.offensive-security.com/metasploit-unleashed/msfrop
21. Nethercote, N., Seward, J.: Valgrind: a framework for heavyweight dynamic binary instrumentation..In: ACM Sigplan notices, ACM (2007)
22. Nguyen, A.Q.: Capstone: Next generation disassembly framework. http://www.capstone-engine.org/BHUSA2014-capstone.pdf
23. Nguyen, A.Q.: Optirop. https://media.blackhat.com/us-13/US-13-Quynh-Opti ROP-Hunting-for-ROP-Gadgets-in-Style-WP.pdf
24. Pakt. Ropc. https://github.com/pakt/ropc
25. Pappas, V., Polychronakis, M., Keromytis, A.D.: Transparent rop exploit mitigation using indirect branch tracing. In: Proceedings of the 22Nd USENIX Conference on Security, SEC 2013, pp. 447–462. USENIX, Berkeley (2013)
26. Roemer, R., Buchanan, E., Shacham, H., Savage, S.: Return-oriented programming: Systems, languages, and applications. ACM Trans. Inf. Syst. Secur. 15(1), 2:1–2:34 (2012)
27. Salwan, J.: Ropgadget. https://github.com/JonathanSalwan/ROPgadget
28. Schirra, S.: Ropper - rop gadget finder and binary information tool. https://scoding.de/ropper/
29. Schuster, F., Tendyck, T., Liebchen, C., Davi, L., Sadeghi, A.-R., Holz, T.: Counterfeit object-oriented programming: on the difficulty of preventing code reuse attacks in C++ applications. In: 36th IEEE Symposium on Security and Privacy (Oakland) (2015)
30. Schwartz, E.J., Avgerinos, T., Brumley, D.: Q: Exploit hardening made easy. In: Proceedings of the 20th USENIX Conference on Security, SEC 2011, p. 25. USENIX Association, Berkeley (2011)
31. Serna, F.J.: The info leak era of software exploitation (2012). http://media.blackhat.com/bh-us-12/Briefings/Serna/BH_US_12_Serna_Leak_Era_Slides.pdf
32. Shacham, H.: The geometry of innocent flesh on the bone: return-into-libc without function calls (on the x86). In: Proceedings of the 14th ACM Conference on Computer and communications security, CCS 2007. ACM, New York, NY (2007)
33. Shacham, H., Page, M., Pfaff, B., Goh, E.-J., Modadugu, N., Boneh, D.: On the effectiveness of address-space randomization. In: Proceedings of the 11th ACM Conference on Computer and communications security, CCS 2004, ACM (2004)
34. Shoshitaishvili, Y., Wang, R., Hauser, C., Kruegel, C., Vigna, G.: Firmalice - automatic detection of authentication bypass vulnerabilities in binary firmware. In: NDSS (2015)

35. Sol, P.: Deplib. https://www.immunitysec.com/downloads/DEPLIB.pdf
36. Souchet, A.: rp++. https://github.com/0vercl0k/rp
37. STIC, P.: Barfgadgets. https://github.com/programa-stic/barf-project
38. Wailly, A.: nrop. https://github.com/awailly/nrop
39. Zhang, C., Wei, T., Chen, Z., Duan, L., Szekeres, L., McCamant, S., Song, D., Zou, W.: Practical control flow integrity and randomization for binary executables. In: Proceedings of the IEEE Symposium on Security and Privacy, SP 2013, pp. 559–573. IEEE Computer Society, Washington, DC (2013)

Author Index

Printed in the United States
By Bookmasters